THE HILL BHUIYAS OF ORISSA

THE HILL BHUIYAS OF ORISSA

BY

SARAT CHANDRA ROY

GYAN

ISBN : 978-81-212-1820-7 (HB)

First Published, 1935

Published, 2018

Published by

Gyan Publishing House
5, Ansari Road
Daryaganj, New Delhi-110002
Phone: 011-47034999, 9811692060
www.gyanbooks.com
E-mail: books@gyanbooks.com

Printed at: G. Print Process, Delhi.

CONTENTS.

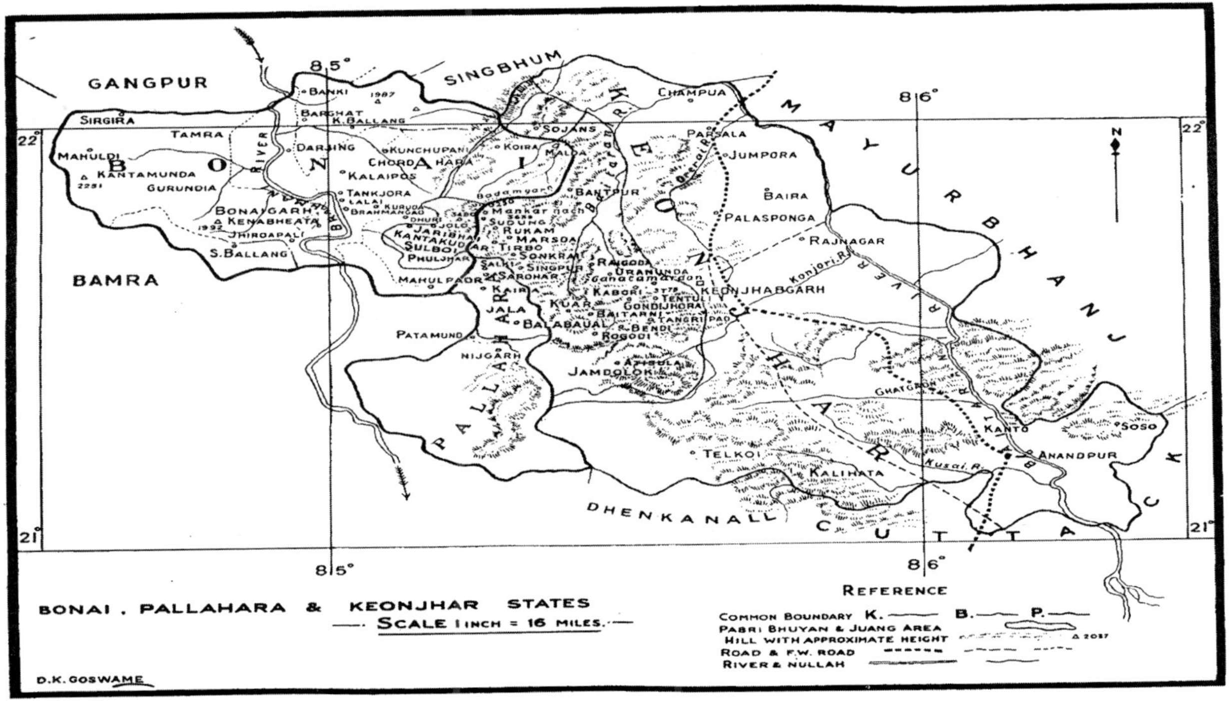

BONAI, PALLAHARA & KEONJHAR STATES

SCALE 1 INCH = 16 MILES.

REFERENCE

COMMON BOUNDARY	K. —— B. —— P. ——
PABRI BHUYAN & JUANG AREA	
HILL WITH APPROXIMATE HEIGHT	△ 2087
ROAD & F.W. ROAD	
RIVER & NULLAH	

D.K. GOSWAME

Preface.

The present work is the fifth volume of a series of monographs on the aboriginal tribes of the Central Hill Belt of India, whose ethnology I have been engaged in studying, off and on, for the last twenty-five years. The Bhūiyās are one of the few tribes whose different branches represent various stages of cultural evolution from the more or less primitive culture of the Hill Bhūiyās dealt with in this volume to the thoroughly Hinduised Zamindar families among the Plains Bhūiyās of Ōṛissā and elsewhere, some of whom now put forward pretensions to Rājput or Kshatriya descent. References have been made in the text to certain points of difference in custom and belief between the Hill Bhūiyās and the Hinduised Plains Bhūiyās. In the foot-notes references have also been made to certain points of agreement and difference in the customs and beliefs of the Hill Bhūiyās and some other Muṇḍā tribes of the Central Hill Belt.

In the preparation of this work, I am particularly indebted to successive Political Agents of the Ōṛissā Feudatory States and their successor the Governor-

General's Agent, Eastern States, for kind permission to work among the aborigines of the States, and for introducing me to the State authorities. My grateful thanks are due to the Feudatory Chiefs of Mayurbhanj, Keonjhar and Bonai for kind hospitality and for giving me the needed facilities for my work. I also desire to convey my best thanks to Dr. P.K. Sen, Bar-at-law, Dewan of the Mayurbhanj State, and Mrs. P.K. Sen, Rai Bahadur J.K. Tripati, Dewan, and Rai Saheb S.B. Sarkar, Civil Judge of the Keonjhar State, Mr. H.D. Christian, Superintendent of the Gangpur State and Mr. Harihar Sahay, Munsiff of that State, for kind hospitality and help.

To my son, Rames Chandra Roy, M. Sc., B.L., who assisted me in my investigations, I owe the photographs and the anthropometrical measurements and their analysis.

Ranchi,
January, 1935.

S. C. R.

THE HILL BHŪIYĀS OF ŌRISSĀ.

CHAPTER I.

INTRODUCTORY.

(i) *Scope of the work.*

The Bhūiyā tribe, although numbering less than two million souls, has a very wide distributior. They are spread over more than half a dozen Provinces of India. They are found in varying numerical strength and social status in Bengal, Bihār, Ōṛissā Chōṭā-Nāgpur, Assam, the United Provinces, the Central Provinces, Central India Agency, and the Madras Presidency. Their principal stronghold at present is in the northern Tributary States of Ōṛissā. Here we may study them in various stages of cultural development, from the almost primitive Pāuṛi or Hill Bhūiyās of Keonjhar, Bonāi, and Pāl Lahera States to the thoroughly Hinduized Bhūiyā Zemindar families such as the Gaṛhatia family of Himgir and the Mahāpātra family of Nāgṛa in the Gāngpur State and some others, and the Pāik Bhūiyās or Khaṇḍāit Bhūiyās and Rājkuli and Prajā Bhūiyās, who hold intermediate positions. According to Risley,[1] "Some of the leading Bhuiya families have come to be Chiefs of the petty States of Ōrissa, and have merged their identity in the claim to quasi-Rajput descent". The Ōṛissā States form the centre of the southern section of the tribe, whereas the Chōṭā-Nāgpur District of Hāzāribāgh and the Bihār District of Gayā form the centre of what may be called the northern section of the tribe.

The Pāuṛi or Pābṛi or Hill section of the Southern Bhūiyās are, as I have said, comparatively more primitive in their customs and manners than the other sections of the tribe. But even among the Pāuṛi Bhūiyās, contact with Hindu culture has, to not a little extent, modified their primitive culture.

It is with these Hill Bhūiyās that the present volume deals. I hope to deal, in a future volume, with the Plains Bhūiyās of Ōṛissa as well as the Northern section of the tribe.

(ii) *Origin and Name.*

The name 'Bhūiyā' and its variants 'Bhūmiā',

1 *Tribes and Castes of Bengal*, Vol. I, p. 111. See also Dalton, *Ethnology of Bengal*, p. 140.

'Bhūihār', 'Bhūiyār', 'Bui' or 'Bhūi', *etc.*, are all derived from the Sanskrit word 'Bhūmi' meaning 'land'. One or other of the variants of the name appears to have been applied, in different parts of India, to widely separated communities, either in the sense of autochthones or children of the soil (*Bhūmi* or *Bhūi*), or in the sense of reclaimers or owners of the land (Bhūmihār) or as implying some connection with land (*Bhūiyā*).

Mr. B. C. Mazumdar, an Indian writer of some reputation, in an article published in 1907 [2] explained the name by saying that the Bhūiyās were so called because they were owners or 'masters of land' (*bhui*). But in the same article he also writes, "Even the thoroughly Hinduized Bhuiyas of Bamra tell us in giving their history and origin that it was Mother Earth who brought forth their first ancestor". In his later writings, [3] however, he opined that the original name of the tribe was 'Bhāiyan' which was rendered into 'Bhūiyā' by the Hindus. The reason he assigns for this view is that in the Buddhist work called *Majima*

2 *Modern Review*, Vol. I, pp. 148-153.

3 *Aborigines of Central India* (1927), pp. 31-42. *Orissa the in Making* (1926), p. 16.

Nikaya, the tribe is mentioned as the 'Bhainyans' or 'Bhayans' of *Ukkala Bassa* (i.e., Utkal or Ōṛissā).

Some pre-Aryan communities of India who call themselves by such titular names as Pāik (soldiers) or *Khaṇḍāit Pāik* (swordsmen) in Ōṛissā, *Ghāṭwār* or Ghāṭwāl (guard of the hill passes) in the Hāzāribāgh District of Chōṭā-Nāgpur, *Ṭikāit* (invested with the *ṭikā* or mark of investiture of landlordship) in the Sāntāl Parganās, and so forth, now resent being called 'Bhũiyās', although cogent reasons appear to exist for regarding them as genuine tribal Bhũiyās in origin.

(*iii*) *Tribal Bhũiyās.*

The process of gradual elevation from a lower social class to a higher, from a despised aboriginal tribe to a respectable Hindu caste, is a familiar phenomenon in India and has been going on for generations among the Bhũiyās as among several other tribes. Thus, of the landholding section of the Bhũiyās of the Santāl Parganās we read in Buchanan's *Bhagalpur Journal* (1810–1811): "Some men of the families of the Thakurs, Thakoits, and Baboos, whom in Captain Brown's time (1772 78) every one called Bhuiyas, and are now commonly called as such by other tribes, said that nobody called them so; that they were Surji Bangs and knew nothing of Bhuiyas or Onwars [4]. They would only acknowledge, that, before they obtained zemindaries, they were called Rai. They have now pure Brahmans as *Purohits* and *Sannyasis* or *Bramhacharis* for spiritual guides, and may form two annas of the population of *Belpata*. They follow the same rule in eating, *etc.*, as the Rajputs. One of the Bhuiyas, not of the blood of the Tekoits, says that both they and he are Bhuiyas and descended from the stock; but that the Tekoits and their kindred are of higher rank, and greater purity. He says the proper name of the tribe is Raj Bhuiyas. Those who are rich have Brahman Purohits (priests), but the poor content themselves with Purohits of their own who pray to the Sun and to Bosomati. They eat fowls, goats, swine, but not beef, and drink spirituous liquors" [5]. In his *Gaya Journal*, Buchanan writes, under date 15th December 1811 :—"In the

---

4 Mr. Oldham in his edition of Buchanan's *Bhagalpur Journal* suggests that "the word is 'Angawar', i.e. pertaining to Anga, the old name of the country adjoining Magadha on the east, just as we find a section of the Bhuiyas called Magahiya, i.e. belonging to Magadha" (Bihar). —*Journal of the Bihar and Orissa Research Society, XV, p.* 340, *Foot-note.*

5 *Ibid.*, pp. 356-357.

evening I was visited by Ohadut Singh, Tikayit of Domni (Dhamni) to whom all the country on this side of the Suknar belongs. He calls himself a Surajbangsi Rajput, and such of his people as live pure are called Ghatwals. Those who adhere to their old impurity, and eat beef, pork, fowls and every other abomination, are called Bhungiyas"[6]

Mr. (now Sir Hugh) McPherson, in his *Settlement Report of the Santal Parganas* (1898–1907) writes thus of these Bhūiyā Chiefs:—"Their Chiefs make the usual Kshattriya pretensions and calling themselves Surjabansis disclaim connection with their Bhuiya kinsmen. But the physical characteristics are all alike Dravidian, and in Captain Brown's time (1772–78) the Chiefs never thought of claiming to be other than Bhuiya. The highest Chiefs of the Bhuiyas are called Tikaits, and are supposed to have the mark of royalty. Inferior Chiefs are called Thakurs, and the younger members of noble Bhuiya families are called Babus"[7].

If some sections of the Bhūiyās now disclaim the tribal name and assume names indicative of a higher

6 *Journal of Francis Buchanan, Patna and Gaya* in 1811-1812 (Patna, 1925), p. 67.

7 *Settlement Report of the Santal Parganas* 1898—1907, pp. 20-21.

social status befitting their present improved position in life, there are others who, sunk lower in social position than most of their congeners elsewhere, deem it a point of honour to call themselves by their real tribal name of 'Bhūiyā'. Thus, the large pre-Aryan and pre-Dravidian population scattered all over Bihār and designated by their neighbours as *Mūsahārs* (*lit.*, rat-killers or rat-eaters), who, however, are but a degenerate section of the Bhūiyā tribe, insist on calling themselves by no other name than that of 'Bhūiyās'. Buchanan in his *Gaya Journal*, under date the 18th February, 1812, writes of village Arkal (Arwal):—"Many Musahars here; they are called Bunghiyas" [8]. To this day, as I have said, most Musahars, as they are called by their neighbours, call themselves *Bhūiyās*.

(*iv*) *Titular Bhūiyās.*

Again, some aboriginal tribes who are tribally quite distinct from the tribal Bhūiyās, as well as a few Hindu castes of high social status, take pride in the designation of 'Bhūihār' which is a variant of the name 'Bhūiyā', but is employed in a different sense from that of 'autochthon'. Thus, the descendants of

8 Buchanan's *Gaya Journal*, p. 163.

the aboriginal founders of villages in Chōṭā-Nāgpur, belonging whether to the Mūṇḍa or Orāon or Khāṛiā or Bhūmij tribes are known as *Bhūihārs*, not as a tribal name but as an honorific class-title denoting holders of a privileged class of tenures in land locally known as *Bhūihāri* tenures. And a sub-tribe of the Mūṇḍās, now found mostly in the Palāmau District, though cut off from the main body of the Mūṇḍā tribe of the Rānchi District by intervening settlements of Orāons and certain other tribes and castes, have long acquired the name of 'Bhūihārs' as a tribal designation, although possessing no Bhūihāri tenures, at any rate at the present day. Dr. Wise tells us that "the term (*Bhūiyā*) is also occasionally used as a surname of the despised Jogi (*Jugi*) weavers (of Bengal), and Bhuiya again is a Mahammadan title" [9].

In higher social spheres, some apparently Āryan landholding communities such as the Bhūihār Brāmhaṇs of Bihār and the Bhūmia Rājputs of Rājputānā take pride in the titular appellation of *Bhūihār* or *Bhūmiā*, as denoting a specially high status in relation to land. It may be noted that Buchanan in

9 *Journal of the Asiatic Society of Bengal*, Vol. XLII, Part I., p. 198.

his *Journal* (both of the Purnea and of the Shāhābād Districts) explains the name of the former as meaning "Bhungiya or Zemindar Bramhans". He says, "Both words imply their being employed in the management of land, the former in the Hindi, the latter in the Persian language...They are fond of being called Raja and Zemindar, and rent land without scruple. They indeed chiefly subsist by farming, although they will not hold the plough with their own hands.. Their manners are very similar to those of the Rajputs. They are fond of military life. They seem to me to be the remains of the Brachmani of Pliny, whom he represents as a people and not as a priesthood." [10]

In Rajputana, as we learn, "the Bhum tenure is very highly esteemed by Rajputs of all classes; so that some chiefs of superior rank think it no dishonour to be styled Bhumias...The Maharajah of Kishengarh, the Thakur of Fategarh, the Thakur of Juni, the Thakur of Bundunwaru, and the Thakur of Tantoi, are among the Bhumias of Ajmere" [11].

---

10 Francis Buchanan, *An Account of the District of Purnea*, 1809-10, p. 208,

11 *Rajputana Gazetteer*, Vol. II, p. 30.

The most notable application of the name 'Bhūiyā' as an honorific designation is that of the well-known 'Bāro-Bhūiyās' or Twelve Bhūiyās of Bengal. These were twelve most eminent and powerful men who possessed or secured extensive dominions in Bengal and rose to be great territorial chiefs during the disintegration and decay of the old Pāṭhān rule in Bengal and the rise of the Moghuls to power, and became famous in history under the name of 'Bāro-Bhūiyās'. They had not the remotest connection with the tribal Bhūiyās, two or three of them having been Mahomedans [12] and the rest high-caste Hindus. [13]

(v) *Confusion through Resemblance of Names.*

Through inadequate information, however, a connection was suggested or rather confusion made between the lowly aboriginal tribe of Bhūiyās in Bihār, Oṛissa and Chōṭā-Nāgpur, on the one hand, and, on the other, the high-class Bāro Bhūiyās of Eastern Ben-

---

12 These were.—Isa Khan Muhammad Ali of Khijirpur and Fazal Gazi of Bhawal and Chand Gazi of Chand Pratap.

13 These were:—Maharaja Pratapaditya Rai of Jasohar, Raja Kandarpa Narayan Rai of Chandradwipa, Lakshman Manikya of Bhulua, Hambir Malla of Bishunpur, Ganesh Rai of Dinajpur, Chand Rai and Kedar Rai of Sripur (Vikrampur), Mukunda Ram Rai of Bhushna, and Kangsa Narayan of Tahirpur. In some accounts one or two names differ.

gal and Assam and the Bhūmihār Brāmhans of Bihār and the United Provinces, by some earlier writers including Buchanan in his *Gorakhpur Journal*, although in the passage already quoted from his *Purnea Journal* [14], he appears to have appreciated the distinction between the aboriginal Bhūiyās and the Bhūmihār Brāmhaṇs. Thus, in Montgomery Martin's "*Eastern India*" which is an abridgement in three volumes of Dr. Francis Buchanan's (afterwards Buchanan Hamilton) Manuscript Journals and Reports known as the *Buchanan Manuscripts*, now in the Library of the India Office in London, we read:—

"The next princes (after Virat Raja who was contemporary with Yudhisthira and assisted him in the Mahābhārata War) of whom any traces remain, had the common name of Pal; and of these many works are to be seen in this district. In the Ayeen Akbery these princes are placed as a dynasty governing Bengal between the dynasties of Adisur, and Bollal Sen, which Abul Fazil considered as distinct. This, however, by no means accords with the common traditions

14 See p. 9 *ante*. *Vide* Buchanan's *Account of the District of Purnea*, 1809-10, J. B. O. R. S. edition, p. 208

of the country. These state that on a certain occasion twelve persons of very high distinction, and mostly named Pal, came from the west country to perform a religious ceremony on the Korotoya river, which formed the boundary-line between the ancient Hindu territorial divisions of Matsya and Kamrup but arrived too late; and as the next season for performing this ceremony was 12 years distant, they in the interval took up their abode here, built palaces and temples, dug tanks, and performed many other great works. *They are said to have been of a tribe called BHUNGIYA, to which also the Raja of Kasi (Benares R.) and Batiya belong.* From inscriptions remaining, and which have been published in the *Asiatic Researches*, it is well known, that the Pals were powerful kings; and according to Captain Wilford (*Asiatic Researches*, Vol. IX, p. 203), the first of them Bhupal or Mohipal, was alive in the year of Christ 1017, when his country was disturbed by the invasion of Sultan Mahmud, who took Kasi, and penetrated far into Bengal. It was probably on this occasion, that Mohipal retired to this remote part of the country with his family and principal officers, and it is probable that according to traditions they returned again to the west after a few years' stay, and after the terror of the Muhammadan invaders had subsided "[15]

Colonel Dalton, in his *Ethnology of Bengal*, published in 1872, on the basis of this statement of Buchanan, wrote as follows:—"At this time (the twelfth century) a part of Upper Assam was under a mysterious dynasty called the Bhara Bhuiya, of which no one has ever been able to make anything, but it is in all probability connected with the following tradition which Buchanan gives in his account of Dinajpur". After quoting the above tradition as given by Buchanan, Dalton writes:—"All the works still existing in the deserted forests on the northern bank of the Brahmaputra are attributed by the people to the *Bhara Bhungyas or Bhuyas*. They were probably connected with the great Bhuya tribe." [16] Later onin the same book, in discussing the affinities of the Koch tribe, Dalton writes:—"I consider they (the Koch of Cooch Behar and Assam) belong to the Dravidian stock and are probably a branch of the great Bhuya family, and we thus obtain a clue of the tradition of the *Bhara Bhuyas*,

15 *Vide* Montgomery Martin's *Eastern India* (comprising Buchanan's account of Dinajpur), vol. II, p. 612.

16 Dalton's *Ethnology of Bengal*, pp. 81-82.

to whose period of rule so many great works in Assam are ascribed". [17]

Again, in his account of the Bhūiyās, Dalton writes:– "In a preceding chapter on the population of Assam, I have noticed that a dynasty called the *Barah Bhuiya* once ruled in that province, and that the country to the north of the Brahmaputra from one end of the valley to the other, is full of great works ascribed to this people, and the origin of their dynasty is probably alluded to in the tradition given by Buchanan Hamilton in his account of Dinajpur, where it is narrated that twelve distinguished persons of the Bhungiya race came to the Koladyne [18] river, the boundary between Kamrup and the ancient Matsyadesh, took up their abode there, extended their sway, and executed great works. In Northern and Eastern Bengal and Chutia-Nagpur, the persons now included in the tribe are in the humblest positions of life, performing offices the most degrading, few of them attaining to the dignity of farmers or cultivators of their own fields; but there are grounds for supposing that some of the noblest families in Bengal

17 *Ibid.*, p. 92.

18 A corrupt form of *Kalindi*. *Vide* McCrindle's *Ancient India as described by Ptolemy* p. 215.

are sprung from this race, and they still hold high positions in the Jungle and Tributary Mahals. . The proprietors of the estates surrounding the Parisnath hill in the Manbhum and Hazaribagh districts, though pretending to be Kshetryas, are Bhuiyas, and they have not been able to efface the characteristic physical traits of their origin "[19]

Dr. James Wise, however, in an article published in the *Journal of the Asiatic Society of Bengal*[20] in the years 1875 and 1876, as Risley points out, " worked out with the patience and thoroughness which mark all his research the obscure history of these twelve Bhuiyas or landlords, and showed that their designation had so little of a tribal character about it that at least one of them was a Mahomedan. They were in fact merely territorial chiefs of portions of Eastern Bengal and Assam ". And the researches of Dr. Wise were so convincing that one should have thought that the question was finally settled.

Cunningham in 1884 in his Archaeological Report for the year 1981-82, wrote:- "I think, Dalton is wrong

---

19 Dalton's *Ethnology of Bengal*, p. 139.

20 *Journal of the Asiatic Society of Bengal*, 1874, Pt. I, p. 197, and 1875, Pt. I, p. 181

when he carries them (the Bhūiyās) to Northern Bengal, and makes them the conquerors of Kuch-Bihar and Assam. He has apparently followed Buchanan in confounding the Bhuihars or Bhumihars of Northern Bengal and Bihar with the Bhuiyas of Shahabad. The latter are an acknowledged aboriginal tribe, while the former profess to be the descendants of Brahmans who took to agriculture as an occupation. Hence their name of Bhumi-hara, or 'Land-tillers'......In Barendra, or Northern Bengal, the people still speak of the *Bara Bhuihar* as the former rulers of the country, and I believe they refer to the wellknown dynasty of the Pal Rajas, whose caste or tribal name is never mentioned in the inscriptions" [21]

This discarded theory of the identity of the aboriginal Bhūiyā tribe with the historical Bāro-Bhūiyās of Eastern Bengal and the legendary Bāro-Bhūiyās of Assam, was temporarily revived by Mr. B. C. Mazumdar as noticed above. Such additional proofs as were put forward by him will not bear criticism as will be seen from a paper published by me in the *Journal of*

---

21 *Archaeological Report*, Vol. XVII, p. 134.

the Bihar & Orissa Research Society[22]. It should, however, be noted that Mr. Mazumdar himself has since discarded this theory [23]. In the following section I shall discuss the racial affinities of the tribe.

---

22 *Ibid.*, vol XVIII, (1932), pp. 57—78.
23 *Vide Man in India*, vol XII (1932), pp. 320—333.

CHAPTER II.

(i) *Affinities and Population.*

In his *Account of Orissa*, published in 1813, Stirling [24] included the Bhūiyās among the Kōl or Mūṇḍā tribes. He wrote:—"The Coles are divided into thirteen different tribes, viz, Kol, Lurka Kol, Chowang, Sarvanti, Dhurowa, Bahuri, Bhumian or Bhumiah, Khandwal, Santal, Sour, Bhumij, Batholi, and Amavat. Their original country is said to be Kolhant Des, which the natives describe as a hilly tract lying between Moharbanj, Singbhum, Jynty Bonye, Keonjher, and Dalbhum; their encroachments on Moherbanj have been felt as serious; some tribes (the Bhumias) are found settled in the back parts of Nilgiri, and from their restless disposition and constant endeavours to extend their possessions, they have proved troublesome to their neighbours even to the powerful Keonjher Raja. The Coles are a hardy and athletic race, black

24 *An Account, Geographical, Statistical and Historical of Orissa Proper, or Cuttack*, pp. 202—3

and ill-favored in their countenances, ignorant and savage to the last degree, but their houses, built entirely of wood, are said to exhibit a considerable degree of neatness and comfort, and they carry on a very extensive cultivation; their arms are the bow and arrow, and small iron battle-axe called *Tangi*, in the use of which they display much skill and dexterity".'

Dalton, [25] however, demurred to Stirling's classification of the Bhūiyās among the 'Kōl' or Mūṇḍā tribes. He wrote:—"Mr. G. Campbell, in his *Ethnology of India* suggests that they (the Bhūiyās) are connected with the 'Buis' of Madras and the Central Provinces. This is probable. The Bhuiya feature is, on the whole, of a Tamulian cast, and it is in the southern frontier of Bengal that we find them in greatest strength and greatest purity. They belong, I dare say, to the southern, rather than to the northern races,—the Dravidian rather than the Kolarian......They form an important element in the population of Singbhum. Tradition says, they were once dominant in the western and southern parts of that country, but were subjugated by the 'Hos' (Kols). In the tributary states of Gang-

25 *Ethnology of Bengal*, p. 140.

pur, Bonai, Keonjher, and Bamra, they are almost the only class possessing proprietary right under the chiefs.

"They are the barons from whom those chiefs originally derived their authority, and are either the support or the sap of that authority, according to the side they take in the politics of the State. They have, in all these little governments that useful institution—an opposition. Mr. Stirling, in his Account of Orissa, classes them among the Kols, but there are no grounds that I know of for so connecting them. As I have said above, they appear to me to be linked with the Dravidian rather than the Kolarian tribes. They were the veritable monkeys that aided Rama in his invasion of Lanka. All the country now occupied by the Bhuiyas is full of traditions of that great hero. He is the favourite god of the Hinduized Bhuiyas......Hanuman, the general of the ape army, was Pawan-ka-put, 'the son of the wind', and the Bhuiyas to the south of Singbhum call themselves Pawanbans, the children of the wind, to this day. That they were the apes of the Ramayana, there can therefore be no doubt". McPherson in his *Settlement Report of the Santal Parganas* (p. 20) probably follows Dalton when he writes, "the

Bhuiyas belong to the same Dravidian Stock as the hill Males".

In his section on the 'Bendkars of Keonjhar, or Savaras', [26] Dalton writes:, "It is difficult to regard them otherwise than as members of the great Bhuiya family and thus connecting them we link the Bhuiyas and Savaras, and give support to the conjecture that the former are Dravidian. The Savaras, occupying the country between the Kandh Maliahs or hill tracts and the Godavery, retain a primitive form of speech, but the BENDKAR Savaras that I have fallen in with have no language of their own and no tradition that they ever possessed one. The form of speech used is Uriya, and those living in mixed villages conform to many customs of Hindu Uriyas of inferior castes. The points of difference are, however, very noticeable; for on those points they follow exactly the customs of the Hill Bhuiyas, and the independent Bendkar communities have all the Bhuiya characteristics....It is in their feasts, festivals, amusements, and methods of bringing about marriage that the points of resemblance between them and the Bhuiyas are most marked".

26 *Ibid* p. 149.

Dalton's admission that the Savaras belong to the same racial group as the Bhūiyās is an admission of the 'Kolarian' or Mūṇḍā origin of the Bhūiyās. For, Sir George Grierson in his *Linguistic Survey of India* [27] has proved beyond doubt that the Savara speech is a Mūṇḍā dialect; and the evidence of customs as well as physical features all point to the Mūṇḍā cultural and racial affinities of the Savaras. In fact, all contemporary authorities agree that the Savaras are one of the Mūṇḍā or 'Kōl' tribes. Thus, Russel, in his *Tribes and Castes of the Central Provinces* comes to the conclusion that "the Savars must be classed as a Munda or Kolarian tribe", and says, "Since Colonel Dalton identified the Bhuiyas with the Savaras of Chota-Nagpur, [28] his evidence appears really to be in favour of the Kolarian origin of the Bhuiyas". In the Indian *Census Report* of 1931, Dr. Hutton too rightly classes the Bhuiyas in the 'Kol' or Mūṇḍā group. Here I may note that in the course of my ethnographical investgations among the Hill Khāṛiās of the Mayurbhanj State in Ōṛissā and also in the Manbhum

27 *Ibid* Vol. XIV, p, 217

28 *Ibid* Vol. II, pp. 308—9

District of Chōṭā-Nāgpur, I was informed by some old Khāṛiās that according to tradition their original ancestors were a couple named 'Sabbar Buṛhā', and 'Sabbar Buṛhī' (the 'Old Sabbar man'; and the 'Old Sabbar woman'), and that the tribal name of the Khāṛiās or at least of one section of the Khāṛiā tribe was 'Sabbar Bhūiyā'. This name obviously points to an ethnical connection of the Bhūiyās with the Mūṇḍā-speaking Khāṛiās and Savars. [29] It is not however, improbable, that in the course of their migrations, some intermixture with the Dravidian-speaking aborigines may have occurred.

Besides the tribe which goes by the specific name of Bhūiyā there are other tribes and sub-tribes who really form sections of the wide spread Bhūiyā people. I have already referred to the Musāhars of Bihār who are generally acknowledged to be a section of the Bhūiyās. Russel is of opinion that "the Baiga tribe of the Central Provinces are really a branch of the Bhūiyas", and that "the Bhaina, Bhunjia and Binjhwar tribes who still reside in this country (Chattisgarh

---

29 It may be noted that there are practically no Savaras in Chota-Nagpur but that their home is in Ōṛissā and in the Ganjam District of the Madras Presidency.

States of the Central Provinces) can all be recognised as offshoots of the Baigas", and that "the Binjhwars or Binjhals are an aristocratic subdivision of the Baigas" [30]. Crooke writes that "the Bhuiyas of Mirzapore seem to be clearly a branch of the Bhuiya tribe of Chota-Nagpur with whom their section-names establish their identity". Crooke further writes that "the Bhuiyas are distinguished with great difficulty from the Bhuiyars with whom they are doubtless closely connected". [31]

Sir Herbert Risley in his *Tribes and Castes of Bengal* [32] gives the following different names or rather divisions of the Bhūiyā people:– "Bhuiya, Bhuinya, Bhuinhar, Bhumiya, Musahar, Naik, Khandait, Khandait Paik, Ghatwal, Ghatwar, Tikayat, Rajwar, Rai-Bhuiya, Sardar, Puran".

It may be noted that the Purāns who are identified by Risley with the Bhūiyās claim racial affinity with the Mūṇḍā tribes of the Khāṛiā and the Savara. Accor-

30 Russel, *Castes and Tribes*, Vol. II, p. 311.

31 Crooke, *Tribes and Castes of the North-Western Provinces*, Vol. I, pp. Vol. II, *Appendix* I, p. 11.

32 Risley, *Tribes and Castes*, Vol. II, p. 180. "Puran......a synonym for Bhuiya in Mohorbhanj".

ding to the tradition of origin of the Hinduised Purāṇ caste which I learnt in Mayurbhanj, "the semen of Bhagwān (God) fell on the earth and produced an egg resembling a pea-hen's egg. From the white of this egg sprang the first ancestor of the Purāṇs, from its membranous coating the progenitor of the Savaras, from its shell the first ancestor of the Khāṛiās, and from the yolk the ancestor of the Bhanja Rājās of Mayurbhanj." This tradition, again, lends further support to the Mūṇḍā affinities of the Bhūiyā tribe.

In the latest *Census Report of India (1931)*, the Bhūiyās are rightly included among the Kōl group and are lumped together along with the Baigās, Bhainās, Binjhwārs, Bhāriās, Bhūmiās, Bhūnjiās, Ghāṭwārs, Kādārs (Bengal), Khetwāris, Naiyās, and Rāos. But presumably by an oversight the Musāhar section of the Bhūiyās has been included in the Tables among the Dravidian-speaking Orāon group [33].

Cultural Affinities.

Although there is very little difference in the physical characteristics and anthropometrical indices

33 *Census of India*, 1931, Vol. I, Part II, *Imperial Tables*, p. 523.

of the 'Kolarian' or Muṇḍā-speaking tribes on the one hand, and the Dravidian-speaking hill-tribes on the other, and both the groups may, I think, be properly classed as Pre-Dravidian, the cultural characteristics of the two groups exhibit marked differences in some respects. And the cultural affinities of the Bhuiyās, as I have said, are with the Mūṇḍā tribes of the Central Belt of India, and not with the Dravidian-speaking tribes of the South. In fact, Muṇḍā or 'Kōl' culture elements are prominently in evidence among the Bhuiyās although they are overlaid more or less by a veneer of Hindu culture varying in density according to the social position of the particular section or family.

The cult of ancestral spirits or 'house spirits' (ōṛā-bōngākō) who are ceremonially conducted to the house after the burial or cremation of a dead person and installed in a special tabernacle (āding or bitar) in the house, preferably in the kitchen, the cult of the spirit of their ancestral hill (*Buru Bonga*) and *Pāt*, the use of stones in burial,—which are among the distinctive features of Mūṇḍā culture,—may still be seen in full vigour among the Pāuṛis or Hill Bhuiyās of the Ōṛissā

States, and in more or less mutilated or attenuated forms among the sophisticated Plains Bhūiyās. 'Elopement marriage' and 'Seizure marriage' which are marked features of Pāuṛi Bhūiyā culture have their analogues among most other Mūṇḍā-speaking tribes. Among other cultural traits which the Bhūiyās share with other 'Kōl' or Mūṇḍā tribes the following may be mentioned:– the general features of village organization and federation of a group of villages, the general features of kinship organization and kinship nomenclature, several customs appertaining to birth, childhood, adolescence, marriage and death, the custom which requires the headman of a group of federated villages to take the first morsel of food in a tribal feast, the practice of taking oath on a tiger's skin or by touching a little earth, and the trial of a suspected dilinquent by the ordeal of dipping the hand in boiling liquid or carrying a red-hot iron on the hands. The worship of Bīrs or hero-gods (such as *Tulsī Bīr*, *Hanumān Bīr*, *Basar Bīr*, *Ladu Bīr*, *Barchhi Bīr*, etc.) among some sections of the northern Bhūiyās would appear to be a special development and extension of the Mūṇḍā cult of ancestor-spirits.

(ii) *Sub-divisions of the Bhūiyās.*

Some old Bhūiyās in the Tributary States of Ōṛissā whom I questioned on the subject gave me the following names of the different sections of the tribe: *Deś Bhūiyā* or *Māṛ* or *Māl Bhūiyā* represented mainly by the *Pāuṛi Bhūiyās; Prajā Bhūiyā* or *Rāutāli Bhūiyā, Bāthūḍi Bhūiyā, Sāntāṛi Bhūiyā* or *Sāntāli Bhūiyā, Ḍonsoṇā* or *Ḍaṇḍsenā Bhūiyā, Rājkuli Bhūiyā* or *Baṛ Bhūiyā, Sāontiā Bhūiyā, Khaṇḍāit Bhūiyā* or *Pawanbaṁs Bhūiyā, Khāṭhi* or *Kāṭṭi* or *Kāṭṭiāri Bhūiyā, Naksiyā Bhūiyā, Hākē*[34] *Bhūiyā, Dākē Bhūiyā, Rikhiāsan Bhūiyā, Musāhar Bhūiyā,* and *Ghāṭwār Bhūiyā.*

A few of these names such as *Hākē Bhūiyā, Dākē Bhūiyā, Meṛhā-tāṛi* and *Naksiyā Bhūiyā,* are probably descriptive names or nicknames not definitely applied to any particular tribe or section. The term "*Deś Bhūiyā*" appears to be a generic term for the more primitive sections of the Bhūiyās of which the genuine Pāuṛi Bhūiyā of the hills is the typical—perhaps now the only—representative. They distinguish themselves from the other sections of the Bhūiyās by adopting the

34 *Hākē*, it is interesting to note, is a Mūṇḍā word meaning 'axe'.

'bānghy' or wooden carrying-pole for their *santak* or distinctive tribal emblem whereas other sections have either the sword (*Khaṇḍā*) or the axe for their *Santak.* The bulk of the Plains Bhūiyās are known as *Rāutāli Bhūiyās* or *Prajāli* [35] *Bhūiyās* (particularly in the Gāngpur State) most of whom have agriculture for their occupation. In the Hāzāribāgh District they are sometimes called *Bhūmin Bhūiyās.*

Those Plains Bhūiyās some of whom still form, and whose ancestors had once formed,—part of the militia of the States they respectively inhabit are known as *Pāik* (soldier) *Bhūiyās* or *Khaṇḍāit* (swordsmen) *Bhūiyās* or *Khaṇḍāit Pāik Bhūiyās.* They go by such titles (*pāris*) as *Nāik, Ohdār, Pardhān, Ganzhu, Kōṭwār, Rāut, Baṛāik, Amāt*, etc. The *Prajā Bhūiyās* and in some places the *Pāik Bhūiyās* have sub-divisions amongst them known severally as *Eksai-ghariā* (100-family-groups), *Panchsai ghariā* (500-family-groups) etc. The *Rājkōli* or *Rajkuli Bhūiyās* are reputed to have originated from the union of Bhūiyā women with male members of the Rāj families. Many of them are employed as

35 'Prajāli' and 'Rautāli' would appear to be local variants of the same class-name.

personal servants in the Rāj families and other respectable families.

The title 'Pawanbaṁś' or Pabanōs' (*lit*, offspring of Pawan or 'the God of the Wind') is claimed by some Bhūiyās in assertion of their descent from Hanumān (the son of the Wind-god Pawan) the devoted follower of Rāmchandra—the hero of the Rāmāyana.

The tribal name '*Rikhiāsan Bhūiyā*' is again claimed by many Bhūiyās of the northern section who derive the name from the fact that their ancestors lived on the roots or from of the jungle, like the ancient Hindu *Mūnis* and *Rishis* (holy sages). Some Bhūiyās claim that their original ancestors were actually the ancient *Mūns* or *Mūnis* (holy Hindu sages). And more than one origin myth of the Bhūiyās is based on this supposition. Thus, one such myth which was recounted to me by some Bhūiyās of village Māṇḍu in the Hāzāribāgh District runs as follows: "*Rikhmun* (corruption of *Rishi Muni*), our tribal ancestor, was one and the same as *Tulsī Bīr* to whom worship is still offered by us Bhūiyās. *Tūlsī Bīr* lived at Maner (now in the Patna District). He was the youngest of seven brothers of whom Bhagwān (God) was the eldest. One day while Tūlsī Bīr with his wooden sandals on, was going to bathe in the Ganges he saw a dead calf in front of the house of his brother Bhagwān. As Tulsī Bīr was the youngest of the brothers he was asked by his eldest brother Bhagwān to throw away the carcase of the calf. Tulsī Bīr at first declined to do so on the ground that it would mean ceremonial pollution, and social degradation. Whereupon Bhagwān said, "No; if you take a bath after throwing away the carcase, you will be purified and we shall eat with you". And so Tulsī Bīr did as he was told to do. On his return after a bath he found that a plantain tree had shot up over the spot where the carcase had been thrown away. And before he could leave the spot the tree attained its full growth and bore fruit and the fruit ripened. Rikh-mun ate the fruit and went back to his brothers and told them what happened. The brothers told him, "You have eaten beef. So we won't eat with you". Tulsī Bīr protested and said he had not eaten beef. Bhagwān said, "All right; let me test you". And Bhagwān placed five fruits on his neck. And thereupon five lumps of beef came out of Tulsī Bīr's mouth. Since then nobody would eat with him, and he became 'Rikhmun' whereas his other brothers became higher *Mūns* such as *Sūruj Mūn* (the Sun God), *Chandramā* (the Moon-deity), and *Devī*. Rikhmun's descendants, the Bhūiyās, migrated from Maner to different places, and became Sūrujbaṁśīs, Chandra-baṁśīs, *etc*. *Tulsī Bīr* is the highest of the *Bīrs* or ancestral gods of these Bhūiyās.

The Rājwārs, it may be noted, have a similar origin myth. Buchanan informs us that the Rājwārs of Bihār told him "that their common ancestor was a certain Rishi who had two sons. From the eldest are descended the Rajwars, who became soldiers and obtained their noble title; from the younger are descended the Musahars, who have obtained their name from eating rats, which the Rajwars reject".

Some Musāhars of village Hāsānpur in thana Fūlwāri of the Pāṭnā District gave me the following tradition of their origin: "We are the descendants of Rikhmūn. Rikhmūn dived into the ocean in search of something. He came out with some dirt. Out of that dirt were born the Musāhars. Our ancestors originally lived on hill-ranges".

The name *Sāntāṛi Bhūiyā* would appear to refer to the Sāntāl tribe whose racial affinity with the

Bhūiyās is thus recognised by the Bhūiyās themselves. Similarly the name '*Bāthūḍi Bhūiyā*' obviously refers to the Bāthūḍi tribe (numbering 72,893 in the Census of 1931) found mainly in the Mayurbhanj (45,049) and Keonjhar (23,637) States besides some (4,202) in the Nīlgiri State and two stray individuals in the Āṭhmalik, two in the Bāmrā and one in the Gāngpur States of Ōṛissā. Regarding the *Bāthūḍis* the only information given by Risley is that they form "a small aboriginal tribe of uncertain origin found in the Tributary States of Ōṛissā".[36] Their population has not been separately enumerated in the Census. My own investigation into the religion and customs of the Bāthūḍis of the Mayurbhanj State have led me to the conclusion that the Bāthūḍis are really a Hinduised branch of the Bhūiyā tribe. They have come sufficiently under the influence of Hinduism to accept the services of Brāmhaṇ priests at their marriages. They also recognise a tribal head styled *Mahāpātra* and his assistant styled *Baṛa-Nāyak*, both appointed by the State and a similarly appointed Brāmhaṇ 'spiritual' superior styled 'Bramhā' whose directions must be followed as to the method of expia-

36 *Tribes and Castes of Bengal*, Vol. I, p. 77.

tion for the sinfulness which a family may incur by such 'sins' as the death of a female member in pregnancy (*stri-badh*) and the accidental death of a cow (*gō-badh*).

The *Sāontiā Bhūiyā* of the list given above obviously refers to the agricultural tribe or sub-tribe of *Sāontis* who, too, though locally regarded as a separate tribe would appear to be another Hinduised section of the Bhūiyās. Neither Risley nor the Census Reports make any mention of them. From my investigations amongst them in the Tributary States of Ōṛissā, I am led to the conclusion that the Sāontis, like the Bāthūḍis, form a branch of the great Bhūiyā tribe. In physical features they exhibit no marked difference from the Bhūiyās. In characteristic cultural traits, too, they resemble the Bhūiyās. Both the Sāontis and the Bāthūḍis have the same *Chāngu nāṭ* or characteristic dances to the tune of the *Chāngu* drum as the Bhūiyās have. Sāonti and Bāthūḍi maidens, like their Pāuṛi Bhūiyā sisters, go to neighbouring villages, to dance with the youth of those villages. The Sāontis and the Bāthūḍis, like the Pāuṛis, are fond of eating the small flying insects locally called 'kalāi pōk'. Their tribal heads called 'Beherās' are appointed by the State. But the Sāontis have been Hinduised to such an extent that they claim to belong to the Zemindār 'hūdā'. In social matters they are governed by the decisions of an officer of their own tribe appointed by the Rājā and styled 'Berājāl'. The office descends to the eldest son of the last holder. The Berājāl has the unique privilage of riding a palanquin within the State. In social customs and in worship the Sāontis have much in common with the Bāthūḍis and the Hinduised Bhūiyās. The Rājwārs are generally recognised as a branch of the Bhūiyās.

Buchanan records a tradition that he obtained from certain Rājwārs in Bihār that "their common ancestor was a certain Rishi, who had two sons. From the eldest are descended the Rājwārs, who became soldiers and obtained their noble title; from the younger are descended the *Musahars*, who have obtained their name from eating rats, which Rajwars reject"

Leaving aside such communities as the *Sāontis*, the *Bāthuḍis* and the Hinduised Rājwārs and the depressed and lonely Musāhars who are now all well on the road to recognition as separate tribes or castes, the

Bhūiyās proper may be roughly classified into the following divisions:— (1) the primitive *Deś Bhūiyā* represented mainly by the Pāuṛi or Hill Bhūiyā of the hills of Keonjhar, Bonāi and Pāl Laherā States; (2) the quasi-military *Khaṇḍāit Bhūiyā* or *Pāik Bhūiyā* of the Ōṛissā Plains and the southern parts of Chōṭā-Nāgpur; (3) the mixed *Rājkōli* or *Rājkuli* Bhūiyās of the Ōṛissā States; (4) the *Prajā Bhūiyā*, or *Rāutāli Bhūiyā* of Ōṛissā and south-eastern Chōṭā Nāgpur who live by agriculture or in some cases agricultural labour; and (5) the land-holding *Ghāṭwār Bhūiyā* or *Tikāit Bhūiyā* or *Rāe Bhūiyā* of the Santāl Parganās, Hāzāribāgh, Gayā, Monghyr and Bhāgalpur Districts, who generally wear the sacred thread and call themselves Surujbaṁśi Rājputs.

(iii) *Population and Distribution: Census of 1921.*

In the Tables Volume of the *Census of India* for 1921, the total Population of the Bhūiyā tribe is put down as 633,222, and that of the Musāhars who form a branch of the same tribe is given as 635,102. Of the former it is noted that they are found in Assam and in Bihār and Ōṛissā, and of the latter that they live in the

Province of Bihār and Ōṛissā. The Table Volume of Bihār and Ōṛissā for the same Census gives the Bhūiyā population of the Province as 578,864 and the Table Volume for Assam shows a Bhūiyā population of 54, 358, thus making up the total of 633,222. But over and above this we find in the Tables Volume of the Census of Bengal for 1921 that the Bhūiyā population of that Province is put down as 60,422. In the Central Provinces, too, there is a considerable population of Bhūiyās. Russel in his article on the "*Bhuiya, Bhumihar, Bhumia*" in his *Tribes and Castes*, published in 1916 wrote:—"The Bhuiyas numbered more than 22,000 persons in the Central Provinces in 1911, being found in the Surguja and Jashpur States". The exact figure given in the *Central Provinces Census* Tables for 1911, is 27,620, out of which as many as 12,581 were found in Surguja, and 7,311 in Jashpur, and 2,600 in the Korea State. The name of the tribe is given as '*Bhūinhār*'. In the Central Provinces Census Tables for 1921, however, the figure has gone down to 11,970 for the whole Province of which 1,389 were in Surguja, 5,733 in Jashpur and 3,041 in Korea. In the Central India Agency, the population of 'Bhumias' is giᴧen as

2,985 in 1921. None of these figures appears to include Bhūiyā converts to Christianity. Besides these, 635,102 Musāhars were enumerated in Bihār and Chōṭā-Nāgpur in 1921; and the Musāhars are recognised as a degraded section of the Bhūiyās. Russel is of opinion that "the Baiga tribe of the Central Provinces are really a branch of the Bhuiyas", and that "the Bhaina, Bhunjia and Binjhwar tribes who still reside in this country (Chattisgarh States of the Central Provinces) can all be recognised as offshoots of the Baigas", and that "the Binjhwars or Binjhals are an aristocratic subdivision of the Baigas". Crooke writes that the Bhūiyās of Mirzapur seem to be clearly a branch of the Bhūiyā tribe of Chōṭā-Nāgpur with whom their section-names establish their identity". Crooke further writes that "the Bhuiyas are distinguished with great difficulty from the Bhuiyars with whom they are doubtless closely connected".

In the Census Tables for the United Provinces, no population figures for Bhūiyās are separately given.

The Bhumias of the Jeypore Zemindari in the Agency Tracts of the Madras Presidency, are identified with the Baigas of the Central Provinces, and appear to be a section of the Bhūiyā tribe. Mr. Russel, as we have seen, gives 'Bhumia' as a variant of the name 'Bhūiyā' in the Central Provinces.

Census of 1931.—In the Census of 1931, the Bhūiyā tribe in Assam has not been separately returned but has been included under the heading "others". So figures are available only for Bengal, Bihār and Ōṛissā, the Central Provinces, Central India Agency, and the Sikkim States. I am indebted to the Census Commissioner of India (Dr. J.H. Hutton) for the following Statement regarding the Bhūiyā population in 1931:—

Figures for the Tribe (or Caste) Bhūiyā are returned by the following provinces:– Bengal, Bihār and Orissa, Central Provinces, United Provinces, Central India Agency and Sikkim State. Assam has not returned this Caste nor has Madras. The total figures by religion are as follows:—

Religion.	Persons.	Males.	Females.
Total	*702,474*	*347,686*	*354,788*
Hindu	691,988	342,371	349,617
Tribal	10,450	5,296	5,154
Christian	36	19	17

The above figures *include* those returned as "Bhūihār" by the Central Provinces and Central India Agency (where the term Bhūiyā has not been used): these figures of Bhūihār by religion are given below :—

Religion.	Persons.	Males.	Females.
Total	*26,242*	*13,391*	*12,851*
Hindu	21,553	10,957	10,596
Tribal	4,689	2,434	2,255

The Āgāriyā figures returned by the United Provinces include those of Bhūiyā. And as the Bhūiyā figures cannot be separated, these are not included in the above total but given below for reference :—

Religion.	Persons.	Males.	Females.
Total	*69,141*	*34,271*	*34,870*
Hindu	68,044	33,685	34,359
Muslim	1,097	586	511

They include the following tribes or castes :—

Āgāriyā, Bhūiyā, Bhūiyār, Cherō Ghāsiyā, Khairāhā, Khāṛwār, Mājhwār, Pānkhā, Pārāhiyā, Pātari."

Although in the Madras Report no separate figures are given for the Bhūiyās, we find that in the Vizagapatam and Ganjam Agencies, the population of *Bhūmiās or Bhaiyas* is given as respectively 31,473 and 181, or 31,654 in all.

For the other Provinces, the population figures as gleaned from the Census Reports of 1931, are as follows :—

BHUIYA POPULATION IN 1931

Province.	Total			Hindu		Tribal		Christians.		Muslims		
	Persons.	Males.	Femals.	M.	F.	M.	F.	M.	F.	M.	F.	
Bengal.	50,405	28,159	22,246	27,611	21,759	548	487	...	...	...	...	
Sikkim.	3	3	...	3	...	...	...	...	...	...	...	
Bihar & Orissa.	625,824	306,133	319,691	303,800	317,262	2,314	2,412	19	17	...	...	
Central I. Agency	614	310	304	310	304	...	...	...	...	...	...	Bhūin-
Central Provinces and Berar.	26,242	13,391	12,851	10,957	10,596	2,434	2,255	...	...	...	...	hārs.
Total ...	703,088	348,096	355,092	342,781	339,927	5,296	5,154	19	17	...	...	*
United Provinces.	69,141	34,271	34,870	33,685	34,359	...	...	...	...	586	511	

MUSAHAR BHUIYA
(all Hindus)

	Persons.	Males.	Females
Bihar & Orrisa.	720,057	361,825	358,226

* Bhuiyas included with Agariyas, Cheros etc.; proportion and total not known.

Thus, the total population of the Bhūiyā tribe in all its branches may be approximately estimated at about one and a half millions and they are found to extend from Sikkim and the Bengal District of Jalpāiguṛi on the north to the Ganjām District of Madras (portion of which will shortly be included in the new Province of Ōṛissā) in the South, and from the Tripura State of Bengal in the north-east to the Cawnpore, Lucknow and Sitapur Districts of the United Provinces in the north-west. The distribution of the Bhūiyā population thus ranges over different districts of Bengal, Bihār, Ōṛissā, Chōṭā-Nāgpur, the United Provinces, the Central Provinces, Central India Agency, and Madras.

CHAPTER III.

HABITAT; PHYSICAL AND MENTAL CHARACTERISTICS

(i) *The Pauri Bhūiyā Country and its Natural Features*

The Ōṛissā Feudatory States of Kēōnjhar and Bonāi adjoin Chōṭā-Nāgpur on their north; and the State of Pāl Laherā lies wedge-like between these two States on their south-west and south-east respectively. The extensive mass of tangled hills and elevated valleys that run from north to south in the form of a crescent along the western borders of the Kēōnjhar State and stretches into the Bonāi State on its north-west and the Pāl Laherā State on its south-west forms part of the southern extension of the Central Hill Belt of India. This range is the watershed of the Baitarani river on the north and the Brāmhaṇi on the south. These jungle-clad hills and high wooded valleys in the north-west of the Kēōnjhar, north-east of the Bonāi and north of the Pāl Laherā States form the home of the Pāuṛi or Hill Bhūiyās. And in the plains at the foot of these hills may be seen the Hinduised and semi-Hinduised Plains Bhūiyās who have spread north through Chōṭā-Nāgpur and the Santāl Parganās to Bihār, and west through Sambalpur and the Ōṛissā States to the Central Provinces.

The habitat of the Hill Bhūiyās or Pāuṛi Bhūiyā section, in particular, lies, roughly speaking, between 21° and 22° North Latitude and 85° and 86° East Longitude.

For their neighbours the Pāuṛi Bhūiyās have in close proximity to most of their settlements a few families of animistic Hos and Orāōns who are comparatively recent immigrants from Chōṭā-Nāgpur besides families of pastoral Hindu Gouṛ-Goālās who have long made the country their home.

The land of the Pāuṛi Bhūiyās rises several hundred feet above the central valley of the Brāhmaṇi and consists of a series of inaccessible hill ranges covered with tangled forests in which the tiger, the panther, the hyena and the wild dog prowl about for their animal prey and, if possible, for some stray human victim, where the wild elephant, the bison, the wild pig (*Sus Indicas*) and the bear roam about in search of food and occasionally cause great damage to the scanty maize and other crops and vegetables grown on the hill slopes by the Pāuṛi Bhūiyā. The *nilgāi* (*Portex pictus*), the *sambar* (*Rusa aritotelis*), the *chithal* or spotted deer (*Axis maculatus*), the mouse deer (*Meminna Indica*) and the four-horned antelope (*Fat-recerus quadricornis*) are pretty common in these heavy jungles, and constitute occasional game for the Hill Bhūiyā. who, however, live chiefly on vegetable diet.

During my stay in these parts I heard frequent complaints of wild elephants and wild pigs damaging the vegetable crop of my Pāuṛi friends, and in my journey through these jungle-covered hill ranges, foot-prints and fresh excrement of wild elephants were on several occasions pointed out to me as indicating the recent presence of those animals. Of an evening one may expect to meet with bears on his way through the Pāuṛi country, and one afternoon in the Pāuṛi parganā of Bonai, one of my party bagged a huge wild pig which came in our way and, when killed, required four strong men to carry its carcase. Pea-fowls and jungle fowls abound in these forests.

The *Sāl* (*Shorea robusta*) predominates in these forests, and among other important trees are the *Sisu* (*Dalbergia sissoo*), the *Asan* (*Terminalia tomentosa*), the *Kusum* (*Schleichera tringa*), and the *Peāsāl* (*Pterocarpus marsupium*). Jungle fruits, edible roots and wild herbs of a few varieties found in their native jungles are utilized by the Hill Bhūiyās to supplement their scanty stock of food; and certain herbs and roots of their jungles are used by them for medicinal purposes.

Climate.

The home of the Pāuṛi Bhūiyā lies, as I have said, on a much higher elevation than the plains of Keōnjhar, Bonāi and Pāl Laherā and is consequently much cooler and pleasanter. The hills rise to an elevation of from 2,000 to over 3,500 feet above sea level. Owing, however, to the presence of heavy tangled forests, the climate is at certain seasons unhealthy and malarious, although the indigenous population resist malaria much better than outsiders. Spleen among children is not uncommon and most people are liable to attacks of fever, especially after the rains.

(ii) Physical Features of the Hill Bhuiyas.

Physical Features. Men and women are well-proportioned, muscular, of medium height and rather light build. The hair is black and plentiful on the head, but generally scanty on the rest of the body, though men with good beards and whiskers are occasionally seen. The hair is ordinarily wavy, but straight hair is occasionally met with and, on the other hand, in some instances the hair has a tendency to curl, and I met one or two men with distinctly curly or rather wooly hair. The mouth and teeth are well formed and the eyes are straight and of medium size, sometimes small. Their heads are dolicocephalic, their noses are broad but not so broad nor so depressed at the root as among some other aboriginal tribes of Chōṭā Nāgpur and Ōṛissā. The skin of the Pāuṛi Bhūiyas also shows a much lighter brown tint than that of the average Dravidian and Mūṇḍā-speaking aborigines. This is a trait which at once strikes the observer. The women are even of a lighter colour than the men. But the Pāuṛis are mostly pregnathous, the projecting cheeks and jawbones giving a certain squareness to the face. The lips are generally rather thick. Both men and women are in their young age comely in appearance. Both sexes are very agile and can stand fatigue well and travel great distances. The weekly market, held every Saturday at village Khūṇṭgāon, on the westernmost extremity of the Pāuṛi area of the Bonāi State, where the Hill Bhūiyās exchange grains and vegetables for salt, tobacco and cloth with the lowlanders, is attended by women as well as men from the Pāuṛi Parganā, a distance of twenty miles. And I have seen several Pāuṛi Bhūiyās bearing heavy loads on carrying poles slung across their shoulders walk at a fair pace across the jungles and hills of the Kuiṛā and Pāuṛi *parganās* to the Bonai State a whole day with only a couple of hours' rest on the way.

The result of an analysis of the anthropometrical measurements of one hundred adult Pāuṛi Bhūiyās of the Keōnjhar State taken by my son Ramesh Chandra Roy is summarised in the following note, and the actual measurements are given in Appendix I.

"The anthropometric measurements of 100, adult Bhūiyās given in Appendix I. were taken by me at the instance of the author and in company with him among the Pāuṛi Bhūiyās of the Keōnjhar State.

I have followed Mr. R. Martin's *Lehrbuch red Anthropologie*, (Jena, 1914) in taking these measurements.

General Physical Features.

Their bodies are well proportioned, of medium height, though not so strongly built as those of their neighbours,-namely,—the Hos, the Santals, the Juangs, and some other Pre-Dravidian tribes. Their skin-colour varies from brown to light black. As remarked by the author, "the skin of the Pāuṛi Bhūiyā shows a much lighter brown tint than that of the average Dravidian and Mūṇḍā-speaking aborigines." The women are of a lighter skin colour than the men. The hair is black and thick on the head and generally scanty on the rest of the body, though men with beards are occasionally seen. The women keep long hair and so do many males. The hair is generally wavy.

The fore-head is usually slightly retreating and the supra-orbital ridges are often moderately developed but a straight vertical fore-head with ill-developed supra-orbital ridges is not very uncommon.

The nose is broad and often concave, being depressed at the root, but not so deep as that of most of their other aboriginal neighbours. The eye-slit is generally straight, but slightly oblique eyes are also found. The tendency to form the epicanthic fold is, however, rare.

The malars are often well developed with prominent zygomatic arches. The chin is either square, oval or, intermediate between them. The alveolar region is often prognathous and the thick lips are either everted or have often the tendency to be everted. The face is often prognathous and square or pentagonal, but the oval face is also found. So on the whole the Pāuṛi Bhūiyās may be marked out from the other aborigines of Chōṭā-Nāgpur and Ōṛissā.

From the analysis of the metric data of one hundred adult individuals, with their ages varying from 25 to 45 years, we find that.:—

The head is long, the average length being 186.8 mm.

Their mean Cephalic Index is 73.29 and the Standard Deviation (S.D.) is 2.64, the range being 67 to 79.

The total number of Dolichocephalic heads is 91, and Mesocephalic 9, there being a complete absence

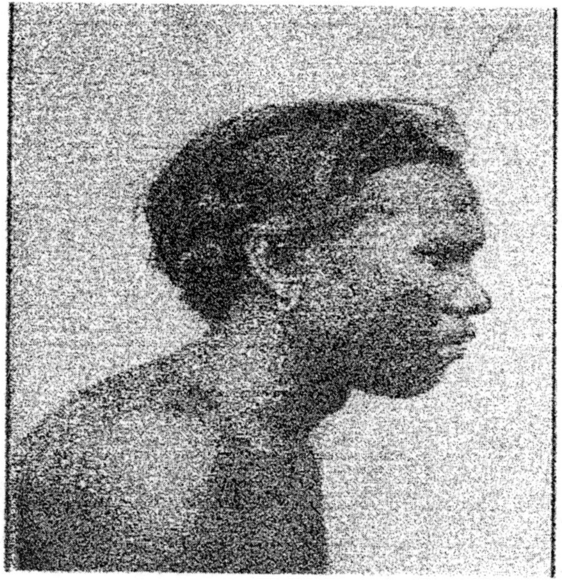

Fig. 2. Type of a Pāuṛi Bhũiyā male (profile of Fig. 1).

Fig. 1. Type of a Pāuṛi Bhũiyā (male).

of the Brachycephalic element.

The average Altitudinal Index is 62.31 with S.D. 3.27. The total number of Hypsicephalic is 47, Orthocephalic 44 and Platycephalic 9.

The Nasal Index shows an average of 87.93 with S.D. 9.75. The total number of Platyrrhine is 64 and Mesorrhine 36, and there is a complete absence of Leptorrhiny.

The average superior facial Index is 86.19 with S.D. 5.02.

The stature varies from 1460 mm. to 1690 mm.

According to Dr. Dixon's classification, most of the Bhūiyās measured by me may be called mainly of the Proto-Australoid type.

By combining the Cephalic, Altitudinal and Nasal Indices we arrive at the following actual result:–

Dolichocephalic	Hypsicephalic	Platyrrhine ...	... 20
Do	Chamaecephalic	Do ...	... 6
Do	Orthocephalic	Do ...	... 31
Do	Hypsicephalic	Mesorrhine ...	... 19
Do	Chamaecephalic	Do ...	... 3
Do	Orthocephalic	Do ...	... 12
Mesocephalic	Hypsicephalic	Do ...	... 2

Do	Do	Platyrrhine... ...	6
Do	Orthocephalic	Do	2
		Total ...	100

Now, the question arises, what is the cause of the small element of mesocephaly and mesorrhiny in the dominant dolichocophalic and platyrrhine type? Is it due to the mixture with some brachycephalic and leptorrhine people in the past or a natural variation of the dominant type?

Before I attempt a provisional solution, I would like to mention the fact that the Pāuṛi Bhūiyās were never measured before. About 100 individuals of the Hinduised section of the Bhūiyās were measured by Risely[37]; and lately Mr. P.C. Bose[38] measured some Hinduised Bhūiyās of Mayurbanj. Mr. Bose took 81 measurements and found 14.9 p.c. leptorrhine and 14.9 p.c. brachycephalic elements among them.

Thus we find that the two foreign elements, *viz*, leptorrhiny and brachycephaly which are found among the Hinduised section of the tribe are completely absent in the Pāuṛi section. So it may be reasonably

---

37 Risley — *Tribes & Castes of Bengal*, Vol. I, pp. 29.

38 *J.A.S.B.* Vol, XXV, No. I, pp. 158.

Fig. 3. Type of a Pāuṛi Bhũiyā (male) (Front View).

presumed that the Pāuṛi section absorbed the two foreign elements which gave rise to mesocephalic and mesorrhine types.

The absorbed leptorrhine element is probably due to the close contact with the Gouṛs, a Caucasian-featured low Hindu caste and also the Hinduised section of the Bhūiyās. But I cannot agree with Col Dalton [39] in thinking that the brachycephalic trait may be attributed to the presence of a submerged Mongoloid strain in this region, for I found no Mongoloid trait among them. To solve the problem, the neighbouring tribes must be studied. Such a study is now in progress and we hope to publish the results in the not distant future."

(iii) *Mental Characteristics.*

The Pāuṛi Bhūiyā is cheerful, light-hearted, good-humoured and even gay in the presence of acquaintances, although shy and timid before strangers. At my first visit to the Khūṇṭgāon bāzār in the Bonāi State a number of Pāuṛi women and some young men fled at sight of the stranger, and it was with difficulty that a few could be induced to remain and allow me to photo-

39 Referred to by P.C. Bose in *J.A.S.B.*, XXV, no. 1, p. 158.

graph them. On a closer acquaintance with them I found them frank, friendly and hospitable and in this respect they resemble the Hōs and the Khāriās among the Mūṇḍā-speaking tribes. Although they are respectful to people in authority and to those they consider worthy of respect, they are not servile, and an air of equality comes natural to them in their intercourse even with the highest authorities they know. They assume an air of superiority to the Kōls—as they call the Hō, Mūṇḍā, Orāon and other immigrants from Chōṭā-Nāgpur and elsewhere. These "Kōls" who have settled in or near the Pāuṛi villages with the permission of the Pāuṛi headmen have to carry burdens and render certain other services at their bidding.

The men among the Pāuṛi Bhūiyās are rather indolent and lazy, though they can bear hardship well and can work hard when required. Pāuṛi Bhūiyā women are more iudustrious than the men. Almost every day groups of Pāuṛi women may be seen in the Pāuṛi country and in the plains villages at the foot of their native hills carrying on their heads loads of wood and bundles of thatching grass, baskets of mustard seeds and other jungle produce to the nearest market or to

Fig. 4. Profile of Fig. 3.

the comparatively prosperous Hindu settlements, several miles away from their own settlements, for sale or barter.

Under the influence of Hindu ideas of purity and cleanliness, both sexes bathe daily and they keep their houses clean and tidy, but wash their clothes only once or twice in a month. In intelligence, they compare favourably with most other hill tribes. The *Dihuri* or priest of one of the Pāuṛi villages I visited impressed me as exceptionally intelligent. On certain points about which the Pāuṛi Bhūiyās decided to withhold information from me, he remained firm even when he was in a state of drunkenness, though he was otherwise extremely voluble and talkative. Like aboriginal tribes not spoilt by contact with a superior civilization, the Pāuṛi Bhūiyās are, on the whole, simple, truthful, and honest, but timid, stubborn, and easily excitable. They value chastity in the married of both sexes. A male or a female, married or unmarried, going wrong with a person of a different tribe is regarded as a heinous social offender and is punished with excommunication. The men are addicted to drink but women abstain from it.

CHAPTER IV.

ECONOMIC LIFE.

Village Sites.

The settlements of the Hill Bhuiyās nestle in the valleys between successive hill ranges, generally close to one of the numerous tiny boulder-covered hill-streams that trickle down the valleys. Most of the settlements cover each a large tract of forest land within the limits of which the village site is shifted from time to time. The Pāuṛis leave one site when all the trees on it have been cut down and the lands prepared for shifting cultivation (*kōmān* or *dāhi*) are exhausted, and remove to another site within the area. They again return to the old site when new trees have grown up to some height. In some villages this shifting of sites is done once every ten years. Each Pāuṛi village or group of two or three villages is separated from other villages by three, four or more miles of long and winding paths through jungles and ravines or difficult passes.

Arrangement of the Houses.

Each village consists of from about a dozen to about 40 houses, and each house consists of from one to four huts. The huts are generally rectangular in shape with two sloping roofs. The walls are generally made of logs of wood planted vertically on the ground and plastered over with mud from inside; and the roofs are thatched. In the middle of the settlement is a decent and commodious hut called the *Maṇḍa Ghar* [40] or *Darbār ghar* which is the dormitory for bachelors and also serves as an occasional guest house and council house for the village elders. Arranged round the inner walls of this hut are the *chāngs* or tambourines, played upon by the young men in their dances. Some of these *chāngs* are supported against the wall, while others are suspended with string from pronged deer-horns affixed to the walls. In front of the *Maṇḍa Ghar* is a spacious yard which is called the *Darbār* or meeting ground where dances are held in the evenings and where the tribal *panchāyats* sit when occasion arises. In some villages the houses are arranged in rows, leaving a wide space in between two rows so as to form a long

40 *Maṇḍa* is a corruption of *mandap.*

yard or a very wide street.

Gai-Sri Khunta.

On one side of this yard is a round rudely carved wooden post from 3½ to 4½ feet high affixed to the ground which is called the *Subha Khūṇṭā* (auspicious post) or the *Gāin̐-Srī-khūṇṭā* or post representing the tutelary goddess of the village. When a new village site is selected, this post is first stuck up in the centre of the chosen site with ceremonies which will be described in a subsequent chapter; and the prosperity or otherwise of the village is bound up with this post. If it is blown down by the wind or is otherwise uprooted, the village site must be forthwith changed as otherwise dire misfortune, it is believed, will overtake the settlement.

The Chhatra Khunt.

In many Pāuṛi villages in the Keōnjhar State, this *Subha Khūṇṭā* is also known as the *Chhatra-Khūṇṭ* (*lit.*, umbrella-post). On occasions of religious festivals, this *Chhatra-Khūṇṭ* is painted white with rice-flour diluted in water, and to it is fastened with a rope a long bamboo pole, 20 to 30 feet high, crowned with a circular shield representing an umbrella made of plaited bamboo and covered over with cloth and ornamented with mirrors and combs

Fig. 5. Inside a Pāuṛi village (Suakāṭi).

and other tinsel, and decked with garlands of vegetable-pith and wreaths of flowers and leaves above and below it; and, on top of all, streams in the air a long flag with garlands and tassels made of pith hanging down from it. The long pole thus arrayed is called the *Ṭhākurāṇī-chhatra* or umbrella of tho goddess known as the Ṭhākurāṇī, and is carried in procession to the hut-temple of the goddess on occasions of her periodical *Pujās* or worship.

Near tho *Maṇḍa Ghar*, generally a little apart, there usually stands another smaller hut which serves as the seat or temple of the mother-goddess Ṭhākurāṇī. Close to the *Darbār* or *Maṇḍa Ghar* are the houses of the village headmen–the Nāek or secular, and the Dihuri or sacerdotal, headman. All around are the huts of the other families of the settlement. Narrow lanes and by-paths run between rows of houses. Outside the older settlements are a number of jack-fruit trees, and close to the settlements are hills on whose slopes the villagers have their scanty cultivation. On the comparatively more level ground between the hill slopes and the group of huts the villagers grow some vegetables, such as pumpkins, beans, and yams.

Although rice is esteemed as food by the Pāuṛi or Hill Bhūiyās, the poorer among them have but little paddy cultivation and own no ploughs or plough-cattle but use a digging-stick called *Ānkusi bāṛi* for sowing seeds with. A *Khūnṭā* or iron-blade fitted into a socket in a wooden handle is to be found in most houses for digging up yams and tubers and for other purposes. Most Pāuṛis obtain rice in exchange for such crops as they grow in their *Komāns* and for the spoils of the chase or jungle produce, or purchase rice with the sale-proceeds of such crops or game or jungle produce including fuel-wood and sāl-leaves, leaf-platters and leaf-cups. Besides leaf-cups and leaf-platters and leaf-mats, some Pāuṛi Bhūiyās make bamboo-baskets by plaiting bamboo splinters.

General Economic Condition.

The energies of the Hill Bhūiyās or, as they are locally called, Pābṛis or Pāuṛis or Pābṛi Bhūiyās,—are directed mainly to the solution of the food-problem. With their activities almost wholly directed to the collection and production of food in their inhospitable hill-fastnesses, they are still in a very low state of material culture. Though their economic life would appear to be more primitive as compared with that of the more settled agricultural cognate tribes, such as the Mūṇḍās, the Hōs, and the village Khāṛiās of Chōṭā Nāgpur and the Plains Bhūiyās of the Ōṛissā States, this difference would appear to be mainly due to unfertile soil of the Pāuṛi country and their rude physical and social environment. Shifting cultivation is the main occupation of the Pāuṛis, and the food thus obtained has to be supplemented by hunting wild animals and birds and collecting edible roots and fruits in their native jungles and occasional fishing in their native hill-streams. Wet cultivation of rice and terracing of fields for such cultivation has not yet been generally adopted. The production of fire by friction has not yet been altogether abandoned, and once a year a ceremonial kindling of new fire by friction takes place in every village. Lucifer matches are, however, fast supplanting the old methods. As wood and thatching-grass are plentiful in their native jungles, the houses of most Pāuṛi Bhūiyās are fairly substantial structures. A few of the more well-to-do amongst them own block-wheel carts for transport, and plough-cattle for agriculture.

The furniture, utensils, weapons and tools and

other belongings of the average Pāuṛi Bhuiyā family mainly consist of a few earthen-ware vessels for cooking food and drawing and storing water and for brewing beer, a few earthen-ware lamps, a stone-roller and grind–stone for pounding turmeric and other substances, palm-leaf mats to sit or lie upon and also to spread out grains to dry in the sun, a few pumpkin-gourds for carrying water, leaf-baskets and bamboo-baskets of different sizes to hold their store of grains or maize or other articles, one or more carrying-nets (*sika*) and carrying-poles (*bahinga*) to carry grains or other articles, one or two winnowing baskets, one or two brooms made of wild grass, one or more rain-huts and umbrellas made of leaves or split bamboo, one or more bamboo-traps for fishing, one or more knives and axes and, in some cases, a spear or two, a few bows and arrows, one or more bamboo-flutes, besides such minor objects as wooden combs and tobacco-powder boxes. Some families may possess one or two rude bamboo-boxes which are really bamboo-baskets with lids fitted with iron chains in front and back. The more well-to-do Pāuṛis generally own a few brass-plates, cups and *lōṭās* (water-jugs) and rude wooden vessels, a string-bed (*chārpoy*) or two, one or more bamboo umbrellas or even cloth-umbrellas, and tiny kerosine-oil lamps made of tin or even a cheap hurricane lantern. Wooden mortars and pestles for pounding rice or even a husking pedal (*ḍhenki*) may be seen in some Pāuṛi houses.

Contents of the Houses.

The following description of the house of a headman of a Pāuṛi settlement will give an idea of the material condition of a comparatively well-to-do Pāuṛi familly. The house of the Dihuri of village Rāoṅta in the Bonāi State consists of four huts. The main hut, which runs from north to south, is divided into two compartments by a partition of wooden posts placed perpendicularly one against another, leaving an opening at one corner. The entrance to this hut is through a wooden door moving on a socket in the eastern wall. The northern compartment is used as a combined kitchen and sleeping room, the hearths being in front of the door and close to the western wall. The southern compartment is used as the *bhitar* or "inner tabernacle" where the ancestor-spirits are believed to have their seat and where offerings are made to them. No outsider is admitted into this room, and here are stored valued possessions of the family, in the shape of money, clothes, utensils and store of maize, rice and other grains. Coins and clothes are kept in a bamboo box. The richest family rarely owns more than three or four brass utensils, but the generality, as I have said, have none whatsoever. But one or two cheap aluminium plates, cups, glasses and *lōtās* may now-a-days be occasionally seen in the houses of a few *Pāuṛis.* They generally eat from leaf-plates and drink from leaf-cups or pumpkin gourds. Cooking vessels are all of earthenware. Palm-leaf mats form their only bed. In a large settlement of nearly forty houses, only two string beds could be found. The second hut, which is to the north of the first and also faces east, is called the *Melā-ghar* in which I found a few earthen vessels for the brewing of rice-beer, two bamboo umbrellas with handles and one umbrella made of *siāli* leaves and having no handle, two brooms, some *chōp* (*Bāuhinia scandens*) fibres, some ropes, a few empty bamboo baskets, a small *puṛā* or straw-rope receptacle containing rice (which the headman collects from contributions by the villagers), for supplying *rasad* or rations to public officers or other honoured guests visiting the village, one winnowing basket, three

Fig. 8. A Pāuṛi Bhūiyā family in front of their house. Some of their weapons and household utensils are also shown.

pumpkin gourds, one palm-leaf mat, one earthen jar of *ghee* (clarified butter) also meant for the *rasad* of public officers, one *bisāh* or weighing apparatus consisting of a small bamboo basket suspended with strings at one end of a wooden beam on which notches have been cut to indicate a *seer* (two pounds) and fractions of a *seer*. There were also in this room one rope-sling (*ghūr pūni*) for discharging stones at small birds that eat up grain put out to dry in the sun, one *kōṭrā* or curved axe for cutting undergrowth in the jungle, one axe (*būdiā* or *ṭāngi*), one ploughshare (*lohā*), one bow and four arrows, and one bugle made of a pumpkin-gourd for scaring away elephants in the jungles. This hut has also a door made of planks of wood joined together and moving on a socket. In this hut are sometimes accommodated relatives of the family, such as a married daughter and her husband, when they come on a visit. The bachelors of the village also sleep in it when the *Manḍa Ghar* is occupied by guests. In front of these huts are two other huts, one used as a cattle-shed and the other as fowl pen and *ḍhenki ghar* where rice is husked with a mortar and pestle. The cattle-shed has a floor made of logs of wood placed perpendicularly side by side over the earthen floor. These two huts have doors made of split bamboo. The average Pāuṛi Bhūiyā has no separate *ḍhenki ghar*, and only a few Pāuṛis own cattle and require a cattle-shed; only one, two or three men in a big settlement own cattle and ploughs, and the others who require the occasional use of a plough borrow it from some neighbour. A hole for husking grain with the wooden pestle is usually made in the floor of the compartment used as the kitchen. The average Pāuṛi has no separate store-room and the *bhitar* or inner compartment serves also as the store or lumber room. It may also be noted that in many villages it is in the *Manḍla-ghar* or *Darbār* house that stores of rice, pulse, and other articles supplied by the villagers for the use of guests are kept slung in straw receptacles from the roof. Decorations to the houses or drawings on the wall are practically unknown, but the walls are sometimes coated over with a kind of yellowish earth with which the Pāuṛi's scanty clothes are also dyed.

Dress.

The dress of Pāuṛi Bhūiyās is of the simplest. At home most of their men wear only a very short loin cloth round the waist, and the

Fig. 7. Bachelors' Dormitory.

poorer men wear only a strip of perineal cloth kept in its place by a string round the waist. Boys and girls up to the age of twelve or thirteen almost invariably wear such perineal cloth which the girls change for a longer cloth only when strangers visit the village or when they dance in the evenings. Young men at their dances and festivals wear long loin cloths with one end hanging down below the knees. Except the poorest, each man has two full-sized cloths, one worn round the waist and another as an upper garment. These, however, are used only on special occasions and during visits to other places. A very poor man uses a napkin for an upper garment on such occasions. The clothes of men and women are generally dyed a light yellow with a kind of yellowish earth which is abundant in the country.

An adult Pāuṛi female uses a cloth about twelve cubits long which is worn as a combined skirt and shawl. Poorer women have each only one such cloth, which is used while going out, whereas a smaller waist-cloth is worn in the house. The hair is parted in the middle of the head. Women have generally a separate bathing place a little apart from that of the men. As most women have only one cloth, they take it off before entering the water. Not unoften a stranger, plodding his way at about mid-day along the winding paths through the jungles and ravines of the Pāuṛi country, is startled at the sudden sight of Pāuṛi women—sometimes a whole bevy of them—bathing in absolute nudity in a hill-stream. On perceiving the stranger, they either hastily seize and put on their clothes lying on the bank, or, if there be no time left for it, remain immersed up to their necks in the water.

Ornaments.

Girls and young women wear a number of thick brass bangles (*bera*) on both arms, brass *Kankans* one on each wrist just below the *Khāṛu*, and more than one brass ring (*mūḍi*) on the fingers—a larger number on the left hand than on the right, a number of toe-rings (*jhūṭia*), one brass anklet (*pahūṛ*) on each leg, one or two wristlets (*tāṛ*) made of brass or lac or both, on each wrist, and one or more bead necklaces (*māri*). Some women wear ear-rings with pendants (*phirphira*) and also nose-rings (*guṇā*). Most young men too wear bead necklaces. Neither tattooing of the body nor cicatrization is practised. The headmen of villages use no head-dress and are not

Fig. 9. Types of Pāuṛi Women in gala dress.

distinguished by any particular insignia of office. But the Pāuṛi Gaṛh-Nāek of village Kuiṛa in the Bonāi State who is the headman appointed by the Rājā for the whole of the Kuiṛa Parganā consisting of twenty-nine villages, has been presented by the Rājā of Bonāi with a costly silk dress consisting of *paijāmā*, *chāpkān*, turban, belt, sword and shield, and the Pāuṛi Mahā-Nāek or headman appointed by the Rājā for the entire Pāuṛi Parganā has also been presented with a robe of honour by him. These men are not the recognized social headmen for their respective *parganās*, but they wield great influence as the intermediaries between the people and the Rājā.

Daily life.

The daily life of the men is largely devoted to the production of food by the *kōmān* and the *dāhi* system of cultivation. The *dāhi* process of clearing land is as follows: A portion of a hill slope, more or less level, is selected for clearance and all the trees on it are cut down and piled one upon another in rows and a large number of bushes and shrubs are also cut down and placed round these felled trees. These are left for some time to dry and then they are set fire to. When the trees are all reduced to ashes the land is dug up and made ready for the cultivation of upland (*gōṛā*) rice.

The *kōmān* process of preparing lands for cultivation is as follows: A plot of hill slope is selected for the purpose and all bushes and shrubs growing on the site are cut down and placed in heaps at the foot of each tree on the selected plot, and left to dry for a month or so. If in the meanwhile other bushes or shrubs have sprouted up they are also cleared, and fire is set to all these heaps of bushes and shrubs so as to burn all the branches and twigs of the trees, leaving only the scorched and naked tree-trunks standing. The ashes are now spread all over the plot, and the *kōmān* is ready for cultivation. Generally in one portion of a *kōmān* upland rice is sown, and on another such crops as *makāi* (maize), *māṛuā* (*Eleusine corocana*) and *kāngu* are grown, and on the ashes at the feet of the standing trunks of trees, vegetable creepers such as *sīm* (beans) and *dhūk* are planted so that the creepers may go up the trees.

As I have said, wet cultivation of paddy is rare in the Pāuṛi country which is full of hills and jungles. In a few villages at the foot of the hills a little wet

Fig. 10. A Pāuṛi Bhūiyā women with ornaments on.

cultivation of low-land paddy, known as *Bil dhān*, is now practised.

From the month of Māgh (January) to Baiśākh (April), men are engaged in the preparation of *dāhi* and *kōmān* fields. Between Fālgun (March) and Baiśākh (May) both men and women carry cattle-dung manure to their fields. It is not permissible to cut down trees or to manure the fields until the new mango blossoms have come out and the Māgh-jātrā festival in January as well as the *Am-nua* ceremony which follows shortly afterwards, have been performed; and paddy cannot be sown unless the *Tirtiā-muṭi* ceremony has been celebrated in Baiśākh (April). These ceremonies will be described in a subsequent chapter. Women are not allowed to cut down trees or plough the fields, but they may break clods of earth in the fields; this is generally done with axe-handles. In these months also the men cut down from the jungles trees which are taken to their fields and burnt for ash-manure; and men, and more particularly women, dig for edible roots, yams and tubers. As soon as there is a shower of rain the men plough up their fields; and then again when the weather is dry they bring to the fields wood for burning into manure or apply cattle-dung manure to the soil. In the months of Chait and Baiśākh (March to May) men also go out to the firests hunt deer, wild pigs or other animals. Between March and May, when the streams are almost dry, boys and men catch fish with their hands. Boys and girls give such help to their parents as they can in household and field work. They also draw water and look after the cattle. Between the months of Māgh and Baiśākh the work of repairing and building of of houses is also undertaken. In Baiśākh and Jaiṣṭha (April-June) the fields are sown by the men with paddy, the uplands being sown after the low-lying, fields, if any. At this season, in a year in which sufficient mangoes are available, the women in some Pāuṛi families squeeze out the juice of the fruit in a small wooden canoe (*ḍōngā*) made for the purpose, and the juice is put out on mats to dry in the sun, and made (into *ambā-sarā* Hindi, *āmāwat*; Bengali, *āmsatva*). In Aṣāṛh (July) paddy-seedlings are transplanted in the *bīl* lands, if any, men and women both taking part in the operations, but the subsequent reploughing and levelling of the fields are the business of the men alone. In

Śrāvan and Bhādo (August-September) both men and women weed the rice fields. In Bhādo (August) *gōṛā* or upland rice is harvested and *rāsi* (*sesamum*), *makāi* (maize) and a few other grains and vegetables are sown on the uplands; and the wet lands, if any, are embanked to store rain-water in them. In Āśvin (September-October) both men and women harvest the *gōṛā* (upland) rice and, in Kārtik (October), the *bīl* (lowland) rice, if any. In Aghān (November), the harvested lowland rice, if any, is threshed and winnowed. Such is the yearly routine. The period between the sprouting of the crops and the harvesting is one of great anxiety and sleepless vigilance. Most of the male population of a village have to be in their fields at night to protect the crops from the ravages of wild elephants, bears and other animals. A kind of rude scaffolding is perched on some tree in the field to serve as the resting-place of the watchers, and logs of wood are kept burning at the foot of the tree where the men by turns warm themselves. In the day-time women too may be seen helping the men to protect the ripening corn from birds and beasts. On a day in October when I arrived at noon at a Pāuṛi settlement of about forty families, I found practically the whole adult male population and many of the women thus engaged in their fields.

This arduous round of duties is, however, relieved now and then by *pūjās* and festivals which mark the termination of one stage of labour and the beginning of another and show how the economic life of the tribe, like their social life, is permeated by religion. Such is the *Māgh-jātrā* festival in January when, among other rites, old fire in all the houses is extinguished and new fire is ceremonially kindled by friction of two pieces of wood by the *Dihuri* with his eyes covered over with rice-flour cakes; all the villagers kindle their own new fire from this sacred fire and rice is boiled in milk over it and offered to the ancestor-spirits. It is only after this ceremony that the forest trees may be felled. The *Ām-nūā* festival of the new mango blossoms is celebrated in February, after which alone the fields may be manured; the *Tirtiā-muṭi* festival is held in April on which day sowing operations have to be commenced with a ceremonial sowing, and the *Ashāṛi Pūjā* in July when sacrifices are offered to the tutelary deities (*Grām-Srī*, etc.) for rains and good crops, and the *Bihiṛā*

Fig. 11. Pāuṛi Bhũiyā producing fire by friction.

Pūjā at the same time after which alone transplantation of lowland rice may be undertaken; the *Gāmhā Punāi* festival in August when the Pāuṛi celebrates his temporary respite from agricultural labours by making a feast of rice-flour cakes and other delicacies and giving absolute rest for two days to the cattle of the village, washing their hoofs, besmearing their foreheads and horns with *sesamum* oil and pounded turmeric and giving them raw rice as well as fried rice (*khai*) to eat and burning earthen lamps at night in the cattle-sheds; the *Bār* and *Nuā-khāi* festivals in September when, with appropriate ceremonies, the first sheaves of upland rice are reaped by each cultivator from his field and new rice eaten after offering the same to the gods; and finally, in some villages, the *Karam-jātrā* festival in October or November and the *Pouṣ-jātrā* festival in December, the former after the harvesting but before the threshing of the rice crops and the latter after the rice has been harvested, threshed and garnered. These feasts and festivals will be described in detail in a subsequent chapter.

During respite from field labours men make pumpkin-gourd drinking-vessels, bamboo sticks and bows, wooden pestles and mortars and the threshing apparatus called *ḍhenki*; and in the winter and spring their girls weave mats of wild date-palms (*Felix sylvestris*). The girls of a village go in a body to the jungles and collect date-palm leaves and *sāl* leaves, and gather yams for food and dry leaves for fuel. Women make cups and plates of the *sāl* leaves. From Māgh (January) to Baiśākh (April), bachelors and maidens often visit other villages for dancing. When at home they dance at the *darbār* ground after the evening meal. Bachelors sleep together in the *Maṇḍa-ghar* save in the months of Bhādra, Āśvin and Kārtik (middle of August to middle of November) when they have mostly to guard their *kōmān* cultivation.

The following is the programme of a day's work that was gone through by a small Pāuṛi family during one of my visits to their village in October, 1918. The family consisted of Chandan Pāuṛi, his wife and baby and a younger brother. As they had already harvested their *gōṛā* paddy and had no wet cultivation, they were not required to guard their fields. At cock-crow the two brothers got up, washed their faces, lighted a *sāl*-leaf cigarette (*phikā*) in the fire that is always kept burn-

Fig. 12. Hut temple of Ṭhākurāṇi.

ing in the house so long as there is anyone in it. Then Chandan and his brother took a plough-bullock and went to the threshing floor and there they threshed their *gōṛā* paddy. Chandan's wife, who had a baby in her arms, got up shortly after her husband, washed her face and went with a winnowing basket to the threshing floor, and husked the threshed rice. The men tied up the rice in a bundle (*bet*) which the woman carried home on her head. Chandan's wife then prepared the mid-day meal which consisted of boiled rice and *baitāṛu* or pumpkin sliced and boiled in water. After all had had their mid-day bath the men first took their meals, and then the women did so. Chandan and his wife then went to the jungle, the former to collect fuel-wood and the latter to dig for yams, of which different varieties are used for food, and to gather such fruits as *dumar* (jungle-figs), *parai*, *jaulua*, etc. On their return home, the woman boiled rice and *sāg*-leaves for the evening meal. After taking their meals they went to sleep,—the husband apart from the wife, as custom forbids a Pāuṛi Bhūiyā to sleep with his wife so long as she continues to suckle her baby.

CHAPTER V.

SOCIAL ORGANIZATION.

(i) *Family Organization.*

The Family. The elementary social unit of the Bhūiyā tribe is the family consisting of parents and their children. The Pāuṛi Bhūiyā family, like that of other Mūṇḍā tribes and other sections of the Bhūiyā tribe, centres round the father through whom descent is traced. Besides being patrilineal, the Pāuṛi famliy is also patripotestal, the father exercising supreme authority in the family. In a few instances, a Pāuṛi Bhūiyā having no male issue adopts as his son a boy from one of his agnatic families. Such an adopted son is treated as a true-born member of his adoptive parents' family and enjoys all the rights and privileges of a son, including the right of inheritance.

Position of Women.

Females among the Pāuṛi Bhūiyās, as among other Mūṇḍā tribes, do not inherit property. Ownership to all property, except the wearing apparel and jewellery of the female members of a family and articles made or acquired by them for her own use, vests in men. On her husband's death a woman is only entitled to maintenance, out of the assets left by her late husband, till her death or re-marriage. Daughters too may not inherit their father's property, but a maiden daughter is entitled to maintenance out of her deceased father's assets, until her marriage. Except for occasional visits to her parents' place, a Pāuṛi woman ordinarily lives in her husband's house. Marriage is ordinarily monogamous, though the husband of a barren woman may take a second wife. With rare exceptions, women are generally well treated, and have considerable influence in matters of domestic economy.

Division of Labour among the Sexes

Pāuṛi Bhūiyā women have their allotted functions as the men have theirs. And of the two, the woman appears to be the more hard-worked. Thus, cooking, drawing water from springs and streams, digging for yams and tubers and gathering edible leaves and jungle fruits, weaving mats with the leaves of the wild date-palm, and helping the men in such agricultural operations as manuring the fields, breaking clods of earth in the ploughed fields, reaping crops, and threshing grains, are among the regular duties of the women-folk. Pāuṛi women, like their sisters among other Mūṇḍā-speaking tribes and among their Dravidian-speaking neighbours such as the Orāons, must on no account drive the plough or get up on the roof of a hut. The main work of making *beorā* or *dāhi* by cutting down and burning jungle trees and bushes for preparing patches of jungle land for shifting cultivation, the collecttion of food by hunting and occasionally fishing, and the construction and repairing of houses and sheds,—these devolve on the men, though fishing is not taboo to women.

(ii) *Village Organization.*

Village organization. The Pāuṛi Bhūiyās are one of the few Mūṇḍā tribes among when though exogamy exists, totemic organization is absent. In place of clan-exogamy, they practise what may be called village-exogamy. The unit of their social organization is the village consisting of families supposed to be descended from a common ancestor and all regarded as "Kuṭumbs" or agnates. And so a Pāuṛi Bhūiyā must seek brides for his sons and husbands for his daughters from outside his own village. Cognatic relations are known as 'Bandhus' and villages with which a Pāuṛi Bhūiyā of a village may enter into marital connections are called his 'Bandhu' villages. In almost every village, however, one or more families of marriage-relations or "Bandhus" of men of that village have settled. Such traces of totemism as exist among the Plains Bhūiyās are not accompanied by any exogamic restrictions and would appear to be due to culture contact and borrowing rather than to survival.

Village Headmen.

For every Pāuṛi village there is a secular headman called the *Nāek* in the Bonāi State and *Padhān* in the Keōnjhar and Pāl Lahera States, and a sacerdotal headman called the *Dihuri* or *Diuri*. The rest of the villagers are called *Parjās*,–that is to say, the commonalty. The *Dihuri* or *Diuri* is said to belong to the elder branch, and the *Nāek* or *Padhān* to a younger branch of the original village-family. The Dihuri is alloted some land called "Dihuri"-land in the village to enable him to meet the expenses of the public *pujās* or sacrificial ceremonies performed for the benefit of the villagers. The Dihuri, besides having charge of the public worship of the gods, is, along with the *Nāek* or *Padhān*, the leader of the villagers in all social, socio-religious and socio-political matters. The *Nāek* or *Padhān* is the guide and representative of the villagers in their relations with the authorities and with the outside world generally [41].

Succession to Dihuriship.

These posts are both hereditary. Within a fortnight after the death of a Dihuri, the villagers assemble at the *darbār* or village-meeting-ground and hand over a new bamboo basket [42] to his eldest son, and each villager presents him with a leaf-cup filled with unhusked rice. The new Dihuri now bathes himself and husks the rice which he offers

---

41 Compare the similar position of the secular and sacerdotal headmen among other settled Muṇḍā tribes, such as the *Mūṇḍā* and *Pahan* headmen of a Muṇḍā village, the *Mānjhi* and *Dihri* of a Santāl village, the *Mūṇḍā* and *Diuri* of a Hō village, the *Mūṇḍā* or *Mahtō* and *Kālo* of a Khāṛiā village in Chōṭā Nāgpur. Among the less advanced Muṇḍā tribes, the functions of the secular and the sacerdotal headmen are combined in one and the same person, as, *e.g.*, in the 'Naya' of the Birhōṛs.

42 The bamboo basket or winnowing-fan is also the insignia of the office of a village-priest among the Muṇḍās, the Khārias, *etc.*

along with some *pālo* and frankincense to *Gāi-srī* or the tutelary deity of the village. He then boils some *āruā* rice into *jāu* which he eats alone. Henceforth he is the recognized Dihuri of the village. There is no bar to a bachelor being appointed a Dihuri.

Election of a successor to a sonless Dihuri.

A village messenger called Ṭāṇḍkār is also appointed by the villagers. There is no land-grant or other emolument attached to this office, which is wholly honorary. When a Dihuri dies without a male issue, the adult males of the village assemble at the darbār and a new Dihuri is elected by the following method. The darbār-ground is cleaned with cowdung and water. Every villager present brings a handful of unhusked rice. All this rice is taken and husked by an elderly man of the village after he has bathed and has washed the basket and winnowing-fan to be used in husking the rice. The rice thus husked is now placed before the assembled villagers. Any one of them who desires to do so, takes up some grains of rice in the joined palms of his hands and drops them on the ground naming some villager whom he considers suitable for the post. The grains so dropped are called *pūnjis* and the *pūnjis* dropped by different men are all dropped close to one another. All the *pūnjis* thus placed on the ground are then covered over with a new earthen vessel. The villagers then disperse. Next morning the villagers after bathing themselves assemble there to ascertain which *pūnji* has remained entirely separate from others so that not a grain has got mixed up with the *pūnjis* on any side of it. The man in whose name such a *pūnji* was dropped is declared to be the elected Dihuri. Some elderly man now hands over the basket containing rice and flowers to the Dihuri thus elected, and says, "From to-day you become our Dihuri." The new Dihuri, thus elected, takes the basket home and keeps it suspended in a *sikā* so that none else may touch it. In the Keōnjhar and Pāl Lahera States, when owing to some calamity in the village, the question of changing the village priest arises the following method is employed in selecting a new Dihuri if necessary. Three *pūnjis* or small heaps of rice besmeared with turmeric powder are placed side by side on the open space (*āngan*) in front of the Dihuri's house. One of these *pūnjis* is called the *Ṭhākūr Pūnji* or *Ṭhākūr kūṛi*, that is to say, the heap representing the gods

(*Ṭhākūrs*), another is called the *Dihuri Kūṛi* or *Hākim Kūṛi* or the heap representing the *Hākim* or person in authority (that is to say, the *Dihuri* himself), and a third is called '*Prajā Kūṛi*' or the heap representing the 'subjects', that is to say, the whole body of villagers. The *pūnjis* are covered over with a new earthenware vessel and left undisturbed till the following morning when the earthenware cover is removed. If the grains in the *Ṭhākūr Kuṛi* or in the *Hākim Kuṛi* are found disturbed or displaced, however slightly, the old *Diuri* will have to be replaced by a new one who must, however, be a member of the old Dihuri family, if possible. Three similar *pūnjis*, one in the name of the *Ṭhākūrs*, another in the name of the proposed new Dihuri, and a third in the name or the *Prajās*, are similarly covered over with a new earthen-ware vessel and left over for the night and examined in the morning. If again the rice in the *Ṭhākūr-Kuṛi* or the *Dihuri-Kuṛi* is found disturbed, another name is proposed and the same test applied, and so on until the three *punjis* are found intact when the person last proposed is elected as the new Dihuri. The Dihuri thus selected offers to the village deity sacrifices of a goat and a fowl, purchased at the cost of the villagers. And the assembled villagers make a feast of the sacrificial meat and boiled rice.

The Village Panchayat and the judicial functions of the Dihuri and he Naek.

The *Nāek* and the Dihuri preside over the *panchāyat* or assembly of village-elders by which ordinary offences and disputes are decided, and the *Nāek* and the Dihuri pass orders and sentences in accordance with ancient tribal custom. Formerly, it is said, a murderer caught in the act might be killed while engaged in the murder; othewise he would be given a severe beating which might cause any injury short of death; and a man proved to have stolen another's goods was punished by making him remain seated for three days with his legs buried in holes made in the ground. A husband catching his wife and her paramour in the act of adultery was entitled to cut down both of them with his axe. But if, before being caught, they succeeded in going a few steps apart from each other they had to be handed over to the authorities for punishment. In such a case the woman is now made over by the *Panchāyat* to the adulterer if he is not a *kutumb* of the woman's father;

otherwise she is made over to her parents. An erring female is not punished unless she has gone wrong with a man of another caste or tribe, in which case she is excommunicated. Disputes about partition or inheritance of property are decided according to customary tribal law by the village *panchāyat* under the guidance of the *Nāek* and the *Dihuri*. When important questions arise which they cannot decide, or when their decision is not accepted, the matter may be referred to the *Panchāyat* of the *Bār*, for convening which, however, the disputing party has to provide a costly feast.

Oaths and ordeals.

The orthodox method employed by a Pāuṛi Panchāyat in deciding disputes or finding out a culprit where there is no convincing evidence, is the use of oaths and ordeals. Oaths are taken by touching the earth [43] and saying,—"May I become one with the earth (*mātiba*)—(i.e. die and rot in the earth)—if my statement (or my claim, as the case may be) is not true or correct"; or by placing the hands on the head of one's son and saying, "May my line (*baṁśa*) be extinct if

43 Compare the custom among the Muṇḍās of swearing by the earth from the deponent's hearth or ancestral grave. (*The Muṇḍas*, p. 424), or, in the case of a boundary dispute, swearing by a little earth from the disputed field. (*Ibid.* p. 426)

my statement (or my claim, as the case may be) is not correct"; or by invoking the gods by name and saying, "If I am guilty, may I be destroyed by you, ye gods". A more elaborate method is the following:—A portion of the *darbār* or open space in front of the *Maṇḍa-ghar* of the village is cleaned with cowdung and water, and on the spot thus cleaned some *benuā-māṭi* or earth from an anthill [44] (representing the Earth), a tiger's skin, [45] and a twig of the *kunu* plant are placed. The village Dihuri now invokes *Dharam-Deotā* or the Supreme God, and offers *āruā* rice to Him. The deponent then touches the ground and says,—"If I be guilty, may my line be extinct or my chest (*chhāti*) burst open."

One or other of three different modes of ordeal are employed to find out the truth or otherwise of an accusation made against a man or a woman of being a *Pāngni* or sorcerer or witch. These are the cowdung (*Gobar-hāṛi*) test; the iron test, and the ladder (*Bāro-āḍḍā*) test. The *Gobar-hāṛi* test is as follows:— A coin is placed in a vessel full of boiling hot cowdung. The person accused of being a *Pāngni* is asked to dip his

---

44 Compare the Muṇḍā's ordeal of burying the legs (*Kaṭa topana*) in holes (*Ibid*, p. 425)

45 Compare the Muṇḍā's oath on a tiger's skin (*Ibid*, p. 424).

right hand into the boiling cowdung and take out the coin. If the hand remains uninjured in the process, the accused is declared innocent. If the hand is burnt or scalded the person is declared to be a *Pāngni*[46]. In the *iron* test, the accused person has to take up a pound's weight of red-hot iron three times on his right hand. If the hand is not scalded the person is declared innocent; otherwise he is held guilty. The *Bāro-āḍḍā* test is the following:—A ladder of twelve rungs is set up and on the ground below the ladder a small circle (*manḍal*) is inscribed. Inside the circle the Dihuri makes offerings of *āruā* rice to *Dharam Deotā*. The accused gets up on the topmost rung of the ladder on which a cup of milk, a mango twig, and some *āruā* rice have been placed. The accused is required to drop these one after another into the circle. If these all fall inside the circle, the accused is declared innocent. If anything—even a single grain of rice—falls outside the circle he is declared guilty. The punishment for a *Pāngni* is expulsion from the village.

---

46 Cf The hot-water (*lolo-da*) ordeal of the Mūṇḍās in which boiling hot water is used for the test instead of boiling hot cowdung. (*The Mūṇḍās*, p. 425).

Other functions of the Dihuri and the Naek.

When a Pāuṛi of the village is found guilty of having killed, either intentionally or through neglect or by accident, a cow, ana calf or ox, or of having kept a non-Pāuṛi female as a mistress, the Nāek or Padhān and the Dihuri pass the sentence of excommunication on him and fix the quantity of rice, goats, fowls, salt and other requisites for a feast which must be supplied for the Panchāyat of the *Bār* organization when they first meet, for the purpose of restoring him to the community; and they also inform the offender that he has to pay a fine of twelve rupees to the *Bār* to be spent as follows:—One rupee each to be paid to the Bhāṇḍāri and the Pāuṛi Behārā of the *Bār*, a rupee or half a rupee to be paid to the Dhōbā Behārā, and the balance to meet the expenses of a second feast when the Panchāyat would finish their deliberations. When hunting expeditions (*Pārdhi*) are contemplated by the villagers—as is usually done between the months of Chait and Jaiṣṭha (March to May)—the Dihuri fixes the date and notifies it to the villagers. On the appointed day he performs a *pūjā* of the village gods in the morning. Then the Dihuri leads the people to the forests. Arriving at a cross-road on the borders of the village, the hunters offer *āruā rice, māṛuā*, molasses and frankincense to *Gāi-srī* and also take a vow of offering her a fowl, if any deer or *sambhar* or wild bear or other game is bagged. They also throw handfuls of rice upwards towards the sky for Dharam-Deotā (the Sun-god or the Supreme God) and downwards for Bāsuki-mātā or Basu-mati (the Earth-goddess). The party return home in the evening.

The Dihuri and the Nāek also allot to different men of the village the duties they have respectively to perform when the Rājā or his officials or other important personages visit the village; they select persons who are to carry burdens or palanquins, etc, for such visitors, and collect contributions in money or in kind for supplying provisions to honoured guests of the village and to meet other public expenses. The Dihuri and the Nāek have also a general supervision over the bachelors' dormitory although, within the dormitory itself, two of the older boys act as leaders, decide upon the order in which they will visit different *kūtūmb* villages to dance with the maidens of such villages, punish the younger boys for neglect of their duties, such as cleaning the dormitory, bringing fuel from the jungle, obeying their elders, attending to the village guests and fagging for the elder boys of the village by running their errands and shampooing their legs and so forth. When any member of the dormitory goes wrong with a *kūtūmb* (agnatic) girl, he is expelled from the dormitory. In many villages there still exist common dormitories for the maidens of the village. The elder girls instruct the younger girls in the different styles of dancing. The girls weave mats for the bachelors' dormitory as well as for their own. As the girls supply the mats on which the boys sleep in their dormitories, so the boys in their turn supply fuel-wood for the girls' dormitory. Logs of wood are kept burning the whole night during the cold months in the dormitories.

When owing to some common tribal grievance against the State authorities, a general rising of the tribe is decided upon at a meeting of the leaders convened by some prominent Bhūiyā leader, such as the Gaṛh Nāek of Kuiṛa or the Sāont of Kolāiposh, and, by way of a secret signal or message, sesamum seeds are sent round to the headmen of the different Bhūiyā villages indicating the number of combatants each village has to supply, it is the Dihuri and the Nāek who decide which of the young men must go to fight; and out the selected youths go, with alacrity, armed with their bows, arrows, and axes under the leadership of their Nāek on the appointed day.

Thus the Pāuṛi village community is not only bound together by a bond of blood-relationship and common worship of the village deities; but it is also an economic, social and quasi-political organization.

(iii) Social Organizations Higher than the family.

Superimposed on this village organization is the larger organization of the Bār. The villages of the Pāuṛi country are grouped for socio-political purposes into several *Bārs*, each "bār" consisting of from three to twelve or more villages [47]. Thus, villages Kunu, Kundra and Derura of the Pāuṛi Parganā of the Bonāi State form what is called a *Tin-Khaṇḍa Bār*; villages Siligura, Bhutra Losi, Batanga, Kensara, Simna and Remta form a *Sāt-khaṇḍa Bar* known as the *Parbat-khaṇḍa Bār*; villages Nawagāon, Kalakudar, Talbahala, Raikura

The Bar Organization.

47 Compare this with the federal *Pārhā* organization of the Mūṇḍās (*The Mūṇḍās*, pp. 417-9) and the Hōs (*District Gazetteer of Singbhum*, p. 94)

and Barsawa form a *Pānch-Khaṇḍa* Bār known as the *Dodhon-Bār*; villages Usgura, Phuljhar, Soso, Palamuṇḍā, Laghirā, Giniā and a few others together form a Bār known as the *Battish-padā-bār*. For purposes of social government, the elders of the different villages constituting the Bār meet in *Bār-Panchāyats*. The objects for which the Panchāyats of a Bār now ordinarily meet are to take back into the community a man who has been excommunicated by his village Panchāyat either for having kept a female of a tribe or caste other than Bhūiyā or Goūr, or for having killed a cow, calf, or ox; and to divide the property of a heirless Pāuṛi of the Bār; and to incorporate into the Pāuṛi community a man of the Goūr caste or a non-Pāuṛi Bhūiyā of a class at whose hands Pāuṛi Bhūiyās may drink water, when such a Goūṛ or Bhūiyā has kept a Pāuṛi female as his mistress.

Public functionaries of the Bar and their functions.

Every Bār has the following public servants: A Pāuṛi male of one of the villages of the Bār is appointed its *Bhāṇḍāri* or barber who is required to shave a social offender when he is ceremonially taken back to the community or to shave a non-Pāuṛi when the Panchayat of the Bār ceremonially incorporates him into the Pāuṛi community. The Bhāṇḍāri also acts as a messenger to notify the date of a meeting of the Panchāyat of the Bār and to summon the people to attend it. Another Pāuṛi of one of the villages of the Bār is appointed as the Behārā of the Bār. His duty is to perform the purifactory rite of sprinkling from a wooden *mān* or grain-measure a little cowdung diluted in cow's urine on the head of a social offender when he is taken back into the community or on the head of non-Pāuṛis who are taken into the Pāuṛi community. Besides this Bhūiyā Behārā, a Dhobā or man of the Washerman caste living in some village of the Bār is also appointed as the *Dhobā Behārā* of the Bār. His duty is to wash the clothes of a person or family when they are taken back or incorporated into the Pāuṛi community, and also the clothes of a family when they undergo ceremonial purificatian after a death or birth in the village. Ordinarily a Pāuṛi family wash their own clothes; and at birth, death or marriage and also on ordinary occasions, the functions of a barber are performed by a fellow tribesman living in the village. For their services on each ceremonial occasion, the

Bhāṇḍāri is given a cloth or a rupee in cash, the Bhūiyā Behārā gets a rupee or so and the Dhobā Behārā gets from half a rupee to one rupee.

Procedure of the Bār Panchayat.

The method of convening a meeting of the Panchāyāt of the Bār and the procedure followed by the Panchāyāt are as follows:—When the social outcaste informs the Dihuri and Nāek of his village that he has collected the amount necessary for restoration to the community, the Dihuri and Nāek summons the Bhāṇḍāri of the Bār and, through him, sends a message to the different villages of the Bār that such and such a date has been fixed for the *udhrā*, or ceremonial restoration of such and such an outcaste to the community. Sometimes men of some neighbouring Bārs are also invited. On the evening preceding the appointed day, as many Pāuṛis as possible assemble at the village of the outcaste. On their arrival, the women of the village come with jugs of water and wash their feet. The guests each present one or two pice to the women. A feast is provided for the assembled guests at the cost of the outcaste. Next morning when the Panchāyat is assembled the Bhāṇḍāri shaves the outcaste and pares his nails, and

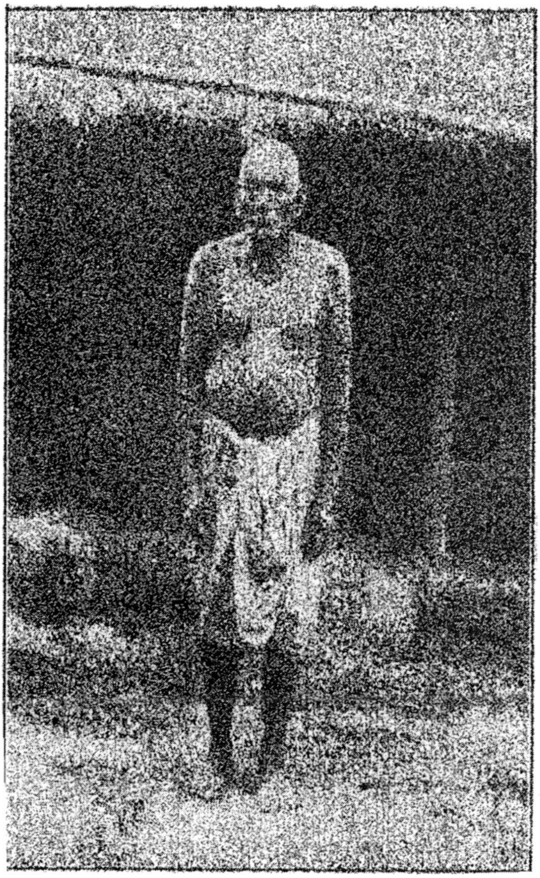

Fig. 13. A Pāuṛi Bhũiyā Headman of a group of villages.

the Bhūiyā Behārā of the Bār by way of purification sprinkles on his head a little cow's urine mixed with a little cow-dung. The same mixture will also be sprinkled over his huts. The man thus restored to the community takes a bath and, by way of a token of his restoration to caste, touches the heap of boiled rice which will then be served to the assembled men of the Bār, with whom he now sits down to a dinner. When they have finished their meal, they go to some stream or pool to bathe. People from adjoining villages return home the same evening, others go back next morning. The same method of purification is adopted to purify, and incorporate into the Pāuṛi community, a Goūr female who has been kept as a mistress by a Pāuṛi man, or a man of the Goūr caste who has kept a Pāuṛi female.

The Bār Panchāyat is invited in the same manner to a village where a Pāuṛi Bhūiyā has died without any son or nephew or brother or other male heir. The assembled elders of the Bār divide the deceased's property into halves,—one half of which is made over to his widow and daughters (if any), and the other half is taken by the Panchāyat who sell all the effects except rice; and the rice, if any, and the sale proceeds of other property go to provide a feast for them.

Besides discharging these social functions, the Bār Panchāyat also assemble to devise means for the redress of any public grievances of the Bār or of the tribe, and take such measures as may be decided upon at such meeting.

A religious bond is supplied to the Bārs by the common worship of *Pāṭs*. A *Pāṭ* is generally some prominent hill or mountain in the neighbourhood, or rather the spirit of such hill or mountain, which is regarded as the tutelary deity of the Bār in the same way as its *Gāī-srī* is the presiding deity of a village. Thus the *Bāro-khaṇḍa Bār* in the Bonāi State, which includes villages Tāsārā, Kēosārā, Bhutrā, Rāotā, Simua, Barābhūi, Julu, Fuljhar, etc., worships *Bhairi-Pāṭ*. Among other *Pāṭs* in the Bonāi State may be mentioned *Khāṇḍā-Pāṭ*, *Jaṭea Pāṭ*, *Belmārā-Pāṭ*, and *Jāoṛi-Pāṭ* The name *Pāṭ* is not however confined to mountains alone. The Brāhmaṇī river, or rather its spirit, is worshipped under the name of *Brāhmaṇī Paṭ*. For purposes of worship *Pāṭs* are represented by stones.

Such are the general features of the social organization of the Pāuṛi Bhūiyās of Bonāi, Keōnjhar and Pāl Lahera. The Bhūiyās of Kuiṛā Parganā of Bonāi follow exactly the same customs and methods in their village organization and village administration. But instead of different Bārs, the whole of the Kuiṛā Parganā consisting of twenty-nine villages form a single Bār, of which the Gaṛh-Nāek of Kuiṛā is the leader, and *Simesvari Pāṭ* the presiding deity.

Kuira Bhuiyas.

These Kuiṛā Bhūiyās of Bonāi, as they are called, form an interesting and instructive link between the unsophisticated and unadulterated Pāuṛi Bhūiyās and the Hinduized Bhūiyās of the Plains. The Kuiṛā Parganā is a small, fairly well-watered valley on the north-east of the Bonāi State; and, favoured by suitable soil, the Pāuṛi Bhūiyās of this tract have taken to regular wet cultivation of rice and thereby improved their economic condition. Naturally enough they are now seeking to rise in the social scale, as they have raised their economic position, to the level of the Hinduized Plains Bhūiyās. They now claim to be "Pānch Śaiā" Bhūiyās and are fast coming to be recognised as such.

In fact, I found local high-caste Hindus taking water at their hands. Although they are undoubtedly Pāuṛi Bhūiyās in origin and still form marriage alliances with the latter and follow practically the same social and religious customs and ceremonies with certain innovations and additions in some details, the more prosperous amongst them disclaim relationship with the Pāuṛi Bhūiyās and now seek the aid of Brāhmaṇ priests at their marriages. This process of gradual Hinduization of sections of aboriginal tribes and their gradual separation from their congeners and, in some cases, their formation into a separate Hindu caste has been silently going on for ages, and forms an important dynamic factor of Indian ethnology.

Bhuiyas of the lowlands.

The more advanced Hinduized Bhūiyās of the lowlands who call themselves Pānch-śaiā Bhūiyās and also *Khaṇḍit* or *Khaṇḍāit* Bhūiyās, lit. swordsmen Bhūiyās—because they form the militia of the respective states and have the sword for their *Santak* or emblem,[48]—have a larger social and

48 The Bhūiyās of the Kuira Paraganā have also adopted the sword (Khaṇḍā) for their emblem and call themselves Khaṇḍāits. The Pāuṛi Bhūiyās have for their emblem the *bāhinga* or carrying-pole, as they have to supply load-carriers to the Rājā when required.

socio-political organization, although their village organization agrees on all points with that of the Pāuṛis and the Kuiṛā Bhūiyās except in the nomenclature of the village headmen. Bhūiyās of the lowlands call their village priest the "Kālo"; and as for the secular headman of a village, the name "Nāek" is still retained in some lowland villages and has been changed for "Ganjhu" in others. Some of these Hinduized Bhūiyā families have also borrowed from the Hindus such titles or *Sangyās* as Sāhu, Phōt-kār, Mājhi, Ohdār, Behārā, Gartia and Pradhān. These titles however do not indicate any special function in the tribal organization. With their broadened outlook on society, these Hinduized Bhūiyās of the lowlands have come to organize a larger tribal association formed of most of the Hinduized Bhūiyās not only of the Keōnjhar, Bonāi and Pāl Lahera States but also of the adjoining states of Gāngpur, Bāmṛa, Mayurbhanj, etc. Once in two or three years the elders of the tribe all meet in panchāyat at the invitation of some important personage of the tribe. Such a tribal panchāyat of the Pāchśai-ghariā Bhūiyās is known as a *Gāddi*. Information is sent to the headmen of different *parga-*

nās and villages as to the day and place appointed for the meeting. Those who can afford to meet the expenses also invite other sections of the Bhuiyās. Such are the Daśgharia, Pānchśai Ghariā and the Panaraśai Bhuiyās (mostly found in the Gāngpur State), the Kāṭiari Bhuiyās of Keōnjhar, Sāontia Bhuiyās of Bonāi and Keōnjhar, etc.

The Pānch-śaiā or Pānch-śai-ghariā Bhuiyās divide the Bhuiyās into three main sections. They call themselves the *Pānch-śaiā* Bhuiyās,—the unmixed Non-Hinduized Bhuiyās such as the Pāuṛis [49] of Bonāi, Pāl Lahera and Keōnjhar, and the indefinite Hākē, Dākē, Meṛhātāṛi, Naksia, Rāutaṛi, etc., as Deś-Bhuiyās or Bāthua Bhuiyās—and the mixed Bhuiyās such as the Rājkuṛi etc., as *Birdiās* or *Birdiā Bhuiyās*.

Procedure at a Gaddi.

At a Gāddi meeting of the Pānch-śaiā Bhuiyās, matters of common interest to the tribe are discussed, and complaints of grave social offences committed by any member of the Pānch-śai-

49 As has been already noticed, the more or less Hinduized portion of the Bhuiyās of Kuiṛa Pargana now disown the name Pāuṛi and call themselves "*Panch Śaiā Des'*" Bhuiyās in imitation of the *Panch Śai-Ghariā Bhuiyās*. The addition of the word "*Des'*" shows that they really belong to the Pāuṛi section of Bhuiyās, the name "*Des' Bhuiyās*" being applied by the *Pānch Śai Ghariās* to the Pāuṛis.

ghariās are heard, discussed and decided, and social outcastes are restored to caste. No one in particular presides at the meeting, but all meet as equals, although the most intelligent amongst the elderly men take the lead in the discussions. On the day when Bhūiyās from different parts of the country assemble, those of each separate locality, such as Bonāi Bhūiyās, Mayurbhanj Bhūiyās, etc. are accommodated in separate *khāndās*, (literally, compartments or enclosures) to cook and eat their meals. Provisions are supplied by the man or men who convene the meeting. When the discussions are finished and it is decided (as is generally done at such *Gāddi* meetings) to take back into the tribe one or more persons who had been outcasted for some social offence, such as causing the death of a bullock through negligence or otherwise, a grand feast has to be provided, at the cost of such person or persons, to all the assembled Bhūiyās. For this final dinner for all the Pānch-śai-ghariā Bhūiyās, the cooking is done not at different *khāndās* as heretofore but at one big *khāndā* or spot called the *Mahā-khāndā* (or great *khāndā*). The other sections of the Bhūiyās are provided with rations which they cook each in their own separate *khāṇlā*. When the dinner for the Pānch-śai-ghariās is ready, the convener of the assembly requests them to sit down to dinner. The eldest of the Sāonts (social heads of certain parganās), Nāeks and Kālos are seated side by side. When all have taken their seats and dinner is served to them, the eldest Sāont, Nāek and Kālo, first eat each a morsel or two, and then some one asks them, "Have you begun?" On their answering in the affirmative, others begin eating [50]. The person thus restored to the tribe dines with the rest as a token of his restoration.

(*iv*) *Influence of Religion on Social Integration.*

Although all the Pāuṛi Bhūiyās of the Keōnjhar, Bonāi and Pal Lahera States do not yet meet in such large tribal gatherings for social purposes as the Pānch-śai-Ghariās do in their *Gāddis*, yet for the last thirty years or more they have begun in the Bonāi State, at any rate, to associate together in a common religious festival at Bonāigarh once in a year in the month of September or October; and already at such meetings of the elders of all the Pāuṛi villages certain topics of

50 Cf. the Mūṇḍā custom which requires the *Karṭāhā* of a Pāṛhā to eat the first morsel of food at such a tribal feast. (*The Mūṇḍās*, p. 419)

social interest have begun to be informally considered. In fact, this religious festival of the Pāuṛis is of great social significance as it helps in bringing together not only all the Bhūiyās of the Pāuṛi country but also other sections of the Bhūiyās as well as some other castes, high and low, of the Bonāi States. Even the Hindu Rājā of the Bonāi State takes a prominent part in this festival which is known as the festival of the deity 'Konto Kuāri'. The name Konta Kuāri is applied to a roundish fragment of some old metal object which was dug up by some cultivator and taken charge of by the Pāuṛi Dihuri of village Jolo near the Khaṇḍādhār waterfall, about sixteen miles from Bonāigaṛh. From its quaint shape it came to be regarded as the receptacle of mystic power or divine energy and consequently the image of a deity. The Dihuri keeps the so-called image in some secret spot during the whole of the year and brings it out only on the occasion of this festival which has come to be a tribal festival of the Pāuṛis and a territorial festival for all the castes and tribes of the Bonāi State. Pāuṛi Bhūiyās even from the Keōnjhar State may be seen attending the festival. As I had the opportunity of witnessing the festival and accompanying the procession, I shall proceed to give an account of this interesting religious festival.

On some day after the eighth day of the new moon (*Kriṣṇāṣṭamī*) and before the following new moon (*amābasyā*) day the Dihuri of village Jolo comes to the Rājā's *garh* at Bonāi when the Rājā takes out from his Bhāṇḍār (store-room) one earthen vessel filled with unhusked rice of a whitish colour, seven pieces of turmeric, and a little vermilion, and hands these over to the Dihuri. With these the Dihuri returns home. On the following Mahālayā or new moon day, the Dihuri goes to the hiding-place of the image, and after making the customary offerings (including the rice, turmeric and vermilion received from the Rājā), carries the image in a small bamboo-box to his own house at Jolo, where the headmen of several Pāuṛi villages assemble. The next day after bathing the image in cold water, and making offerings of *āruā* rice, fowls, molasses, etc., to the deity, the Dihuri of Jolo carries the image or symbol of Konto Kuāri in the bamboo-box in a procession accompanied by the headmen of different Pāuṛi Bhuiyā villages and followed by a band of musicians playing on their drums and pipes and flutes. That afternoon on their arrival at village Haldikudar—a Pānch-ṣai-ghariā Bhuiyā village,—the Bhuiyā Gāonṭia or headman of the village anoints the image with turmeric paste and offers sacrifices to it. Then the image is taken to the house of every other villager who may wish to make sacrifices and offerings to the deity. Thence the party proceed to village Khuṭgaon and halt that night at the house of the Jāgirdār or landlord of that place known under the title of Mahāpātra, who is a Hinduized Goṇḍ. The bamboo-box containing the image of Konto Kuāri is hung up inside the house.

Next morning the Goṇḍ Mahāpātra sacrifices a goat to Konto Kuāri. From his house the image is taken by the Dihuri of Jolo to other houses in village Khuṭgāon and, at every house where it is taken, either a goat or a fowl is sacrificed to the deity and other offerings are made. As the deity may not spend more than one night at any one village, the party proceed that day to village Bichnāpoit where they halt for the night at the public rest-house known as *ḍerā-ghar*. Next morning the deity is taken first to the house of the Nāek of the village who is a Goṇḍ and thence to other houses of the village where the presence of the deity may be sought. At every house either a goat or one or more fowls are sacrificed to the deity, and other offerings are made. Thence the party proceed to village Pūigāon and there they halt for the night at the public *ḍerā-ghar*.

Next morning the deity is taken first to the house of the Goṇḍ headman (Nāek) of the village and then to the other houses of which the owners request the Dihuri to take it; and the deity receives sacrifices and offerings at each such house. Towards evening the party cross the river Brāhmaṇī and reach village Jokāikelā where they halt for the night at the house of the Kālo or village priest who is a Pānch-śai-ghariā Bhūiyā.

The following morning, after sacrifices are offered at the Kālo's house, the deity is taken to other houses in the village where offerings and sacrifices are made to the deity. In the evening the party proceed to village Jōmkāi and halt at the *Maṇḍa-ghar* for the night. Next morning after pūjā offerings and sacrifices are made to Konto Kuāri at the house of the Gāonṭiā or headman of the village who is a man of the

Kolitā cast, the image is taken to the house of different villagers who may want to offer sacrifices to the deity. Thence the party proceed to village Obodyā, and, if the *ashṭāmi tithi* (eighth day of the moon) has already begun, they proceed straight on towards the Rājā's palace at Bonāigaṛh. If, however, the eighth day of the moon falls on the next day, they halt for the night at Obodyā in the compound of the Rājā's *Khāmār* or threshing floor where next morning a goat is sacrificed to the deity and then the image is taken to different houses in the village and at each such house sacrifices and offerings are made to the deity. Thence, at sunset, the party start in procession and at about nine in the evening reach village Kontmel about a mile from Bonāigaṛh. By the roadside at village Kontmel an earthen altar has been erected on which sacrifices to the deity are to be offered. A canopy has been set up over it, and lamps have been lighted and carpets spread under it and seats placed for the Rājā and members of his family as also for other respectable visitors.

On the party arriving there, the Rājā and his party receive them. The Dihuri of Jolo comes up to the Rājā with the image, salutes him, and enquires of him about the health and welfare, first of himself, then of his *Rāṇī*, then of his children, then of his servants, then of his elephants, then of his horses, and last of all about the welfare of the land (*Prithvī* or Earth). The Rājā answers "yes" to every question; and then, in his turn, the Rājā asks the Dihuri about the welfare of himself and his children and then of the Pāuṛis generally; and to every question the Dihuri replies in the affirmative. Then the Dihuri places the image on a new cloth which the Rājā holds in his hands for the purpose. The Rājā then places it on a small silver throne which is kept in readiness to receive the deity. While the Dihuri hands over the image to the Rājā, he addresses the Rājā, saying—"Here is your deity (Deota); we kept it in the hills. Examine and see if the image is broken or intact." The Rājā looks at it and says, "It is all right", and hands it over to the Amāt, a man of the Sudh caste who officiates as the priest of some of the Rājā's family deities. The Sudh priest or Amāt puts down the image on the mud-altar prepared for the purpose where the Amāt worships the deity with offerings supplied by the Rājā, and sacrifices two goats supplied by the Rājā, both reddish grey in colour and both with horns equal in size and both of the same height. The two goats are made to stand side by side and both are slain with the same stroke of the sword dealt at their joined necks by the practised hand of the Bārik. After these offerings and sacrifices on behalf of the Rājā, a number of fowls and goats brought by men of surrounding villages are offered to the deity, and offerings of pumpkins, *muṛki* (pyramid-shaped cakes made of fried rice or *lāwā* and molasses) and sweets are brought by the people and offered to the deity by the Amāt. Everyone bringing the offerings and sacrifices does so in the hope of being favoured with some desired boon from the deity, and it is asserted that the boons mentally prayed for at the time by the persons who bring the offerings are generally granted. The image is next taken to a cross-road at Konjuli, a *basti* or quarter of the town of Bonāi; and there again several persons of different castes bring offerings and sacrifices which are offered to the deity by the Amāt. The image is then carried in procession successively to the house of a man of the Suṛi (liquor-seller) caste and that of a man of the Kūsāri (brazier) caste, where special offerings are made to the deity.

Then the image is taken successively to the altars of the deities Nilji and Kumāri where, too, sacrifices are offered. Finally the image is ceremonially installed in a shed prepared for the purpose in the Rājā's palace compound where sacrifices are again offered.

The following morning, which is the ninth day of the moon, after sacrifices of a sheep and a goat, the deity is carried by the Rājā himself into the inner apartments of his palace, where the members of his family make offerings of sweetmeats to Konto Kuāri; and finally on an inner veranda of the palace the Amāt bathes the image in liquor and makes offerings of rice, sweets, etc., and sacrifices one or more buffaloes, one or more sheep and sixteen or more goats to the deity. After being taken to the Rājā's *Chhatragambhirā* (room in which State umbrellas are kept) the image is taken first to the houses of the different kinsmen of the Rājā and then to houses of other residents of Bonāigaṛh and finally to the Amāt's house. At every house where the image is taken sacrifices or offerings are made to the deity. The Amāt now hands over the image to the Dihuri of Jolo who in his turn carries it from house to house in Bāhārgaṛh, a quarter of Bonāigaṛh, just beyond the immediate vicinity of the palace. Finally it is taken to the bank of the Brāhmaṇī where the Rājā's *behārā* of the untouchable Pān caste hands over to the Dihuri a goat and a fowl. These the Dihuri sacrifices to the deity, and the Pān Behārā who by reason of his being an untouchable is not allowed to touch the image or even offer flour or rice to the deity with his own hands, offers from some distance seven cakes called *neem chūkli* made of rice-flour and pounded leaves of the *neem* tree. This privilege is allowed to the Pān Behārā as, it is said, an ancestor of this Pān first discovered the image.

Now the Dihuri of Jolo places the image in the bamboo box and, accompanied by the whole body of Pāuṛi headmen, crosses over to the other side of the Brāhmaṇī where they pass the rest of the night at the house of a certain man of the Keōnṭ caste. Such is the rigidity of custom with this people that even if, in any year, the day dawns by the time they reach the Keōnṭ's house, the party must lie down in the house for a short while to keep up the practice which has now acquired the force of an inviolable rite. On getting up, the men bathe themselves and bathe the deity, and the Dihuri makes offerings to the deity of rice, flowers, etc., and, when available, a goat is sacrificed. Then the Dihuri takes the deity in procession from house to house where sacrifices and offerings are made. Thence the party proceed successively to villages Nalai, Tankjura and Brāhmaṇ-gāo, Amātpati, Kurda, Bhugru, Godrua, Dhuri, Kolaiposh, Joṛibāhā, Konta Kudar and finally, on the Kojāgar Purṇimā day, return to village Jolo. At every village the image is taken round and offerings and sacrifices are made to the deity at different houses.

Arrived at Jolo, the image is kept suspended on a tree in the jungle. Almost all the adult Pāuṛi Bhūiyās of the nearly sixty villages of Pāuṛi Parganā of the Bonāi State assemble at Jolo on the Kojāgar Purṇimā day with goats or fowls and rice and other offerings. In the course of the day the deity is taken in procession to the Dihuri's house and placed in the *āngan* which has been cleaned with cowdung and water. There the offerings and sacrifices brought by all the Pāuṛi Bhūiyās of the country are offered by the Dihuri to the goddess. The rice and the meat are then cooked and the people are treated to a hearty feast. They then all disperse. Finally the Dihuri and another member of his family take the image to its hiding-place which is kept secret even from the other members of the Dihuri's family. The reason assigned for taking one member of the family in the Dihuri's confidence is that in the event of the Dihuri's death the other man may know where to find the image. Like the Amāṭ at Bonāi, the Dihuri of Jolo collects a decent sum (about twenty to thirty rupees) as fees paid to him for the pūjā at the different houses where the image is taken during the journey to Bonāigaṛh and back. Part of this is spent in the feast to the assembled Pāuṛi Bhuiyās on the Kojāgar Purṇīma day and part in drink while the assembled Pāuṛis wait on the bank of the Brāhmaṇī opposite Bonāigaṛh to take back the image of Konto Kuāri from Bonāi to Jolo.

This annual tribal gathering although originating in a mere accident, namely, the discovery of a peculiarly shaped piece of metal, bids fair to develop in time into a great socio-political and socio-religious congress of the tribe.

Here, by way of a digression, it may be noted that the Konto Kuāri festival would seem to throw an interesting sidelight on the social history of ancient India. The participation of the Hindu Rājā of the Bonāi State in the worship of Konto Kuāri, the goddess of the semi-savage Pāuṛis, and some other usages of the Rāj family, such as the worship of the deities Āndhāri and Kuāri who are the tutelary deities of the Pāuṛi Bhuiyās of the Kuiṛā Parganā, in temples built near the Rājā's palace and the employment by the Rājā of a family priest of the low semi-aboriginal caste of Sūdhs to worship these aboriginal deities, and of a Keōnṭ spirit at every marriage and *upanayan* (investiture with the sacred thread) in the Rāj family, and the sacrifice of goats and buffaloes offered by the Rājā near his palace to the spirit of an ancient Kōl hero, Mahābīrā,—all this would seem to give us an insight into the politic methods which the ancient Āryan immigrants into India adopted in order to conciliate the overwhelming masses of non-Aryan population and bring them under subjection, and impose something of their Aryan culture on them, although in this process of the Aryanization of the aborigines the originally simple and sublime natural religion of the ancient Indo-Aryans was leavened by admixture with the animistic religion of the indigenous population, and gave rise to the heterogenous pantheon of Hindu gods and goddesses that now constitutes Popular Hinduism—an amalgam of the religion of the Āryan and that of the non-Aryan (Proto-Australoid or Pre-Dravidian and Dravidian).

In this connection it is interesting to note that the village deities are all Devīs or goddesses and at their temples at Bonāigaṛh maintained by the Rājā, the officiating priest or *Amāt* has been a man of the semi-aboriginal Sūdh caste for three or four generations and before that the *Amāt* was an aboriginal *Bhūiyā*. It is said that the old *Bhūiyā* Dihuri family left Bonāi owing to some disagreement with the Rājā and the Sūdh priest was appointed temporarily, in expectation of the return of the *Bhūiyā* Dihuri family, but that as the latter did not return, the Sūdh family has been working as priests since then. Even in the Kumāri temple in the Rājā's palace, the Sūdh *Amāt* along with a Brāhmaṇ priest, performs the prescribed *pūjās*. To this day the *Bānesvara Lingaṁ* or Śiva at the Bānesvar temple at Bonāi is in sole charge of *Bhūiyā* priests.

(v) *Influence of State-Policy on Sociology.*

Certain rites and customs connected with the installation of some of the Native Hindu Ruling Chiefs of the Tributary States of Ōṛissā (Eastern States Agency) give us a further insight into the politic methods by which alien Hindu adventurers succeeded in establishing and consolidating their sway over these aborigines. In the process of conciliation of the aboriginal population, the culture of the immigrant Hindus while influencing the aboriginal culture to some extent could not escape the infiltration of a fair share of aboriginal ideas and customs. The following accounts of the part taken by the Bhūiyās in the installation ceremonies of the Rājās of the Keōñjhar and Bonāi States would appear to be highly interesting and illuminating in this connection.

Installation ceremony of the Raja of Keonjhar.

The installation of a Rājā of Keōñjhar is not regarded as complete until his Bhūiyā subjects have performed their part of the ceremonies. Colonel Dalton who witnessed the ceremony has given a brief account of it in his *Ethnology of Bengal*. These ceremonies as prescribed by old custom and actually practised at the present day were thus described to me in much greater detail by an old retired Officer of the State whose functions included the superintendence of the installation ceremonies, and who served the State for many years and supervised more than one royal installation at Keōnjhargaṛh.

On the appointed day the Pāuṛis or Hill Bhūiyās muster strong at the Rājā's palace under the leadership of a Bhūiyā who holds the hereditary title of Mahā-Nāyak (*lit*, the great leader). While the Rājā is seated on the throne, the Bhūiyās march into the court-yard of the palace with their *chāngu* drums and other musical instruments. Then the Mahā-Nāyak (of village Oṛal) approaches him with a large pumkin on his shoulder and presents it to the Rājā in token of the allegiance of his tribe. He then solicits the Rājā's permission to perform the identical ceremonies with which the Bhūiyās are reputed to have installed the first Bhanj Rājā of Keōnjhar. On such permission being granted, the Mahā-Nāyāk, stooping on his hands and feet and thus representing a horse, carries the Rājā on his back to the *Siṁhāsan Melā* or throne room. There another Bhūiyā officiant styled the Kāṭoi (of village Bāṅspāhāṛ) is seated on a cotton quilt. A new earthenware pitcher filled with water is kept close by. The Bhuiyā Mahā-Nāyak in the guise of a horse, carries the Rājā on his back to the throne-room and seats the Rājā on a new cloth spread over the knees of the Kāṭoi. Another Bhuiyā (the headman of Village Bargoru) who is Styled *Rōṛā* then makes offerings of flowers to the deity represented by the new earthen pitcher (*mangal-ghaṭ*), and sprinkles a little sanctified water from the pitcher on the Rājā. He then places a crown, made of a long flexible creeper called *suālatā*, on the Rājā's head, and also invests him with a *paitā* (sacred thread) made of the "Seem" creeper, and marks a 'Rāj-ṭikā' or mark of royalty on the Rājā's forehead with vermilion and sandal-paste.

The headman of the Sāñoti tribe (probably a Sub-tribe of the Bhuiyas) who is styled the Berājal Mahāpātra then ties a silk [51] turban (Pāgṛi) on the Rājā's head, and another headman of the same tribe who is styled *Gharpo* stands by the side of the Rājā, fanning him with a bunch of *Sīāṛi* fibres fastened together in

51 It is said that the silk turban has been recently introduced in place of the cotton *pāgṛi* formerly used.

the shape of a *chāmar* or whisk, and the headman (*Kabāṭ*) of the Khoṇḍ tribe holds over the Rājā's head an umbrella made of *siāṛi* leaves.

A number of Bhuiyās stand all around the Rājā, holding in their hands clubs made of tree-branches with leaves and barks on, to represent maces of gold and silver, and also other imitations of the insignia of royalty such as flags and banners, canopies and *chāmārs* or fanning whisks, royal umbrellas etc. Then the headman of the Rājkuli Bhuiyās, who bears the title of *Daṇḍa-sena* sounds a gong and the Mahāpātra of the Sāōnti tribe marks the Rājā's forehead with a mark of *dahi* (curdled milk). Then the Kabāṭ of the Khōṇḍ tribe makes over his umbrella to a Bhuiyā to hold it over the head of the Rājā, and lies down with his face to the ground before the Rājā and personates a *Meṛiāh* (or victim for human sacrifice). The Bhuiyā (headman of village Bargōṛā) who bears the designation of Roṇā hands over a sword to the Rājā and tells him, "I invest thee with the right of beheading people. Do thou thy will". The Rājā touches the neck of the 'Meṛiāh' with the sword two times and hands back the sword to the Roṇā. The Roṇā, in his turn, similarly touches the neck of the mock Meṛiāh with the sword, and puts it back. Then the Khoṇḍ Kabāṭ who personated a Meṛiāh gets up and beats a hasty retreat, as custom requires that he must not be seen for three days, after which he is to appear again before the Rājā, as if restored to life by a miracle, and fall at the feet of the Rājā by way of obeisance; whereupon the Rājā presents him with a new cloth. When the Meṛiāh disappears, the Bhūiyās approach the Rājā and, in a body, prostrate themselves before him, and crave the Rājā's forgiveness for their past offences. They do not get up until the Rājā tells them that they are forgiven and bids them rise. Then they all get up, and the Mahā-Nāyak steps forward and formally inquires about the Rājā's health and the welfare of his family, of his elephants and horses, and of all the State parapharnalia. These loyal inquiries are duly answered, and the Karaṇ or Writer-in-Chief of the State reads out from a palm-leaf document stereotyped inquiries regarding the health and well-being of the Bhūiyās, their families, cattle, streams and fields. Again the Bhūiyās prostrate themselves before their Rājā, and then take leave of him.

The cotton-quilt and other articles made for the ceremony as well as the garments worn by the Rājā on this occasion are given to the Bhūiyās as their perquisites.

Colonel Dalton, who himself witnessed the installation of the grand-father of the present Rājā of Keōnjhar thus describes the ceremony:—

"A large shed attached to the Raja's palace and ordinarily used as lumber room, was cleared out, swept and garnished, spread with carpets, and otherwise prepared for the occasion. A number of Brāhmaṇs were in attendance in sacerdotal costume, seated amidst the sacred vessels and implements, and articles for offerings used in the consecration of Rājās, according to the ceremonies prescribed in the Vedas.

"Beyond the circle of the brahmanical preparations a group of the principal Bhūiyās were seated, cleanly robed for the occasion and garlanded.

"When the company were all seated and these arrangements complete, the young Rājā Dhanurjai Bhanj entered and distributed *pān*, confections, spices, and garlands, and retired. Then after a pause there was heard a great crash of the discordant but wild and deep-toned wind instruments and drums of the Bhūiyās and other tribes, and the Rājā entered mounted on the back of a strongly-built Bhūiyā Chief, who plunged and pawed and snorted under him like a fiery steed. Moving to the opposite side of the brahmanical sacred circle, followed by a host of the tribe, one of them placed himself on a low platform covered with red cloth, and with his body and limbs formed the back and arms of the throne on which the Rājā, dismounting from his biped steed, was placed. Then the attendant Bhūiyās each received from the Rājā's usual servants extemporised imitations of the insignia of royalty,—banners, standards, pankhas, chaurs, chhatras, canopies,—and thirty-six of the tribe as hereditary office-bearers, each with his symbol, ranged themselves round their chief.

"There was a temporary hitch in consequence of the unexpected absence of the hereditary sword-bearer, but after a slight delay a deputy was found and the ceremony proceeded, not, however, until the Bhūiyās had protested against such an irregularity being admitted as a precedent. Then one of the principal

Bhuiyā chiefs, taking a light flexible jungle creeper of considerable length, binds it round the Rājā's turban as the 'siropa', or honorary head dress, conferred by them. The bands strike up whilst this is done. Bards chant hymns of praise, and Brāhmaṇs recite from the Shama Veda and, the leading chief of the clan, Bamdeo Ranha, dipping his finger into the saucer of sandalwood essence, makes on the forehead of the Rājā the mark called '*tika*'. The Brāhmaṇ priest, the prime minister or *bewartha*, and others then repeat the ceremony of giving the *tika*, so that a considerable amount of such sealing is required to constitute a Rājā of Keōnjhar. The brāhmānical ceremony of consecration had been duly solemnized on a previous occasion by the Brāhmaṇs, but a portion of this ceremony, omitting the anointing with clarified butter, etc., was now again performed by the priests, ratifying and rendering sacred the act of the Bhuiyās. Then the sword, a very rusty weapon, is placed in the Rājā's hands, and one of the Bhuiyās, named Anand Kopāt, comes before him kneeling sideways, the Rājā touches him on the neck with the weapon as if about to strike off his head, and it is said that in former days there was no fiction in this part of the ceremony. The family of the Kopāt hold their lands on the condition that the victim when required shall be produced. Anand, however, hurriedly arose after the accolade and disappeared. He must not be seen for three days; and he presents himself again to the Rājā as miraculously restored to life.

"The Bhũiyā chiefs next make offerings to the Rājā,—rice, pulse, pots of ghee, milk, honey, and other things,—each article being touched by all the sirdars before it is presented. The chief sirdars now solemnly address him, and telling him they have under the authority exercised by them and their ancestors from time immemorial, made over to him the realm and the people therein, enjoin him to rule with justice and mercy. It was a long speech, of which I could catch but little. The ceremony was then concluded with a salute of guns. The Rājā arose and again mounted on his curvetting and frisky biped steed, left the assembly surrounded and followed by all the Bhũiyā office-bearers and their insignia, and was thus escorted to his own apartment in the palace.

"Soon after—it may be on a subsequent date—the Bhũiyās do homage to the Rājā elect. They come in a body bringing in as gifts, produce—gourds, fruits, Indian corn,—and laying them at the Rājā's feet, they ask after his health, his establishment, his horses and his elephants, and in return the Rājā inquires after their crops, cows, fowls, and children. This over, each sirdar prostrates himself, and taking the Rājā's foot in his hand places the royal toe first on his right and then on his left ear, and then on his forehead."[52]

As in Keōnjhar, so in the neighbouring State of Bonāi, the installation or *abhiseka* ceremony of its Hindu *Rājā* is not regarded as complete unless and until a Bhūiyā chief puts the distinctive mark of kingship on his forehead in the manner described below.

Before the advent of the Kadambaṁśī Rājās of Bonāi, who claim to be Āryan Kṣatriyas, the Pāik or Khaṇḍāit Bhūiyās appear at one time to have held the country in sovereignty, and the titles of Sāmant, Phōtkār, Gartiā, Ṭhākur, etc., borne by various Khaṇḍāit Bhūiyā families may not improbably have come down from those days, unless they have been bestowed by some ancestor of the present Rāj family. That the present Rāj family of Bonāi derived their authority

52 Dalton, *Ethnology of Bengal*, pp. 145-147.

from the former Bhūiyā chiefs not wholly by conquest but partly by conciliation appears to be evidenced by the fact that to this day some honorary Bhūiyā officers take a prominent part in the installation ceremony of a new Rājā and also in the periodical installation ceremonies held three times in the year, namely, on the day following the Daśahārā ceremony, the full moon day in the month of Pouś, and the full moon day in the month of Śrāvan. A short account of the ceremony is given below.

The Installation ceremony of a Raja of Bonai.

As soon as a Rājā dies, his heir, in company with the family priest and the Rājā's *Mantri* (Minister) and his near agnates, if any present, approach the corpse before it is taken out of its death bed. Either the priest or the *Mantri* takes a new silk turban in his hands and first places it on the head of the corpse and forthwith takes it off and crowns his heir by placing this turban on his head. The ancient sword of the Rāj family known as the "Kumāri Prasād" (i.e. Blessed by Kumāri, the tutelary goddess of the family), is also placed by the priest or by the *Mantri* into the hands of the new Rājā. The Rājā now sits on the throne (*gadi*) in a *Darbār* held for the purpose, and orders the Mantri,—"Remove the corpse" (*Murdā uṭhāo*). The corpse is then removed from its room and carried to the cremation-ground. The new Rājā may not accompany the corpse to the cremation-ground nor take any part in the Śrāddha or funeral ceremonies,—his younger brothers, if any, or cousins or other near agnates performing the same. Between the day of the demise of the late Rājā and the formal installation or *Abhiṣeka* of the new Rājā, the latter has to live in seclusion in the *Baṛ-darbār-* (Big Darbār-) house of the palace. All this time he must keep holding a sword in his hand. Although he takes no part in the funeral ceremonies, he observes ceremonial pollution for ten days from the day of the late Rājā's death, lives on a purely vegetable diet (*habiṣyānna*) for eleven days, and has his head shaved and his nails pared on the eleventh day. On the morning of the sixteenth day, the new Rājā repairs to the temple of *Bāneśvara* (Śiva) by the side of the Brāhmaṇī river about three miles from his palace. It may be noted that the deity is represented by a phallic emblem made of stone, and the priest of the *Bānesvara* temple is a Bhuiyā. The gold-handled and gold-embroidered

State-umbrella is taken to the temple where the Rājā himself holds it over the head of the Bānesvara *Śiva-lingaṁ*. Then he returns in procession to the palace, the umbrella-bearer holding the State umbrella over the Rājā's head. On his return to the palace, the family priest of the Hinduized Śūdh or Śūdha caste makes offerings of flowers and sweets to the tutelary deity of the family and to the *Pāṭ Khaṇḍā* which is said to be the sword with which the first *Kadamb Baṁśi* Rājā conquered the country and which is therefore also regarded in the light of a tutelary deity. The Brāhmaṇ priests of the Rāj family perform the *Hōm* ceremony at the same time. The Rājā remains all the time seated where these ceremonies are going on, armed with five kinds of weapons, namely, the *Kumāri Prasād* sword, one dagger, one knife, and three bows and arrows. After these *pujās* are finished, the Rājā rides an elephant and goes in state to the Bānesvara temple once more. Two Bhūiyās styled *Ankuliā Baktriās* act as his body-guards and walk before the Rājā, each armed with a battle-axe. Arrived at the temple, the Rājā prostrates himself before the *lingaṁ*. Then he visits successively all the important temples of the town, namely,—

the Kōpesvara temple, the Gopāl-ji temple, the Kumāri temple and the Jagarnāth temple, and prostrates himself before the images. On his return to his palace, he sits in Darbār where a Bhūiyā landholder who is known by the title of *Sāmanta* makes *ṭikā* or a mark of sovereignty on the Rājā's forehead with earth and then addresses him as "Rājā" and says—"I grant thee such-and-such (names) a village". The Rājā in return says, "I grant such-and-such (names) a village to you, and make you my Sāmanta" (General of the forces). Now-a-days, however, the same village which the Sāmanta "grants" to the Rājā is in return "granted" back to the Sāmanta. Then other "vassals" of the Rājā, such as the Mahāpātra, the Daṇḍapātra, and the Gāoñṭiās salute (*salām*) the Rājā and make certain presents to him. Finally Brāhmaṇ priests pronounce benedictions on the new Rājā. As I have already noticed, the same *Abhiṣeka* or Installation ceremonies are gone through three times every year. The only difference in these periodical installation ceremonies is that the *ṭikā* ceremony is omitted. I had an opportunity of witnessing the ceremonies on one of these occasions.

In the Pāl Lahera State the Bhūiyās have no

special function to perform at the installation ceremony of the Rājā. It is the tribal chief or headman of the allied tribe of Sahars (Savaras) who takes the leading part in the Rāja's installation. He takes the new Rājā on his lap, and ties a certain jungle creeper round his head by way of crowning him king.

Such periodical associations of the principal tribes of a State either for a common religious cult or for a common State ritual do not appear to have helped, to any appreciable extent, in welding the different castes and tribes of the State into a centralised people with anything like a common national feeling. These occasional gatherings round some deity or round their King have, however, the beneficial effect of stimulating their religions emotions—their feeling of dependance on supernatural agencies for protection and prosperity, and of fostering their feelings of loyalty and respect for the constituted head of the State. As for social organization, it would seem as if the highest real integration to which the Bhūiyās have so far attained was the socio-political federation of a group of villages known as the Bār or the Piṛ under a common headman. Only on occasions of extreme tribal exasperation or a real or supposed common danger, however, the tribe, as a whole, come together to right a real or fancied wrong. A knotted string or "ganthi" of tree-fibre is passed round from village to village in the names of the tribal chiefs with a message to assemble in arms at an appointed place on an appointed day, and the message is strictly obeyed and the whole country is thrown into commotion. Such was the Bhuiyā rebellion of the year 1891 in the Keoñjhar State due to grievances regarding enhanced rents and forced labour, which had to be quelled with a strong hand and the people pacified by a fresh rent-settlement.

CHAPTER VI.

KINSHIP ORGANIZATION.

Kutumb and Bandhu Villages.

For purposes of marriage, the Pāuṛi Bhūiyā country, as I said in the last chapter, is divided into groups of exogamous village-communities called *Kutumb* villages, the members of which are supposed to be of one blood and, as such, may not intermarry. In relation to each group of *Kutumb* villages, the remaining villages of the particular Parganā are called *Bandhu* villages, that is to say, villages with the members of which individuals of the former group of *Kuṭumb* villages may enter into matrimonial alliances. This classification of villages for matrimonial purposes as *Kuṭumb* villages and *Bandhu* villages obtains not only among the unsophisticated Pāuṛi Bhūiyās of Keonjhar, Pāl Lahera and the Pāuṛi Parganā of Bonāi but also among the more sophisticated Bhūiyās of the Kuiṛā Parganā of Bonāi. Thus in the Kuiṛā Parganā, villages Kuiṛā,

Kādōdi, Nuāgāon, Teherāi, Sunuā, Ḍumarḍi and Kōlmōnga form one group of *Kuṭumb* villages; Kasirā, Bhōjpāli, Nadi Kasiṛā and Kōmōnḍō form a second group of *Kuṭumb* villagss; Tōntrā, Raikerā and Bōndōl form a third group; Tintō, Indpur, Bōrḍih, Pōnmōg and Khajūrḍih form a fourth group; and Pāṭmūṛā, Bar Pāṭūli, Sān Pāṭūli, Mithardyā, Sarigar, Ganua and Pāmpōsh form a fifth group. Each of these groups are exogamous so far as its own group is concerned but endogamous so far as other groups of Pāuṛi villages are concerned. It is doubtful whether the alleged common descent of all the Bhūiyās of one *Kuṭumb* group of villages is an actual fact or the result of deliberate arrangement and make-believe [52].

52 It may be noted that, like the Pāuṛi Bhūiyās, their neighbours the Juāngs (one of the most primitive among the Mūṇḍā tribes) also regard all the old Juāng families of a settlement to be descendants of a common ancestor and, as such, *Kutumb* or agnates among whom no intermarriage is permissible. But the Juāngs of a village in the Keonjhar State, unlike the Pāuṛi Bhūiyās regard all other Juāng villages as their Bandhu villages and may marry in any of those villages. This would appear to have been the original custom which permitted marriage in any settlement outside their own. It is interesting to note that in some Pāuṛi Bhūiyā villages, in the Pāl Lahera State and in the neighbouring villages (e.g. Kuār) of the Keonjhar State, the Pāuṛi Bhūiyās have adopted certain titles or honorific designations like *Mantri*, *Parihār*, *Koṭa*, *Jena* etc., which they call *Khili* (cf. *Kili* or clan among to Mūṇḍās, Hōs, etc.), and which have practically developed into exogamous clans; and even among these *Khilis*, some are regarded as having developed out of one original *Khili* and, intermarriage amongst them are prohibited. Thus the Pradhān *Khili* may not intermarry with the Kaṭai, Jena and Parihār *Khilis*,

As among other Proto-Australoid Mūṇḍā tribes, the father is the guardian of his children, the system of reckoning descent is patrilineal; and the wife is brought to her husband's family; in other words, marriage is patrilocal, and the type of family is patrilineal and patripotestal.

Although theoretically a Pāuṛi Bhūiyā may marry any Bandhu female—and formerly this seems to have been the rule,—with the advance of time, regard for certain near consanguinous relationships among members of *Bandhu* families together with the "classificatory" system of reckoning kinship, imposed a few restrictions on this simple rule of marriage and kinship. Thus, the widow of a maternal uncle, although a *Bandhu* woman, cannot be taken in marriage.

The Classificatory system and Kinship Nomenclature.

Under the classificatory system of reckoning kinship, the same relationship term is used in addressing most, though not all, persons of the same generation and sex. Thus every one whom the father of a Pāuṛi Bhūiyā calls "didā" or elder bro-

---

and the Mantri or Matri *Khili* may not intermarry with the Mōndamth and Sōnwai *Khilis*.

ther (or cousin), is his own "baṛu" and his mother's "deṛsūr" and every one whom his father calls "nāno" or younger brother (or cousin) is his own "kōkā" and his mother's "dhongrā", and every one whom his mother calls "didā" (elder brother or cousin) or "nāno" (younger brother or cousin) is his own "māmu". In several cases, there are two distinct groups of terms to express relationship, one in speaking *of* relatives and another in speaking *to* him. In the following terms of relationship and mutual address, the terms "brother" and "sister" are used in a classificatory sense and include cousins, however remote. As the terms of address are used in a much more general sense and are of more extended application, they are necessarily fewer in number.

List of Relationship Terms.

English term of relationship.	Pāuṛi's term for the relationship.	Pāuṛi term for addressing such relative.
Father	*Buā*	*Eh Buā !*
Mother	*Mā*	*Eh Mā !*
Father's younger brother ...	*Kōkā* ...	*Eh Kōkā !*
Father's younger brother's wife...	*Kōkī* ...	*Eh Kōkī !*

English term of relationship.	Pāuṛi's term for the relationship.	Pāuṛi term for addressing such relative.
Husband	*Ghaitā or gusiā*	(*Eh* father of so-and-so).
Wife	*Bharyyā* ...	*Eh bo!* (or *Eh* mother of so-and-so).
Elder brother's wife	*Bahu* ...	*Eh Bahu!*
Father's elder brother ...	*Baṛu* ...	*Eh Baṛu!*
Younger brother's son ...	*Baṛu* ...	*Eh Baṛu!*
Mother's elder sister's husband...	*Baṛu* ...	*Eh Baṛu!*
Great grandfather ... } Great-grand-uncle ... }	*Baṛu* ...	*Eh Baṛu!*
Wife's younger sister's son ...	*Putrā* ...	*Eh Putrā!*
Wife's younger sister's daughter	*Mosā* ...	*Eh Mosā!*
[A woman's] younger sister's son or daughter	*Jhiāri or Nāni*...	*Eh Nāni!*
Younger brother's daughter ...	*Baṛāi Jhi* ...	*Eh Baṛāi!*
Father's elder brother's wife ...	*Baṛāi* ...	*Eh Baṛāi!*
Mother's elder sister... ...	*Baṛāi* ...	*Eh Baṛāi!*
Wife's father	*Śasūr* ...	*Eh Śasūr!*
Husband's father	*Śasūr* ...	*Eh Buā!*
Husband's elder brother ...	*Deṛsūr* ...	*Eh Deṛsūr!*
Husband's mother's brother ...	*Mouṛā Śasūr* ...	(not approached, named or addressed).
Wife's mother's brother ...	*Mouṛā Śasūr* ...	*Eh Sasūr!*
Wife's elder brother	*Baṛ-sārā* ...	*Eh Dādā!*

English term of relationship.	Pāuṛi's term for the relationship.	Pāuṛi term for addressing such relative.
Wife's mother	*Śās*	*Eh Śās'u !*
Wife's elder sister	*Baṛ Śāri or Deṛ Śās u* ...	*Eh Deṛ Śās u !*
[Woman's] elder sister's husband	*Bhĕnāi* ...	*Eh Bhĕnāi ! Eh Goi !*
Husband's mother	*Śās*	*Eh Mā !*
Husband's elder sister ...	*Deṛ Śās u* ...	*Eh Deṛ Śās u !*
A co-wife	*Santōṛ* ...	*Eh Ninā !* (Elder) *Eh Nani !* (younger)
Elder brother	*Didā* ...	*Eh Didā !*
Elder sister	*Ninā* ...	*Eh Ninā !*
Husband's elder brother's wife ...	*Ninā* ...	*Eh Ninā !*
Great-grandmother ... / Great-grand-aunt ...	*Bāi*	*Eh Bāi !*
Wife's younger sister's husband	*Saṛhu* ...	*Eh Saṛhu !*
[Man's] elder sister's husband ...	*Bhĕnāi* ...	*Eh Bhĕnāi !*
Father's father ... / Father's uncle ...	*Ajā*... ...	*Eh Ajā !*
Father's mother	*Bāi*	*Eh Bāi !*
Mother's brother	*Māmu* ...	*Eh Māmu !*
Father's sister's husband ...	*Māmu* ...	*Eh Māmu !*
Father's sister	*Atā*	*Eh Atā !*
Mother's brother's wife ...	*Māi*... ...	*Eh Māi !*
Mother's younger sister ...	*Mousī* ...	*Eh Mousī !*

English term of relationship	Pāuṛi's term for the relationship.	Pāuṛi term for addressing such relative.
Mother's younger sister's husband	*Mousā* ...	*Eh Mousā !*
Wife's elder sister's son ...	*Baṛu* ...	*Eh Baṛu !*
Younger brother's wife ...	*Buhāri, Bhāsuni*	*Eh Bhāsuni !*
Husband's younger brother's wife	*Bhaini* ...	*Eh Nani !*
Mother's father (or uncle) ...	*Ajā*	*Eh Ajā !*
Mother's mother (or aunt) ...	*Bāi*	*Eh Bāi !*
Son's wife's father	*Samdhī* ...	*Eh Samdhī !*
Daughter's husband's father ...	*Samdhī* ...	*Eh Samdhī !*
Son's wife's mother ... Daughter's husband's mother	*Samdhani* ...	*Eh Samdhanī !*
Younger brother	*Sān' bhāi* ...	*Eh Nāno !* (or addressed by name).
Younger brother's wife ...	*Bhāsuni* ...	*Eh Bhāsuni !*
Wife's younger brother ...	*Śaṛā* ...	*Eh Saṛā !*
Elder sister's husband ...	*Bhēnāi* ...	*Eh Bhēnāi !*
Elder brother s daughter ...	*Jhiāri* ...	*Eh Nani !* (or by name)
Daughter	*Jhia* ...	*Eh Nani !* (or by name)
Son	*Pō*	*Eh Non !* (or by name)
Elder brother's son	*Putrā* ...	*Eh Non ! Eh Putrā !* (or by name)
Husband's elder brother's son ...	*Putrā* ...	*Eh Non ! Eh Putrā !* (or by name)

English term of relationship.	Pāuṛi's term for the relationship.	Pāuṛi term for addressing such relative.
(Woman's) elder sister's son ...	*Baṛu* ...	*Eh Baṛu !* (or by name)
Husband's youger brother ...	*Dhōngrā* ...	*Eh Dhāngra !*
Daughter's Husband	*Jōwāe* ...	*Eh Jōwāi !*
Sister's daughter's husband ...	*Bhānji jōwāi* ...	*Eh Jōwāi !*
A woman's brother's son ...	*Bhāñjā* ...	*Eh Non !*
Younger brother's daughter ...	*Baṛāi* ...	*Eh Baṛāi !*
Husband's younger sister ..	*Dhōngṛi* ...	*Eh Dhōngṛi !*
Sister's daughter	*Bhāñji* ...	*Eh Māi !*
Sister's son	*Bhañjā* ...	*Eh Bhañjā !*
Wife's brother's daughter ...	*Bhānoj* ...	*Eh Bhāñji !*
Husband's sister's daughter ...	*Bhānoj* ...	*Eh Bhañji !*
Sister's son's wife	*Bhāñja bō* ...	*Eh Bhañji !*
Child's or nephew's or niece's son	*Nāti* ...	*Eh Nāti !*
Child's or nephew's or niece's daughter	*Nātin* ...	*Eh Nātin !*

From the above list it will be seen that—(1) Two different terms are in some cases employed for each class of relatives of the same generation and sex according as they are older or younger than the person speaking.

(2) Different terms are employed in many cases

for relatives by marriage on one's own side of the family or one's wife's or husband's side of the family.

(3) A few reciprocal relationships (Eg., 'baṛu' for a man's father's elder brother and also for a 'younger brother's son) are designated by a common term.

(4) Such social correlations of terminological features as the employment of the same kinship term for two relationships which may be combined in one and the same person, occurs: E.g. the term '*māmu*' for the mother's brother and also for the father's sister's husband, and the term 'baṛai' for mother's elder sister and father's elder brother's wife.

(5) Some of the terms of address given in the foregoing list are further used in addressing another, even an unrelated, person of the same sex and generation as the relative or relatives to whom the term of address is appropriate.

Cross-Cousin Marriage.

As among most other tribes of the Mūṇḍā stock, cross-cousin marriage between the offspring of a brother and a sister is in vogue. The children of two sisters may also intermarry, provided one party belongs to a *Kutumb* group and the other to a *Bandhu* group. As I have already pointed out, it will be seen from the kinship nomenclature given above that the same kinship term "māmu" is employed for the mother's brother as also for the father's sister's husband. No jests or jokes are permissible with one's father's sister or mother's brother's wife who are both regarded in the same light as one's mother. It is different in the case of a person in his relations with his grand-parents and grand-uncles and grand-aunts. Two brothers may also marry two sisters so that a man's elder sister (*baṛu*) may also be his father's elder brother's wife (*baṛu*).

Joking Relations between Grand-parents and Grand-children.

In common with most other Mūṇḍā tribes as also the Dravidian-speaking Orāons, jests and jokes and forms of speech suggestive of conjugal familiarity (*Huriā*) are freely indulged in among persons related to each other, either actually or in the classificatory sense, as grandparent and grandchild. This is probably a survival of the same social regulation which is said to exist even to this day in the island of Pentecost and amongst the Dierri tribe of Australia. It may be pointed out that similar jests and jokes and familiar modes of speech are also permitted between a Pāuṛi Bhūiyā and his elder brother's wife, and nothing is thought of any liberties that may be taken by the one with the other. And as a matter of fact, the younger brother of a deceased Pāuṛi Bhūiyā has the first choice of the hand of his deceased elder brother's widow.

Kinship Taboos.

The following relations, actual or in the classificatory sense, are said to be "Gour" or taboo to each other; namely, Deṛsur (husband's elder brother) and his *Buhāri Bhāsūṇi* (younger brother's wife); *mauṛā-śaśur* (husband's mother's brother) and his *bhānjā-bau* (sister's son'e wife) *baṛ-śāṛi* (wife's elder sister) and a man's *bhōnāi* (younger sister's husband). A *Deṛsūṛ* (husband's elder brother) and his *bhāsūni* (younger brother's wife) must avoid each other, and must not approach or even name each other, and so must a *mouṛā śāśur* and his *bhañjā bau*, and a *mouṛā śāś* and her *bhāñji jōwāi*. The *baṛ*

54 A comparison of the kinship system of the Pāuṛi Bhūiyās with that of most other tribes of the Muṇḍā group will show that there is not only a general resemblance but also close similarity in most of the important particulars such as, correspondence in kinship nomenclature, to kinship taboos, cross-cousin marriage, joking relations between grandparents and grandchildren in the classificatory sense, functions of certain kin, and the rights and privileges of certain relatives,—the only striking difference being the absence of totemism amongst the *Pāuṛis*. Compare the similar custom of the Birhōṛs—*The Birhors* (Ranchi, 1925), pp. 135-136.

śarī and her *bhēnāi* may talk to each other but must keep at a respectful distance from each other and not mix on familiar terms.

The Functions of Certain Kin.

At the birth of a Pāuṛi child a paternal grandmother (either own or one in the classifactory sense) has to sever the umbilical cord. The maternal uncle of a child is required to shave the child's hair at the first hair-cutting ceremony, and either of the parents of the child has to throw away the hair into some stream. Either the father or father's brother or cousin, or the father's father or uncle, of a Pāuṛi male must put on the betrothal ring on the finger of the latter's fiancée: Neither a maternal uncle nor any other relative may do so. The eldest son first sets fire to his father's corpse at cremation and puts the first handful of earth into his grave.

The Rights and Privileges of Certain Relatives.

The Pāuṛi father has absolute right over his minor children, and retains custody of them when the mother deserts him or is divorced by him. At a marriage of a Pāuṛi girl, in the Māṅgi-bibhā form her mother is entitled to receive a cloth from the bridegroom and so are the girl's younger brother, father's father, and her father's mother. At the burial of a deceased Pāuṛi, his eldest son has to put the first handful of earth into the grave before the other sons and then the agnates, and finally relations by marriage may do so.

Kinship Organization among the Plains Bhuiyas.

The Bhũiyās of the plains—the Pānch Saiā or Khaṇḍāit-Pāik Bhũiyās, as they call themselves, have adopted a few *gotra* names, apparently in imitation of their Hindu neighbours. The tribe, as a whole, style themselves *Pawan-banś* or descendants of the Wind. The *gōtra* names adopted by different families are *Nāgas* (snake), *Gajas* (elephants) and *Kachhap* (tortoise) or *Kāsyap gotra* and *Kabutar* (pigeon). The adoption of the same *gotra* name by two or more families is however no bar to intermarriage between such families. On the other hand, such intermarriages appear to be preferred and these *gotras* have a tendency to become endogamous. The only restriction on marriage is that there can be no marriage between a man and a woman if any agnatic relationship can be traced between them. Nor may a Khaṇḍāit-Pāik

Bhuiyā, or a Rāj-Kuli Bhuiyā, like the Pāuṛi, marry the widow of his maternal uncle. Cross-cousion marriage, and marriage between the children of two sisters, are approved. The division of villages into *Bandhu* and *Kuṭumb* villages is not recognized. Different Khaṇḍāit Bhuiyā families are known by different titles called *Sāngyās* (Sanskrit *Sāngyā*) such as Shāhu, Phōtkar, Ṭhakūr, Sāont, Mājhi, Ohdār, Pradhān, Sārlia, Gartiā. Although there may be no intermarriage between members of the same *Sāngyā* belonging to the same village, as they are actually or presumably descendants of the same ancestor, there is no bar to intermarriage between families having the same *Sāngyā* but living in different villages—provided no genealogical relationship can be traced between the two families. The *Māngi Bibhā* form of marriage is the orthodox form in vogue amongst the Khaṇḍāit or Pānch-śai-deś Bhuiyās, though it is comparativly rare among the Pāuṛis. Brāhmaṇ priests are called in by the Plains Bhuiyās to perform the *Hōm* ceremony at their weddings. Girls are married before they attain puberty, and the parents of the boy make the selection of a bride for their son. Clothes are presented by the bridegroom to the parents and the younger brother of the girl. Although the bride is brought home after the wedding, she goes back to her parents a few days later and finally comes to live with her husband a few months after she attains puberty. The Brāhmaṇ priest is again called in to perform the *Bandhan* ceremony, on which occasion a new ornament is, if means allow, presented by the bridegroom to the bride. Relatives are entertained to a feast as at the wedding ceremony. Remarriage of widows is permitted. Their kinship nomenclature and rules of inheritance and adoption are practically the same as among the Pāuṛi Bhūiyās.

It is interesting to note that the term 'khili' which is sometimes used by the Bhūiyās as synonymous with 'gotra' is reminiscent of the Mūṇḍā term '*kili*', meaning —'clan', and goes to support the Mūṇḍā affinities of the Bhūiyā tribe.

CHAPTER VII.

MARRIAGE AND INHERITANCE

(i) *Marriage Customs.*

Marriage, among the Pāuṛis is endogamous so far as the tribe is concerned and exogamous so far as Kutumbs or agnates, actual or reputed, are concerned. The only exception to tribal exogamy is said to have been not long ago made in favour of their neighbouring Hinduized community of Gouṛ Goalās. A Gouṛ woman might be kept, though not formally married by a Bhūiyā man without the latter losing caste and the offspring will have all the rights of legitimate children. Similarly a Gouṛ man desiring to take a Bhūiyā woman as his wife or mistress might, not long ago be taken into the Bhūiyā caste on his providing a feast to the 'Deś' or tribe-fellows. But such instances appear to occur rarely, if at all, at present.

The Pāuṛi Bhūiyās recognize four forms of marriage known respectively as *Dhari paṛā*, *Jhikā*, *Phul-*

Khōsi and *Māngi Bibhā.* Of these the first form is the one most prevalent and the last two are rather infrequent. The *Dhari paṛā* and *Jhikā* marriages [55] are love marriages between adults; the *Phul-Khusi* marriage is a compulsory marriage; and the *Māngi Bibhā* [56] is in some cases a love marriage between adults and in other cases an early marriage in which guardians of the bride and bridegroom select a partner for their boy or girl. The Māngi Bibhā marriage is an imitation of the Hindu custom and occurs only in a few exceptionally well-to-do families aspiring to rise in the social scale. Widow-marriage known as Rāṇḍi-bibhā is also in vogue. Exchange marriages, or the marriage of one's son and daughter with the daughter and son respectively of another man, is not practised, as such marriages, it is apprehended, may lead to family quarrels. The procedure followed and the ceremonies observed in the different forms of marriage in vogue amongst the Pāuṛi Bhūiyās are described below.

---

55 These may be compared to the *Digar-peṭāi* or *Digar-pā* marriage of the Juāngs, *Udraudhi cholki* or elopement marriage among the Khāṛiās, the *Udraudhi bāplā* of the Birhōṛs, and the *Āpangir Bāplā* of the Sāntāls.

56 This form of marriage may be compared with *Sadar bāplā* of the Birhōṛs, the *Māngni bihā* or *āsli bihā* of the Khāṛiās, the *Āṛāndi* of the Muṇḍās the *Andi* of the Hōs, and the *Kiring bahu bāplā* of the Sāntāls.

(1) Dhari-para Marriage. Girls are wooed by young men when the latter visit a *Bandhu* village and dance with the girls there. The boys of a village after their evening meals take their rude tambourines or drums, called *chāngus*, and go to some *Bandhu* village to dance with the girls there. Generally the people of the latter village have information beforehand, and either before the party arrive or just on their arrival the young men of this village disappear in a body and, on such occassions, they in their turn generally go to some *Bandhu* village to dance with the girls there. The young visitors go straight to the *darbār* of the village and there warm their *chāngus* in the fire that is kept burning at night, [57] and play on them. Thereupon some elderly woman of the village, who usually looks after the girls, ask the girls to go to the *darbār* and dance with the young men from the *Bandhu* village. No male members of the

---

57 It may be noted that the mere primitive Juangs keep fire burning day and night in their *Maṇḍaka* (as they term their *darbār* or bachelors' dormitory). This fire is ceremonially renewed every year on the full-moon night of the month of Māgh. Any Juāng of the village requiring fire must take it from the *Maṇḍaka* and not from a neighbour's house. And it is reasonable to infer that Pāuṛis, whose customs in many essential matters, ressemble those of the Juāngs, once used to keep similar perpetual fire in their *darbār* or *maṇḍa-ghar*.

village will show themselves so long as these visitors remain in the village. The girls join the visitors and dance to the music played by them. In the intervals of the dances and songs many a jest and joke pass between the boys and girls, and peals of laughter and sounds of merriment frequently punctuate the music. Thus they go on dancing and singing till a late hour of the night and somtimes till daybreak. If in the course of the dancing any boy and girl feel a growing attachment for each other, they sometimes retire to a distance. One token of growing affection is for a girl to present a young man with the tender cob of the maize. The elderly lady who does not show herself to the dancers, is however always on the look-out to see if there are any indications of growing attachment between one or more boys and girls. If in the morning she sees any prospect of matches being formed, she requests the boys to stay on for the following night, and the boys do so with alacrity. The girls in their dormitory prepare a hearty breakfast for the guests while the latter sit beside them engaged in joyous conversation. While the meals are being cooked, the girls give the young men some parched rice or other fried grains to eat. When the meals are ready the young men are served, and after finishing their meals:they go to the *Maṇḍa-ghar*, which is the bachelors' dormitory as well as the village guest-house. The girls then take their meals and join the young men at the *darbār* or dancing-ground in front of the *Maṇḍa-ghar*, and dancing and singing go on until sunset. In the evening, again, the girls prepare a dinner for the visitors who sit beside the girls while they are engaged in cooking and preparing the meals. And again, after the evening meal they take up their dances and songs. When the attachment between a young man and a girl has ripened in the course of the dances, the young man presents one of his own necklaces (usually made of beads) to his sweetheart. The acceptance of the necklace by the girl constitutes them *Phul-mitras* (literally, 'flower-friends'), and thereafter no other boy will make love to the girl, as she will henceforth be considered as betrothed to the boy. And in the course of the night perhaps some other attachments are formed,—in which case, the invitation to stay on is repeated next morning, and the same routine is repeated by the girls and young men. Thus it not infrequently happens that a party of *Bandhu* boys stay on in a *Bandhu* village for four or five days or until the old duenna sees that there is no further prospect of more attachments being formed.

On the last day of their visit, the boys receive a formal invitation from the girls to a dinner. Fowls or goats are killed for the feast and the girls prepare a sumptuous dinner for the guests. Hitherto the guests were not supplied with oil while they took their daily bath, and they gathered their own toothpicks. On that day however the girls bring them toothpicks and give them oil to anoint their bodies with. Then some of these young guests go to search out one or two young men of the girls' village and bring them to the dining place and make them sit at dinner with themselves.

Dinner over, the guests slowly wend their way home, playing on their drums. The girls bear them company up to the boundary of their village. Here they all halt for an hour or so, each party singing to the other by turns. Such songs are known as *jhāṛ-gīt*. A short specimen of the songs sung on such an occasion is given below:

Girls :— *Gāgāilā kau !*

Nāṭgit karibārē, ār dinkē thāu.

Phuṭi galā kāsi !

Tōmāṛ āmār, Bhāi, phūlbāsibā[58] *āsi.*

Boys :— *Kānkṛir kāsi !*[59]

Ār din jāibo, bhāi, berā gelo basi.

Kankṛir kāsi !

Translation.

Girls :— There crows the crow !

To sing and dance, stop one day more.

Kāsi flowers have blown !

Between thee and me, flower-friendship we'll form.

Boys :— Tender fruit of cucumber !

Some other day to sing we'll come;

The day advances; Farewell! Thou tender fruit of cucumber!

When a number of such songs have been sung, the girls lightly bow to the boys and the boys return the salutations and depart. Not long afterwards, the girls

58 "Flower friendship" is a literal rendering of *Phul-maitra* which is equivalent to a "betrothal."

59 This is an expletive.

return the visit and are received by the young men of the village in their *darbār* ground. The girls of the village itself must not be seen so long as these girl-visitors remain in the village. The young men spend one or more nights in dances and songs in the company of these visitors and, after entertaining them to a hearty meal on the morning of their departure, escort them to the boundary of the village, playing on their *chāngus* and singing. At the boundary of the village they halt for a while, each party singing to the other as before; and then after due salutations they part. A specimen of such songs is given below:—

Boys:— Phūl dhāu dhāu; chali jāu jāu;
Git padē māri dēbē, chali jāu jāu.

Girls:— Nāi jānoi, Gintō!
Sāg toṛilē chintō!
Mui nāi jānoi, Gintō.

Boys:— Nui pāni ānanti, Gintō!
Bhāi, ai na jānonti!

Girls:— Pitaṛaṛa khari jānoi nā jānoi, Bhāi.
Jathākathā kari
Pitaṛaṛ khari! Jāthākathā kari;
O, Bhāi, jāthākathā kari.

Translation.

Boys:— Whilst hastening home, ye Flowers!
Sing one more song, whilst ye go.

Girls:— No songs I know, O Friend!
Whilst I gather herbs you'll see, no songs I know.

Boys:— Water from the stream you draw,
O Friend, [yet] you say no songs you know!

Girls:— Bracelet of brass![60] Whether I know or not,
Some song [for thee] I'll sing;
Bracelet of brass! Somehow or other, Friend,
Somehow or other [I'll manage to sing.]

Such visits are interchanged from time to time. And, in the intervals between these visits, the affianced. young persons meet at markets when the girls present their sweethearts with eatables such as cakes, fried grains, cucumbers, etc., and the boys present their sweethearts with wooden combs made by themselves.

---

60 This is an unmeaning expletive.

Such interchange of love-tokens goes on for a year or more.

At a later visit to the girls' village, one of the boys seizes his sweetheart by the hands and elopes with her, the other boys having under a previous arrangement gone a little ahead. When the lovers reach the boundary of the boy's village, the girl is asked to wait awhile while the boy goes home and informs some female member of his family, such as a sister or a sister-in-law (but not the boy's mother), who thereupon goes to escort the bride home. The woman goes to the bride and tells her,—"Come, *Bau* (bride), come home". She follows her to her sweetheart's place. Some elderly woman of the family marks the forehead of the bridegroom and then of the bride with turmeric powder. While this is being done, other women make the benedictory sound of *huṛ huṛā* by waving the tongue with its tip against the palate.

Hanri-Sara Ceremony.

The same day, or one or more days later, the *Hāñṛi-sarā* ceremony is performed as follows:— Relatives are invited to a bridal feast. A preparation of rice called *jāu* is prepared in a new earthen vessel (*hāñṛi*) with a new earthen lid (*sarā*) either by the bride herself, or by some other woman of the family with the bride sitting beside the hearth. The bride first offers a little of the *jāu* to the ancestor spirits of the family inside the *bhitar*, and then distributes it to the invited guests who are further treated to rice and meat and other delicacies. The bridegroom sits to dinner with the men, and the bride with the women. According to custom, the bride may not sleep with her husband until after her first menstruation in her new home and the purification that must follow by bathing and having her clothes sent to the washerman to be washed. During the interval she is required by custom to sleep with other girls or in a neighbouring house of some relative of her husband's. But, in practice, she generally sleeps with her husband during those days with the connivance of the women. In the *Dhari-paṛā* form of marriage, no bride-price is payable at the time; but either on the birth of a child to the couple or at any time within twelve years from the marriage, the customary present of three oxen, five *khaṇḍis* of unhusked rice or two rupees in cash, and one or more pieces of cloth are presented by the bridegroom to the bride's parents.

(2) Jhikâ or Ghichâ Marriage.

In the Jhikā or Ghichā marriage, the boy woos the girl at a dance in a *Bandhu* village as in the *Dhari-paṛā* form of marriage. This form of marriage appears to be a compromise between the *Dharipaṛā* and *Māngi-bibhā* forms. The boy informs his parents that he wishes to marry such and such a girl. If the boy's parents are not able to pay at once the customary bride-price of three oxen, five *khaṇḍis* of unhusked rice or its cash value estimated at two rupees, and one or more pieces of cloth, but expect to be able to pay the same within a year or so, they send some relatives of theirs to the parents of the girl to inquire if they would give their daughter in marriage to the boy. If they agree, as they always do, they say "*Ghichi kari lai jeba*" (seize her and take her). The relatives return to their village and inform the parents of the boy accordingly. Then, on a suitable day, the boy with a party of youthful friends consisting of both *kutumbs* and *bandhus* goes towards the village of the bride. Arrived at the jungle on the boundary of the village, the party come to a halt and send two of their number to inform the parents of the bride of their arrival. The latter send their daughter in company with some other girls to the jungle on the pretext of their gathering fuel or leaves from the jungle or drawing water from a stream. When the girls enter the jungle, the bridegroom comes up to them and seizes his bride-elect, the other men of his party hiding themselves behind trees or bushes at the time. The companions of the bride make a feigned attempt at striking the bridegroom. In the meanwhile the companions of the bridegroom come out of their hiding-place and make a show of striking the companions of the bride, and they in their turn seek to retaliate by pelting stones or clods of earth at these boys. While the two parties are thus engaged, the bridegroom makes good his escape with the bride-elect, and takes her straight to his own home. The boys push the companions of the bride to some distance towards the bride's village, and then return to their own village. The girls on reaching their village inform the men, in mock seriousness, that a tiger has carried off their companion, whereupon the missing girl's parents and relatives arm themselves with sticks and go to the jungles as if in search of the girl, and make a pretence of searching the jungle for traces of the missing girl. One exclaims—"Here is a bit of her cloth;" another exclaims—"Here are marks of her foot-steps," and so forth. Finally, if the bridegroom lives in a neighbouring village, they go to his house that day; otherwise they go there on the following day, make a show of a quarrel and claim "blood for blood" for their girl. The elders of the village are all assembled and are asked to surrender the offending young man "to the vengeance of the girl's Kin." The boy's people, with befitting submissiveness, plead for compassion and say, "*We* have done it. Now deal with us as you like." Then all become quiet, the guests are entertained with a hearty dinner, and a formal promise is made to pay the customary bride-price within a year.

The bride and bridegroom on their arrival at the bridegroom's house are anointed on the forehead with oil and turmeric-paste by some elderly female relative of the boy, while other females go on making the benedictory *huṛ-huṛa* sound. Bride and bridegroom put on clothes dyed yellow with turmeric. Then an offering of *jāu* pudding is made to the ancestor-spirits and the *Hāṇṛisarā* ceremony is performed as in the *Dhari-paṛā* form of marriage, and friends and relatives are treated to a feast. In addition to the Hānṛi-sarā ceremony, another ceremony known as the *Juhār-pāni* ceremony is gone through on the same day as follows :

Juhār Pāni-ceremony.

The married couple stand on a yoke, the bride to the left of the bridegroom, while female relatives pour over their heads water mixed with turmeric paste, and make the *huṛ-hurā* sound. Wives of the bridegroom's brothers and cousins besmear bride and bridegroom with mud brought from a flowing stream. When the bride has been purified after her first menstruation in her husband's house, a room is set apart for the couple to sleep in. Until then they are supposed to sleep separately. A few days later the mother and sisters of the bride come to see her. An interesting part of merry-making on the night of the marriage is to make the bride ride on the back of a woman standing on all fours and imitating a horse. This may be magical, being probably meant to symbolise the wish that the bride may have power over the groom. A year or so later the parents of the bride are invited to take the promised bride-price, and a feast is arranged for the purpose, to which friends and relatives are invited.

(3) Phul-Khusi. In some instances, a Pāuṛi young man whose suit is not accepted by the maiden of her choice manages to insert in her hair a bunch of white *thheuṛ* flowers or, failing that, some kind of blood-red flowers. And this is taken to amount to betrothal, so that no other youth may claim the hand of that girl [61]. When the girl and her parents are reconciled to the inevitable, marriage is solemnised as in the *Jhikā* form described above. If in any case the marriage cannot take place and the girl is to be married to some one else, this can only be done by going through ceremonies appropriate for a widow-marriage.

(4) Mangi-Bibha. In the Māngi Bibhā form[62] of marriage which is comparatively rare, being adopted only by a few very well-to-do families, ordi-

---

61 Compare the similar custom among the Santāls *(Itut)*, the Khāṛias *(sundrum tāppā)*, the Birhōṛs *(Sipundur Bapla)*, the Hōs *(opar tipi)* and the Mūṇḍās *(sindri tāppā)*. I have known of a case of murder out of revenge for a Mūṇḍā youth forcibly anointing *sindur* on the forehead of a Mūṇḍā girl.

62 This form of marriage appears to have been borrowed with modifications from the Hindus. Among the Hindusised Plains Bhūiyās, a few days before the marriage, a Brāhmaṇ priest invests the prospective bridegroom with the sacred thread and initiates him by giving him what is called *gurukarṇa*, which consists of whispering into his ears the name of the Hindu deity whom he is to regard and worship as his tutelary deity (*iṣṭa devatā*).

narily the mother and other female relatives of a boy selects a *Bandhu* girl as a suitable bride for him and, if the boy agrees to the match, negotiations are started through a *bandhu* who acts as *Kōṇḍra* or intermediary. In a few instances, however, the boy falls in love with a *Bandhu* girl at the dances, and the parents, if in particularly affluent circumstances, decide to marry the lovers in the Māngi Bibhā form, and a party of male relatives are sent to the girl's parents with about a *maund* of rice, one goat, and a brass ring.

If the party meet on their way with one or more of the following omens, namely,—a small deer (*kuṭrā*) or a tiger or a vulture or a rat passing across their path, or a jackal to their right, or a snake or an empty vessel along the path, or a parrot flying overhead with cries, they will return home. In Keonjhar and Pāl Lahera, the negotiations are then ended; but in the Bonāi State two more trials are given: Another day they will again undertake the journey, but if again they come across any of the bad omens mentioned above they will come back a second time. If even on a third journey a bad omen is again encountered, the idea of the match will be given up. Meeting on the way with an elephant or a white-headed kite (*Sankhā Chil*) or any white bird flying, or a vessel filled with water, is considered a good omen for any undertaking including marriage negotiations.

When the party arrive at the birde's house, if the bride's people are agreeable to the marriage proposal, their feet are washed by the women of the family and their sticks are taken into the house. A mat is spread out for the guests to sit upon; *sāl*-leaf cigarettes are distributed to them to smoke, and finally they are entertained with a hearty meal.

Next morning the boy's father or other guardian or some other relative addresses the father of the girl, saying-"*O Bandhu*, we have come in the expectation of eating a certain fruit, will you give it to us?" The boy's father replies, "If you can bear the burden (meaning, marriage expenses) of both sides, come on, otherwise don't". Then they present the parents of the girl with the rice and goat and ring that they have brought with them, and put on the brass ring (*mudi*) on the right ring-finger of the bride. This engagement ring may be put on either by the father or some near *Kutumb*, such as a paternal uncle or paternal grandfather and grand-uncle of the bridegroom. A maternal uncle or other *Bandhu* may not do so. While putting on the ring, the man tells the girl, " From to-day you become our *bahu*. We shall take you home when the bride-price is ready ". After a formal promise to pay the usual bride-price (*mūla*) for such a marriage, the party return home. The minimum customary bride-price in the *Māngi-bibhā* form of marriage consists of the following items in Bonāi: One cow for the bride's mother; two bullocks, one for the bride's father and another for the maternal uncle; two goats, one castrated and the other not castrated; five pieces of cloth, each fourteen cubits long, one for the bride's mother, one for her mother's sister, one for her father's sister, one for her elder sister, and one for her younger brother; one rupee in cash for the mother as the price of the milk with which she suckled the bride in her infancy; a certain measure (five *khaṇḍis* or more) of husked rice and the same quantity of unhusked rice.[63] In the Kēonjhar and Pāl Lahera States, two bullocks, the one for the birde's father and

63 Among the Plains Bhūiyās, the bride price, which not long ago varied from Rs. 7 to Rs. 9, may now go up to Rs. 50, according to the social position of the parties and the means of the bridegroom.

one for her mother's brother, one cloth for the mother, one goat, five *khandis* ($2\frac{1}{2}$ mds.) of rice, and one rupee as *Khirikhiā* (or eating *Khir* or condensed milk as a consideration for mother's milk), form the minimum bride-price.

Later on, on an appointed day, a party of ten or fifteen, male as well as female relatives by marriage, besides *Kōṇḍhrās* or companions of the bridegroom (but neither his parents nor kinsmen), go to the bride's house to bring her to her future husband's place. The bride is brought to her new home escorted by her *kondhrās* or companions acting as bridesmaids and a large party of her father's relatives by marriage, male and female. Musicians with *ḍhōl* and *chāngū* drums accompany the party. When they arrive at the boundary of the bridegroom's village, which they usually do in the evening, a number of men and women come out to receive them, some of the men carrying lighted torches; and a band of musicians of the Pāṇ caste accompany them. The women wash the feet of the guests on the road. On their arrival at the bridegroom's house, mats are spread out for them to sit on; cigarettes (*phikā*) of rolled *sāl* leaves are distributed and the relatives of bride and bridegroom enter into a friendly chat, while the bride is conducted into the house by the mother and sister of the bridegroom and a number of married female relatives. Among the Pāuṛis of the Bonāi State, widows are not allowed to accompany her at the time. The *Dihuri* or village-priest puts down in three places side by side on the ground a little sun-dried (*āruā*) rice and powdered turmeric as offerings respectively to the Earth-goddess or *Basu-mātā*, to God or the Sun-god named *Dharam-deōta* and to the Ancestor-spirits or *Pitrus*, and invokes their blessings, saying,-"Thou O Earth-goddess that art below, and Thou Dharam Deota that art above, and O ye Ancestor-spirits, here I offer to ye all this rice and this turmeric powder. Do ye bless the bride and bridegroom and keep them in health, happines and prosperity." Then the Dehuri marks the forheads of the couple with turmeric paste and sprinkles, *āruā* rice on them while women make the benedictory sounds of *huṛ-huṛā* or *ulu-ulu*. Among the Pāuṛis of the Bonāi State, marks of turmeric paste are made by some married woman on the bride's forehead and rice is sprinkled on her, while elderly women make the *huṛ-huṛā* sound.

The bride and bridegroom who remain fasting

the whole day have their nails pared in the evening by the *Bhaṇḍāri* or barber who also paints the bride's feet with a red dye known as *āltā*. Then they are conducted to a spot on the *padā* or courtyard which has been cleaned with cowdung and water for the ceremonies. In some villages, particularly in the Kuiṛā parganā of Bonāi, a mud platform is constructed for the purpose. To make this platform, a spadeful of earth is brought by married women and maidens from a cross-road where the village-priest or Dihuri has made offerings of turmeric, rice, molasses and milk to *Dharam* (the Sun-god), *Bāsukī-mātā* or *Basu-mātā* (the Earth-goddess), and *Gāi-srī* (the tutelary deity of the village) to bless the union. This spadeful of earth which is mixed with other earth used in making the platform is dug up by the Dihuri himself. On this platform, or rather the spot where the wedding ceremonies are performed, is placed a new earthen pitcher filled with water and having a few leafy mango twigs sticking out of its mouth.

Soon afterwards, in the Bonāi State, the bride and bridegroom, accompanied by a bevy of married women and unmarried girls, go to a stream; one woman fills a pumpkin gourd or *tumbā* with water from the stream for that night's ceremony, and a few other women take water in gourds and earthen pitchers for use in the *kādō-ghāṭi* ceremony to be performed on the following day. Musicians play on drums and flutes and the women make the *hūṛhuṛā* sound while the water is being taken. The water thus brought at night is called *chuṛ-pāni* or stolen water.

On their return from the stream, bride and bridegroom are seated, the bride to the left of the bridegroom, before a yoke planted upright in the *paḍā* or courtyard, or on the marriage platform in case one has been erected. In some villages, the yoke is laid flat on the ground and the bride and bridegroom are seated upon it. Then they are bathed in this "stolen" water by a married female.

Bride and bridegroom will now put on clothes dyed yellow with turmeric, and their foreheads will also be anointed with turmeric paste whilst some elderly women make the *huṛ-huṛā* sound. This constitutes the actual marriage.[64] Among the Pāuṛis of Keōnjhar and

64 Among the Hinduized plains Bhūiyās, in addition to the triba marriage ceremonies, a Brāmhāṇ priest performs *hōm* by pouring obla tions of *ghee* or clarified butter into fire.

Pāl Lahera States the wedded couple are not taken to a stream nor bathed that night. There the Kādō-ghāṭi ceremony is performed on the next day, not with water thus brought, but with water secured by begging from seven houses by a few married women. The guardian of the bridegroom presents a new cloth to the bride and another to the bridegroom and they put on these new clothes after they are bathed in the '*Chuṛpāṇi*' while seated on the yoke. The *huṛ-huṛā* or *ulū-ulū* sound is not made. Female relatives of the bridegroom now pay each a few coins to the bride as presents.

Then follows a feast in which the bridegroom eats with the male guests and the bride with the women. The younger brother or cousin of the bridegroom, who in the capacity of *Sāngdiā* or best man, and the younger sister or cousin of the bride who in the capacity of *Gharni* or bridesmaid, have both remained fasting the whole day, sit down to dinner respectively with the bridegroom and the bride. Then there is dancing and singing in accompaniment to the sound of the *chāng* drum.

In Bonāi, next morning a few elderly women

bring out to the *padā* or courtyard all the remaining vessels of *Chuṛ-pāni* which they now pour on the ground so as to make it muddy. On this wet and muddy ground, the women, old and young, of both parties dance for a while, and the men of both parties sing songs, and men and women bespatter one another with mud. A specimen of the songs sung on this occasion is the following, which is supposed to be addressed by an old dancer to the young people:—

Ban puṛai puṛai,
Khajur mūl diśai,
Sabri berā dhāngar dhangri,
Amār berā buṛhai?

Translation.

[As] when the forest trees are burnt,
The *Khijur* stump [alone] is left;
So each for partner gets a youth,
For me alone an ancient dame!

A party of women take the bride to the hut-temple of the Mother-goddess Thākurāṇī, singing as they go.

Dancing and feasting go on for three days and nights. On the third or fourth night bridegroom and bride sleep in the same room. But in cases where the bride and bridegroom are adults, they do not sleep together until four or five days after the bride's first menses at the husband's house, when the turmeric dyed clothes they have been wearing since the wedding are made over to the washerman (Dhōbā Behārā) to wash, their nails are pared by the Bhaṇḍāri, and they bathe separately in the neighbouring stream. In the Bonāi State, until this ceremonial purification known as *Āṭmangrā*, the bride sleeps with the maidens of the village in the *Dhāngṛi-bāsā* or Maidens' Dormitory.

Am-bibha.

In Bonāi, a man who has had no children by his first or second wife and is about to marry again, has, a day or two before such subsequent marriage, to be ceremonially wedded to a *mango* tree.[65] This Ām-bibhā or mango-marriage, as it is called, is obviously intended to make him "fruitful" like the mango-tree so that he may be blessed with children by such subsequent marriage.

---

65 It may be noted, that this custom of "mango-marriage" is in vogue amongst the Plains Bhūiyās as also some other castes and tribes of Ōṛissā and Chōṭā-Nāgpur.

(4) Randi Bibha or Sanga or Widow Marriage.

Remarriage of widows[66], called *Rāṇḍi-bibhā* or *Sāngā* is customary amongst the Pāuṛi Bhūiyās. But the younger brother of the deceased husband is considered to have the first right to the hand of his elder brother's widow. If the widow marries some other man, she loses all right and authority over her children, if any, by her former husband, and they live with the people of their deceased father. No particular ceremonies are observed at the wedding of a widow nor need any bride-price be paid or the consent of any relative taken.

(II)—Divorce.

A Pāuṛi Bhūiyā may divorce his wife for any of the following reasons, namely—

(1) For habitual neglect of her household duties, such as not regularly cooking the meals or not giving sufficient food to eat to her husband and his parents, brothers or sisters;

(2) For frequently quarreling with her husband or other member or members of her husband's house;

66 This is customary not only among all the Muṇḍā tribes, but also amongst most Dravidian-speaking tribes of India.

(3) For carrying on an intrigue.

The consent of a *panchāyat* or of the husband's kinsmen is not essential for a divorce; but all that is required is that the wife should be made over to her parents, and the relatives informed of the fact of the divorce. The husband is entitled to the custody of the children. A divorced wife may re-marry. No bride-price has to be paid by a man marrying a divorced woman, nor are any ceremonies required to be performed for such a marriage.

(iii)—Partition and Inheritance.

Sons of a Pāuṛi Bhūiyā have no right to claim partition of the family property during their father's lifetime. Nor has a son even the right to claim maintenance from his father, even if he should choose to expel him from the house during his own lifetime. On his death the property of a Pāuṛi is divided in equal shares amongst his sons; but if after such division any surplus is left over, the eldest son is entitled to it.[67] In Kēonjhar sons may claim partition from

67 Among the Plains Bhūiyās I found in some places (as, e.g., in the Mayurbhanj State), the eldest son receiving the largest share and the second son a smaller share than the eldest but a large sharer than each of his younger brothers, and so on, the youngest son receiving the smallest

their fathers. Thus Jagarnath Dehuri of Suākāṭi had to give shares to his sons, and so also Rām and Lakshman of Donlā. The eldest son gets a slightly larger share than the other sons. If the deceased leaves an unmarried daughter, his sons are required to maintain her until her marriage and are entitled to the bride-price at her marriage, but have to defray her marriage expenses. Sons of a widow or of a divorced woman by a second husband are entitled to inherit their father's property just in the same way as the sons by a first wife. In Keonjhar, however, a son by such a second wife gets only half of what a son by a first wife gets. A sonless Pāuṛi Bhūiyā may adopt a son (*Pōsheā Pō*) from some *kuṭumb* family. Such a son will inherit his adoptive father's property just as a son of his own loins would do. The adopted son must, however, be an agnate, otherwise he cannot inherit his adoptive father's property. No ceremonies are necessary, but the relatives and fellow-villagers (*barō bhāi*) have to be treated to a feast so that the fact of adoption may be thus duly 'notified'.

---

share. In other respects the customary rules of inheritance appear to be the same among the Pāuṛi Bhūiyās and the Plains Bhūiyās. In some places where the deceased has left no sons, either natural or adopted, but only a daughter or daughters, the daughter or daughters may get a small portion of the properties left by the deceased, provided the agnates who are the next of kin agree.

CHAPTER VIII.

BIRTH, CHILDHOOD, AND PUBERTY CUSTOMS.

The commencement of each successive stage in the life of a Pāuṛi Bhūiyā, as of almost all tribes and castes, is marked by ceremonies intended either to relieve the individual from the harmful spiritual influences peculiar to the out-going stage or to assimilate his nature to the new state of life he is entering and making the entry into the new state safe and prosperous. The various ceremonies observed at the different stages of a Pāuṛi's life up till pubesence is attained, are briefly described in the present chapter.

Birth.

An expectant mother has to take certain precautions to protect herself and particularly the child in the womb against evil spirits. She may not go to the jungles and hills and, in fact, she may not leave the *basti* or the inhabited part of the village except to go to the stream for bathing purposes. This prohibition is generally, though not always, regarded in Bonāi; but in Keonjhar and Pāl Lahera this is rarely observed. She is not allowed to see smoke rising from a cremation so that the *masāṇi* and *chūrni* spirits that are believed to haunt cremation-grounds may not do any harm to her and to the child in her womb. In practice, however, the sight of cremation-smoke is not much heeded, but a pregnant woman will neither go to a cremation ground nor touch a corpse.

Difficult Labour.

In cases of difficult labour, vows are made to Dharam Deotā (the Supreme God) and to Basumātā (the Earth-goddess) to facilitate delivery. The head of the family addresses the deity saying, "Thou didst generate the child in the womb; do Thou now bring it out safely. We shall offer Thee *akṣat* (*āruā* rice) and *s'ītal* (molasses) or *poṇḍrā* (fowl) (as the case may be) in case of safe delivery; otherwise (in the event of miscarriage) blame will attach to Thee." A few days after birth, when mother and child have been ceremonially purified, the vow is fulfilled by offering the promised sacrifices and offerings. In Bonāi, in a case of difficult labour, lids of all earthen-ware vessels in the house are taken off and thrown away to facilitate delivery through sympathetic magic. No male is permitted in Bonāi to enter the hut during labour pains and before delivery. The delivery takes place in a portion of the hut set apart as the lying-in compartment.

As soon as a child is born, the navel-string is cut by the father's mother (*āji*) or by some other woman standing in the same relation, in a classificatory sense, to the baby. She is called the *Suṛuni* or midwife. In Bonāi, she receives about half a pound of rice as her remuneration, and on the occasion of the child's name-giving ceremony gets a pot of boiled rice and meat called *sutrā-hāṇḍi*. The navel string is buried by her outside the house [68]. The babe is washed in tepid water shortly after birth. In the case of a male child, the navel.string is severed with an arrow, in the case of a girl with a knife, or sometimes (as I found in Bonāi) with a splinter of bamboo,

For eight days after parturition, the parturient woman gets only rice and fried *nim* (*Melia azadirachta*)

---

68 Among the Plains Bhūiyās of the Mayurbhanj State the custom of burying the navel-string or umbilical cord at a corner of the lying-in room prevails; among the Juangs, near neighbours of the Pāuṛi Bhūiyās, it is buried inside the room, near the doorway.

leaves and salt for her meals. In Keonjhar, however, I feund (*Kūrthi dolichos biflorus*) soup being given with fried salt. She is not permitted to take either pulses, vegetables, fish or flesh. So long as the child cannot sit up, she may not take fish, flesh, pumpkin, and the *biri* (*Phaseolus roxburghii*) pulse as these are believed to cause sickness to the child.

Ceremonial Impurity.

The ceremonial impurity of a parturient woman is removed by instalments. Thus, on the eighth [69] day after delivery, when the clothes and other articles used in the confinement room are purified by washing, and *not* before that, the members of the family may take drinking water at her hands, but she may not yet cook food for them nor enter the kitchen. After the child is named, some time after the eighth day and before the thirteenth day of its birth, members of the other Pāuṛi families may take drinking water from her hands, and cooked food from the other members of the family but not yet from the parturient woman herself. The other taboos con-

69 In the case of the Plains Bhūiyās, this first purification *(nartā)* takes place on the tenth day and the second purification *(ekushā)* on the twenty-first day in imitation of some Hindu castes. At the other extreme, among the primitive Juangs, the only purification takes place generally on the second or third day after birth.

tinue as before. On the day of the name-giving ceremony, old earthen-ware cooking vessels are cast away and new vessels used. It is only after four months from the birth of a son and five months from the birth of a daughter that the final purification takes place. Relatives are entertained at a feast; and from that time she may enter the kitchen, cook food for members of her family and her tribe, and they may all take food and water at her hands. Until this final purification, the husband of the parturient woman, like the woman herself, may not approach the seats of the deities when any pūjā or scrificial ceremony is being performed, nor may he offer any sacrifices himself.

Other customs connected with birth.

A child born with one or more teeth is believed to bring ill-luck to its parents. Among the Pāuṛis of the Bonāi State, I was told that such a child is, in some cases, suffocated and thrown into a stream. But the Pāuṛis of Keonjhar and Pāl Laṇhera deny the existence of any such practice, and I heard of no such case having occurred in recent times. Twins (*johōra chhōwā*) are much prized. To avoid the death of an infant whose elder brothers and sisters died prematurely, the mother of a Pāuṛi infant in the Bonāi State leaves it in a manure-pit saying—" All my children die prematurely. What shall I do with a fresh child? Here I leave it ". Another woman who is there, exclaims " This child is mine ", and forthwith takes it up in her arms and carries it home. Subsequently the mother of the child brings it back from the house of the other woman. In the Keonjhar and Pāl Lahera States, in the case of such a babe, five or six men go to its mother after the first ceremonial purification, and tell her, " This is *our* child and not *yours* ", and one of them takes up the child in his arms and then hands it back to its mother saying,—" We leave this child of ours under your care. Nurse it for us by giving it *dudh-pāni*, (*lit.*, milk and water)".

Name-giving (Nam-Tora).

On a day between the eighth and the twentieth day from the birth of a child, a name is selected for the baby with the following rites. All the Pāuṛi women of the village are invited to the house, and some of them cook rice and pulse in earthen-ware vessels for a feast. No meat may be cooked or eaten that day at the house.

In Bonāi some near *kuṭumb* woman (agnate) from another family prepares a sort of pudding by boiling rice flour with sesamum seeds (*rāsi*). This is offered first to the ancestor-spirits, and then a bit of it is given to the child to eat, and then the rest of it is eaten by all the women present. In Keonjhar, a *Kuṭumb* (agnatic) male boils *āruā* (sun-dried) rice in water and offers the rice with its gruel to the ancestor-spirits of the family. The man who cooks this rice is called the *Brāhmaṇ* for the purposes of the ceremony. The floor of the hut is cleaned with cowdung and water, and on a spot so cleaned a circular diagram is drawn with turmeric powder. Inside this circle is placed a jug of water mixed with turmeric powder. Elderly women sit down in front of this vessel but outside the diagram. One of them in Bonāi drops into the water of the jug a grain of sesamum (*til* or *Khasā*) together with a grain of rice, and at the same time pronounces the name of a certain relative of the child. But in Keonjhar, the agnate who has cooked the rice performs this function. If it is a male child, the first grains of sesamum and rice are dropped in the name of the paternal grandfather of the child. If the rice or the sesamum sinks into the water, the woman says, "No, he (the grandfather) has not come". If the rice and *til* float, then the *til* is taken out and placed on the head of the child, while the woman says, "Yes, he has come." If the first grain of rice sinks down, another grain of rice and a sesamum-seed are dropped into the water in the name successively of one paternal grand-uncle after another. If the rice-grain still sinks, names of the baby's father's paternal grandfather and grand-uncles are tried in succession. When ultimately the rice floats, the woman exclaims, "There! he is come!" And the name of the relative at whose name the rice floats is selected as the name of the child. If the rice does not float at the name of the father's grandfather or grand-uncles, the same process is repeated in the names of other deceased agnatic relations, one after another, while fresh grains are dropped in the name of each; and the name at which the grain of rico floats, is the name selected. In the case of a female child, her father's mother is first named, then the father's aunts in succession, then the father's grandmother and grand-aunts, and so on. In the case of both sexes it is only after the names of dead agnatic relations are exhausted that the names of maternal relations may be taken. All the names taken must be those of deceased relations, for the child is supposed to be the reincarnation of some dead relative.[70]

After a name has been selected, relatives and tribe-fellows of the family may take food in the house, but no food cooked by the mother of the baby will be eaten by them until after four months from the birth in the case of a male child and five months in the case of a female child. In Keonjhar, the person who officiates at the name-giving ceremony ties a new white thread round the baby's neck. Besides the name thus selected some children get pet names or nicknames. After the clothes used by the mother and child have been sent to the washerman's (Dhōbā Behārā's) house, the father of a first child in Keonjhar will fasten a new thread round his wife's neck. The Pāuṛis whom I questioned about the object of this thread-tying could assign no other reason for it except that it is an ancient custom.

---

70 For similar customs among allied tribes, see *The Mūṇḍās and their Country*, pp. 458-9. The Birhōṛs and the Khāṛiās of Chōṭā Nāgpur select a name for a new-born child by the same process. Among the Juāngs, the name is selected by the midwife.

Disposal of Milk-teeth.

Cast milk-teeth of children are thrown away on the roof of a hut, by a parent or a brother or a sister, saying,—"Here! take this old tooth and give a new tooth in its place". This is a wide-spread custom found not only among different aboriginal tribes of Ōṛissā, Chōṭā-Nāgpur and elsewhere, but also among many Hindu castes of Bengal, Bihār, Ōṛissā, Chōṭā-Nāgpur and elsewhere.

First Hair-cutting.

From two to five months after the birth of a child the hair (*janam-bār* or 'natal hair') of the child is shaved for the first time by the *māmu* or mother's brother; and the father or mother in Bonāi but in Keonjhar the mother's brother of the child takes the hair to the nearest stream and casts the hair into the water.[71] The child is then bathed by the mother. The mother's brother too takes a bath and is then regaled with liquor and treated to a feast. He is presented, in Bonāi, with a new cloth for his offices. Neither tattooing nor cicat-

71 The Hinduized Plains Bhūīyās get the first hair-cutting performed on an auspicious day according to the Hindu Calendar; and the first hair is cut in front of an auspicious water-vessel (*mangal-ghaṭ*) filled with water from which a small leafy mango-twig juts out.

rization is practised by the Pāuṛis. But in cases of certain ailments such as colic pain, a copper pice is heated and pressed down over the right side of the stomach; and this results in a cicatrization.

Ear-piercing.

At the age of four or five years, when the child is able to walk about, anyone skilled in perforating ears, preferably a paternal grandmother or grand-aunt, pierces the child's ears with a thorn of the *samudrar phera* or *phani-mansā* bush. When the pain consequent on such ear-piercing abates, either a small reed or a thin piece of wood is inserted into each hole to widen it or brass *mudrās* (ear-rings) are worn. No feast is given to relatives nor are any other rites observed.

Menstruation.

As among most other Mūṇḍā tribes a female is considered ceremonially unclean and is under a taboo for a week after every menstruation. During this period she is not allowed to touch any cooking utensils or water vessels; nor will any male member of her family or tribe, not even her husband, take food or drink water touched by her, nor sit down on the same mat or other seat with her. Women alone may drink water touched by her and sit on the same mat with her, but even they will not eat food cooked by her. She has to sleep on a separate mat by herself. On the eighth day she will herself wash her clothes in ashes and hot water, and then take a bath. Then she will anoint her body with oil and turmeric paste and with a fragrant paste made of pounded *Sabitrī gandhā* and blossoms of the *Champā* flower.

Dormitories for the unmarried.

Most Mūṇḍā-speaking tribes have a Bachelors' Dormitory where all the unmarried young men of a village sleep at night. In most of those tribes, the maidens of a village also sleep together in a separate hut, though in most such tribes the maidens have no separate dormitory-building specifically constructed for them, and they sleep together in some vacant hut belonging to a fellow-villager or in the hut of a lone widow. The Pāuṛi Bhuiyās in the Bonāi State maintain a regular dormitory specially constructed for the use of the maidens, generally by the side of the Bachelors' Dormitory.

Boys and girls sleep with their parents till about their seventh or eighth year after which they are admitted into their respective dormitories. The common dormitory for the Pāuṛi boys of a village is called the *Maṇḍa-ghar* or *Darbār-ghar* and that for girls the *Dhāngrīn-bāsā*. In some villages the *Dhāngrīn-bāsā* is adjacent to the *Maṇḍa-ghar*, and in a few villages the *Dhāngrīn-bāsā* and the *Maṇḍaghar* has only one partition wall between them. In some villages, however, the common *Dhāngrin-bāsā* no longer exists but the girls of the village sleep in the house of some lone widow or are distributed in more than one such house. In Keonjhar the *Dhāngrin-bāsā* as a distinct institution with its own regulations has fallen into decay, but the Pāuṛi maidens of a village sleep together in one or more vacant huts or with some lone widow in her hut. When public officers or other important personages visit the village or a party of Pāuṛi guests come to the village for marriage negotiations or other purposes, they are accommodated in the *Maṇḍa-ghar*, and the boys sleep either in the *Melā-ghar* or some other vacant hut in the village.

In these dormitories, boys and girls are trained in

habits of obedience and instructed in their duties to their elders and superiors and also in dancing and singing. The older boys exercise authority over the younger boys of the dormitory who have to fetch water in the morning and bring tooth-picks for the older boys to wash their faces and clean their teeth; they have to sweep the floor of the *Maṇḍa-ghar* every morning and clean it with cowdung and water, and bring wood from the jungle and keep the wood burning at night so as to keep the *Maṇḍa-ghar* warm; they have to shampoo the legs of the older boys and run their errands. The elder boys allot such duties to different batches of boys in turns. They are instructed by the older boys in their duties to their elders and superiors and in the different tunes and melodies of their songs and in playing upon the *chāng*. One or two of the older boys act as leaders of the dormitory boys, chastise them when they neglect their duties or otherwise go wrong. They may expel a member of the dormitory found in intrigue with a *kuṭumb* (agnatic) girl. It is the leaders who decide as to the village where they are to go for dances on any particular night.

The elder girls exercise similar authority over the

younger girls. The latter have to perform similar duties for their dormitory and for the elder girls as the younger boys have to do for their dormitory and for the older boys. The older girls instruct the younger girls in the different steps of the *chāng* dances, in the different tunes and melodies of their songs, and in the way they should behave themselves to the boys of other villages who come to dance with them in their village and to whose villages they themselves go for dances.

In Keonjhar and Pāl Lahera, however, these customs appear to have suffered more or less decay. There one of the married men is now selected by the Pāuṛis of the village to act as the leader and superviser of the bachelors. He is called th *Pāhāli* or *Dongōā*. Similarly an elderly woman acts as the guide and mentor of the maidens. She decides as to what village they are to go on any particular day for dancing, and she generally accompanies them to such dancing trysts.

"*Āṛ-bandha*" or *the Sacred Thread.*—Occasionally an elderly Pāuṛi Bhūiyā may be seen wearing the sacred thread or *paitā* in the manner of twice-born Hindu castes. At most five *per cent* of the old men among the *Pāuṛis* may be found with a *Pāitā* or sacred cord across their neck. No ceremonies are observed in wearing it, nor is the wearer required to observe any special rules with regard to food and drink or contact with people of other tribes and castes. Like the Pāuṛi Bhuiyās, some Mūṇḍās and Bhumijes also choose to wear the sacred thread.

CHAPTER IX.

DEATH AND ITS ATTENDANT CEREMONIES.

Sickness and Death.

Cause of sickness.

Most diseases are believed by the Pāuṛis to be the infliction of some offended or mischievous spirit. A protracted illness is attributed to the *Masāni* bhuts or the spirits of persons whose manes have not been ceremonially taken back to the house. The ancestor-spirits, though ordinarily beneficent, may cause illness to some member of the family if the *bhitar* or inner tabernacle set apart for them is polluted by the intrusion of some ceremonially unclean person. Other deities may cause sickness if there is any defect or remissness in the periodical offerings or sacrifices to them. *Bāutis* or the familiar spirits of particular individuals may also cause illness and even death, but generally they aflict only members of the house in which they have their seats. They ordinarily cause minor ailments such as sores and abcesses on the neck or feet of persons entering their *āsthāns* or seats while such intruders are ceremonially unclean; but sometimes they may even cause some fatal illness to such intruders. Vows of sacrifices are made to them to secure their forbearance. *Boṛām*, *Gāi-srī* and other village-deities may cause epidemics when offended, but they ordinarily protect the village from epidemics and other misfortunes. *Chitrāngi* is a minor spirit who afflicts people with night-mares. The patient shakes off the *Chitrāngi* spirit by turning round on his bed and thus rids himself of a night-mare.

The friends of a sick man call in a spirit-doctor styled the *Rāuṛiā*, to find out which particular spirit is responsible for the trouble. The methods of the *Rāuṛiā* will be described in a later chapter. In the case of any affliction through a *Masāni* spirit, the *ningchhā* ceremony is performed by the *Rāuṛiā* waving four times over the head of the patient a few grains of rice wrapped up in a leaf and throwing the bundle away while bidding the *Masāni* spirit (who is addressed by name) to depart. In the case of an infliction by the ancestor spirits, they are promised an offering of *jāu* (rice-pudding) cooked in a new earthen vessel and are asked to return into their *hāṇṛia* or earthen vessel in which they are believed to reside inside the *bhitar.* In cases of epidemic, the Dihuri makes offerings of water to *Boṛām* and *Gāi-srī* and to other gods of the village and the adjacent hills. Certain roots and herbs are also administered to the sick. These folk-medicines will be described in a subsequent chapter.

When all remedies fail and the sick man dies, the corpse is laid with its head to the south and is besmeared with oil and turmeric paste. Those who can afford to do so cover the corpse with a new cloth, but do not take off the old cloth which the deceased had on. The corpse is carried out of the house, face upwards and feet pointing north, wrapped in a mat and tied to a wooden pole. While the corpse is being taken out of the house, the women increase their wailing. As soon as the corpse is carried out, one or more women clean the floors and courtyard of the house with cow-dung and water and throw away all earthen cooking vessels. Females do not go to the burial-place or cremation-ground.

A person killed by a tiger is cremated, as other-

Disposal of the dead. wise, it is believed, the tiger which killed the man will carry off the corpse and will return and kill other persons. Persons who die of snake-bite, a fall, cholera or small-pox, must be buried. Children up to the age of seven or thereabouts are buried. Corpses of other persons may be either buried or cremated. Except in the case of a person killed by a tiger, burial is more usual. The agnatic families (*Kuṭumbs*) of a village have their graveyard separate from those of the *Bhandhu* families of the village. A pit about six feet long and three feet deep is dug, and the corpse let down into it. Ear-rings and necklaces, if any, worn by the deceased, are buried with the corpse; but bracelets and other ornaments are taken off among Pāuṛis of the Bonāi State but not among those of Keonjhar who are said to leave even silver bracelets with the corpse in the grave in the pit. The corpse is laid on its left side with its head to the south and face to the west. Then the eldest son of the deceased first throws a handful of earth into the grave and then other sons do the same; next the *kuṭumbs* and then the *bandhus* perform the same rite in honour of the deceased. Three logs of wood are placed over the corpse. Finally all fill in the grave with earth. Pieces of stone (*Pāthar gāddi*) are piled over the grave, and over these stones thorny twigs and bushes are spread so that wolves and other beasts may not disturb the grave. In the case of a cremation the corpse in Bonāi is laid on the funeral pile with its head to the south,[72] the eldest son first puts fire to it and then the other sons, next the *kutumbs*, and finally the *bandhus* put fuel-wood over the corpse. In Keonjhar the corpse is placed over the funeral pyre in a sitting posture and wood is piled up on all sides of it, and a brother of the deceased in preference to a son puts fire into its mouth. When a pregnant woman dies, the child in Bonāi is taken out of the womb and buried at some distance from the grave of its mother; but in Keonjhar only a mark is made on the womb with the end of a paddy grain, and the woman is buried with the child in its womb.

When the men return from the burial-place or cremation ground, as the case may be, they have their

---

72 In this the Pāuṛi Bhūiyās agree with a few Mūṇḍā tribes such as the Birhōṛs, but differ from most other Mūṇḍā tribes (E g. the Mūṇḍās, the Khāṛiās, the Hōs and the Sāntāls) who bury their dead with the head pointing north. The Plains Bhūiyās, too, follow the general custom of placing the corpse with its head to the north. Among the Juāngs the practice appears to vary and Risley does not appear to be correct when he says that the head of a Juāng corpse always points to the south.

nails pared and the hair round the scalp shaved by some *Bandhu*. In Bonāi all *kuṭumb* males in the village, young and old, have their nails pared and the hair round their scalps shaved. But the widow and daughters of the deceased need not get their nails pared. In Keonjhar, however, distant relatives and tribe-fellows in the village are purified by only a cold water bath. The clothes of all the men who attend a burial or cremation as also those of all members of the deceased's family are made over to the *Dhōbā Behārā* for washing; and they all wear new or washed clothes, and those who have none borrow such clothes from some neighbours. The *Dhōbā Behārā* washes the clothes with hot water and ashes, and puts them out to dry. The clothes are brought back the same evening or next morning when rice is given to him to boil and eat. On the eleventh day, a feast is provided to all relatives—*Bandhus* as well as *Kuṭumbs*. In Bonāi only *Bandhus* may act as cooks for this feast, but in Keonjhar *kuṭumbs* too may take part in the cooking. When the relatives take a few days to collect the necessary provisions for a feast, the various purificatory observances such as the shaving of the head and paring of the nails of all people tainted with death-pollution as also of the members of the family of the deceased and the changing of old clothes for new ones are similarly delayed.

Calling back the shades of the dead.

Except in the case of a woman dying in childbirth or during pregnancy, and of persons who have been killed by tigers, or have died of snake-bite, an accidental fall, cholera, and small-pox, the shades of other dead people in Bonāi are conducted back to the house either on the third, fifth, seventh, ninth or eleventh days from the day of death with the following rites[73]. At sunset a party of relatives—either *kuṭumbs* or *bandhus* or both—of the deceased start from the deceased's house and proceed in the direction of the grave or cremation ground. One man of the party carries either two sickles, one in each hand, or a brass cup in his left hand and a stick in his right hand, and another carries a new earthen vessel containing rice-flour, and a third man carries an earthen vessel in which goat's flesh has been cooked. When the party arrives at the boundary of the village, three

73 Compare similar rites among the Mūṇḍās, the Birhōṛs and most other Mūṇḍā-speaking tribes. The Hinduized Plains Bhūiyās have generally given up the custom of calling back the shades.

sticks are planted into the ground in the form of a tripod, and the earthen vessel in which goat's flesh has been cooked is placed over it and smashed into pieces. While the vessel is being broken, the men call the deceased aloud by name and cry, "Come, come! Do thou enter the hut". Then the spirit attracted by the smell of the cooked meat, is believed to come there and enter the earthen vessel containing rice-flour, and is carried home. The man with the brass cup strikes the cup with the stick, or if the man carries two sickles he strikes one against the other. When the party reach home, the people in the house ask them, "How has the spirit come?" Then some one examines the rice-flour and looks out for the footprints of the animal which is believed to have carried the spirit on its back. Something resembling the footprint of an elephant, or of a cow or an ox or a cat or an ant or some other animal is always imagined to be present in the rice-flour, and the man exclaims,—"See! Here is the footprint of the spirit's vehicle!" The rice-flour is now burnt and eaten by the seven men who have conducted the spirit home. A fowl which was left in the *bhitar* or inner tabernacle before the party went to fetch the spirit is now sacrificed and its blood offered to the ancestor spirits. Then some *kuṭumb* or agnate of the deceased puts rice on a leaf-plate placed on the floor of the *bhitar*, and offers the rice first to the spirits of all the ancestors and other members of the family who predeceased the person whose shade has just been brought home, and finally to the new shade or spirit. In Keonjhar, the shade of old men only are called back to the house by the Pāuṛis.

On the day of purification (*suddha*), at noon, a party of relatives go to the crossing of two roads, cleanses with cow-dung a bit of ground at the junction of the roads, and a *bandhu* or cognatic relation of the deceased offers a little *āruā* rice and turmeric powder to the ancestor-spirits, saying—"*Dharam*-God [is] on high and *Bāsuki* (Earth-Mother) below. And O ye Ancestor-spirits! this offering is made to ye." If a red ant or a white ant or some other worm is found on the cleaned crossing, it is taken up and carried home in a leaf; and if no worm or other thing is found on the spot a leaf or a grain of rice is picked up and carried home. One of the party goes on striking a knife against a sickle. Arrived at the deceased's house, they let loose the ant or worm and drop the rice or leaf on the floor of the kitchen. The inmates of the house ask them—"What have you brought?" They reply, "We have banished sorrow, and brought happiness." From the day of burial or cremation until the day when the shade is brought back, every day a son or a younger brother of the deceased carries a leaf-cup (*dōnā*) of boiled rice to the boundary (*gāon-mur*) of the village and puts it down on the ground for the nourishment of the spirit of the deceased. This practice obtains both among the Bonāi as well as the Keonjhar Pāuṛis.

After these sacrifices and offerings have been made to the shade now installed in its old home, the members of the family become freed from death-pollution. Until now they have been under a taboo; no member of the tribe would take food or drink water at their hands. On the first day of pollution, their meals are cooked for them—or at least the cooking-pot is put upon the hearth—by some agnate of theirs not belonging to the family. In some villages during all these days of pollution they are provided with food cooked at the houses of their neighbours.

Birth and Death Customs of the Khaṇḍāit or Plains Bhūiyās.

As already noticed in the footnotes, the Hinduized Bhūiyās of the plains, under the influence of Brāhmaṇ priests, have modified their ancient customs relating to birth and death to some extent. They now observe only eleven days of ceremonial pollution after the birth of a male as well as of a female child. On the eleventh day, only the child's parents have their nails pared, and the clothes of the members of the family are washed. A Brāhmaṇ priest performs a mutilated form of the Hōm ceremony and oblations (*Piṇḍa*) are offered to ancestor-spirits in the manner of the Hindus. On the twelfth day agnates and other relatives are treated to a feast.

To select a name for the child the same method is employed as by the Pāuṛi Bhūiyās.

The Khaṇḍāit Bhūiyās have adopted the Hindu custom of ceremonial feeding of the child with rice for the first time. This ceremony is performed in the fourth month of the child's life or later. Some elderly member of the family puts into the mouth of the child a little *kṣīr* or rice boiled in milk, after a portion has been offered to the gods. A feast is provided to relatives.

On the fifth, seventh or ninth year of its life a Khaṇḍāit Bhūiyā child has its ears perforated. A barber perforates the ears with a metal pin. Relatives are entertained on the occasion but no religious rites are observed.

The more well-to-do Plains Bhūiyās practise cremation whereas the poorer Bhūiyās bury their dead. But, rich and poor, all must bury the corpses of women dying during pregnancy and the corpses of members of their families who die of cholera or small-pox or snake-bite. In the case of the corpse of a pregnant woman, the child is taken out of the womb and buried separately at some distance from its mother, as among the Pāuṛis; in some places the corpses of the woman and of the embryo are buried on opposite banks of a stream, for it is believed that spirits cannot cross a stream. The shade of the deceased is invited back to the house and incorporated with the *pitrūs* or ancestor-spirits with similar ceremonies as among the Pāuṛi Bhūiyās.

CHAPTER X.

RELIGION AND MAGIC.

(i) *Religion.*

The Spirit-World.

The Pāuṛi Bhuiyā, like other rude tribes, attribute all the ills of life—all bad luck in the food-quest, in personal security and in physical well-being—to unseen supernormal powers and beings that fill earth, air, and water. In his estimation the presence of an invisible spirit-world interpenetrating this visible world of man and more or less capable of controlling the forces of nature and the course of human life, makes the Pāuṛi's journey through life full of risks and dangers, particularly at its turning-points, such as birth, puberty, and marriage, and in all new undertakings, such as hunting, fruit-gathering, forest-clearing and agricultural operations. For security against dangers believed to proceed from these supernormal beings and energies, and in order to place themselves in harmonious relations with them and thereby ensure good luck and avoid bad luck, the Pāuṛis, like other communities, have adopted such means as suggested themselves to the tribal mind or was "revealed" to their wise men or "seers" of old, for the propitiation and conciliation, and control where necessary, of these invisible powers. The faith in higher powers and the rites and methods adopted to place themselves in touch and secure harmonious relations with them and thereby revive hope and moral courage when danger threatens and fear invades the soul, constitute their Religion proper. The ways and means adopted to control or press into service the impersonal elements, forces, potencies, powers and tendencies that may harm or help, may be said to constitute what anthropologists would generally term "magic".

Nature of Pauri Gods.

The Pāuṛi Bhũiyās have risen to the conception of a regular hierarchy or gradation among the gods and spirits of their faith. As it is not every evil power or energy that is entitled to be called a spirit, so it is not every spirit that is entitleed to rank among the deities. Only the more powerful amongst the spirits are recognized as such and given fixed local habitations and names and propitiated at regular intervals by the Pāuṛi village communities, so that they may help them in the troubles of their every-day life and ward off dangers that may otherwise befall them, and in general restore confidence and a feeling of security and strength in times of crises. Besides the spirits of their deceased ancestors and the local spirits whose cult looms large in the religion of the tribe, the Pāuṛis, unlike their more primitive neighbours and congeners—the Juāngs, have arrived at the conception of a purely beneficent Supreme Deity called Dharam-Deota—the great Sun-god, the giver of light and life. Like some of the Chōtā Nāgpur tribes, the Pāuṛi sometimes also calls Him the "Sākhi" or 'Witness' of the doings of men and spirits. It is probably after the Pāuṛi took to agriculture that Mother Earth or Dhartī-Mātā, also variously called Bāsukī-mātā, Basuṛi Ṭhākurāṇi, or Basu-Mātā, has been assigned an important position—only next to the Supreme Deity—amongst the Pāuṛi deities. Indeed she is sometimes spoken of as the wife of Dharam-deōtā or the Sun-god. And the Sun god is by better-informed Pāuṛis identified with Boṛam.

When questioned as to the forms of their deities, more than one well-informed Pāuṛi told me:—"The gods are like the wind; our villags-gods go with us unseen when we go to the jungles to hunt or to the *komāns* (clearances on the hill-slopes) to watch our crops". But though the gods are ordinarily formless and invisible they appear before the Pāuṛi in his dreams in definite shapes. Thus the Gāī-srī always appears in the shape of an old lady wearing a reddish silk cloth, and so also does the goddess Ṭhākurāṇī (identified by the better-informed Pāuṛi with the Gāī-srī) appear in the same shape and garb, with hair hanging down in long locks (*jaṭā*); a Pāṭ or Hill-god generally appears as a stalwart man dressed in royal robes and riding a horse. It is asserted that, when moving in the air, a god sometimes appears to men below as a streak of moving fire.

The following account given to me by Jaideb Dihuri, the Pāuṛi priest of village Suākāṭi, in the Keonjhar State, as to how the deity Ṭhākurāṇī revealed Herself to the Pāuṛis of the village in the time of one of his ancestors, throws an interesting light on the Pāuṛi's anthromorphic conception of the gods. One evening, when the Pāuṛis of the village were warming themselves before a fire (*dhūni*) in their *maṇḍa-ghar* the deity entered there in the shape of an old lady. She found the assembled Pāuṛis now putting the thin ends of logs of wood into the fire and now the head-ends. They did not recognize the deity and so she judged the people to be very stupid and decided not to remain there in that shape, and vanished into thin air. That night Ṭhākurāṇī appeared to Jaideb's ancestor and some other villagers in a dream and told them that on the following morning they would find her in the Dihuri's house. In the morning the Dihuri and his wife took a bath and reverently entered their hut where they found Ṭhākurani in the shape of a lively infant disporting herself in a basket. In reverential fear the Dihuri exclaimed: "How shall I, in my impurity and ignorance, be able to serve Thee properly (i.e. without any remissness, though unintentional) in Thy present shape?" Thereupon the Deity said, "Very well, then I shall remain with you in another shape." On this the Dihuri covered up the Deity with a basket. And next morning he discovered inside the basket a short sword made of shining gold. In this new shape which the Deity assumed for the benefit of the Pāuṛis of Suākāṭi the Ṭhākurāṇī was regularly worshipped at the Dihuri's house until, many years later, the Mārhāṭṭa troops came to the village and plundered the houses and threw away the golden image of the Deity into the Teliādah eddy of river Baitaraṇī. The Pāuṛis, too, fled for life from the village. Later, when they returned to their village, the Ṭhākurāni appeared to the Dihuri in a dream and said, "I shall not return in person to Suākāṭi now. Get an iron sword made and instal it in a new hut and make regular offerings to it in my name." And the villagers were relieved in mind and did as the Deity directed. Ever since then two goats are offered to Her every year, one on the occasion of the *Bihiṛa* pūjā in the month of Aṣāṛh and another in the month of Kārtik in front of the new temple of Ṭhakurāṇī.

A brief account of the different deities and spirits, their functions, and the occasions on which and the manner in which their assistance is invoked is given below :—

(ii) *General Tribal Gods.*

Highest in rank and power are Dharam-deōtā or

the Sun-god, and Bāsukī-mātā or Bāsu-mātā or Dhartī-mātā—the Earth-goddess, who may be called the general gods of the Pāuṛis. They are sometimes described as husband and wife. A Pāuṛi Dihuri indignantly told me, "One must be a fool to think that Dharam-deōtā sits on high and Bāsukī-mātā has her seat below. They are here, there, everywhere". They are not represented by any symbols and have no *āsthāns* or fixed seats. The purport of one of the riddles put by one Pāuṛi boy to another is, "Who is the Deity who travels everywhere and has no temple?" The answer given is "Dharam-deōtā". Another popular saying describes Bāsukī-mātā as having "Eyes on four sides, and wings on four sides, and flying about" (*Chārī āṛē ānkhi, Chārī āṛē pānkhi, būlichhē*).

At every religious festival, the Supreme Spirit or *Dharam-deōtā* and the Earth-spirit or *Bāsukī-mātā* or *Bāsu-māta* or *Dhartī-mātā* are first invoked, though not ordinarily with any sacrifices or offerings. "*Tarē Bāsu-mātā uparē Dharam-Deōtā*" is an expression employed not only before all invocations to the deities and spirits but also as the opening formula in an oath or adjuration. While the other deities, if offended, may sometimes cause harm, Dharam-deōtā and Bāsukī-mātā or Dhartī-mātā are always beneficent. A white goat (*pōṇḍrā*) is sacrificed in Asāṛh by the Dihuri to Dharam-Deōtā on the the occasion of the Bibiṛā-pūjā for seasonable rainfall, and a white fowl is offered to Him whenever there is any trouble in a family or a village, and at the same time *āruā* rice (*akṣata*) is offered to Dhartī-mātā. Again, in Baiśākh on the occasion of the Tirtīā Muṭhi Pūjā, *āruā* rice is offered to Dharam-deōtā on a *kōmān* field at the first ceremonial sowing of paddy seeds. Before starting on a hunting expedition on the *Ākhni Pārdhi* day in Chait each hunter offers a piece of turmeric to the Earth-goddess. Offerings of rice, turmeric, milk and molasses are made to Dharam-Deōtā and Bāsukī-mātā at a marriage. Vows are also made to them at times of crises, such as at the difficult labour of a pregnant woman, and fulfilled after the desired boon is granted. At the founding of a new village in the Bonāi State, the Dihuri offers rice, molasses, and milk to Dharam-deōtā.

Konto Kuāri, whose *pūjā* has been described at length in a previous chapter, is a new deity who, from an obscure origin, has attained almost to the position of a national deity in the Bonāi State. She is identified with the Hindu goddess Dūrgā, the manifestation of the protective power of the godhead. The Hinduized northern Bhũiyās, in Chōṭā Nāgpur, it may be noted, offer regular periodical sacrifices to the Sun-god and the Earth-goddess whom they call respectively Suruj-Nārāyan and Dhartī-mātā.

(iii) *Nature Deities.*

Pats or Hill-gods and River-gods.

As I have already noticed, a group of Pāuṛi villages regard some prominent hill[74] or river in the neighbourhood as the guardian deity of such villages, and offerings and sacrifices are offered to the Pāṭ or the spirit of such hill or river. Ordinarily the Pāṭ[75] is represented by some stones in each village, where the pūjā is made by the village Dihuri on a Thursday in *Āsārh*. The Dihuri remains fasting the whole day. A little before

74 Compare the *Buru Bonga* of the Muṇḍās, the Hōs, the Sāntāls, the Birhoṛs, and the Bhumij. The Juāngs, like the Pāuṛi Bhũiyās, offer sacrifices to various *Pāṭs* such as *Koṛā Pāṭ*, *Mahā-Samari Pāṭ*, etc. The Khāṛiās also call their hill-deities as "Pāṭs."

75 The name *Pāṭ* has now been extended to mean a deity in general. In village Donla in the Keonjhar State I found a hut in which a stone is kept to represent *Lakshmi Thakurāṇi Pāṭ*. The Wild Khāriās of the Manbhum District offer sacrifices to the *Dolma Pāṭ* or the spirit of the Dolma-hills.

sunset of the Thursday fixed for the pūjā, the Dihuri rinses his teeth, washes his face, and bathes before he goes to the altar (*merh*) erected for the pūjā. During the pūjā, any one, even the Rājā, happening to pass by the altar must stop there. Such of the villagers as wish to attend the pūjā, must bathe before approaching the altar. The Dihuri burns incense and offers milk, *ghee*, *dahi* and *gūṛ* to the Pāṭ and, while sprinkling *āruā* rice on the stone representing the Pāṭ, prays—"O such-and-such (names) Pāṭ, keep us in health, keep our families and children in health; give us good crops; may tigers and bears disappear." Goats are then sacrificed on behalf of the villagers. Besides this general annual worship, individual Pāuṛis or others sometimes get the Dihuri to sacrifice for them goats or fowls in fulfilment of vows.

It may be noted that a particular village may also worship a special *Pāṭ*[76] of its own as well as the common *Pāṭ* of a group of villages. Thus the *Bāro-khāṇḍa* Bār in the Bonāi State, consisting of villages Toinsa, Kainsārā, Rāonta, Jōlō, Fuljōr, *etc.*, all sacrifice to the *Brāhmāṇī Pāṭ*, or the spirit of the river *Brāhmaṇī*.

76 Compare the *Hātu Buru Bonga* of the Birhōṛs.

But the Pāuṛis of Toinsa also offer sacrifices to a neighbouring hill called *Kuṛāḍi Pāṭ*, and those of Tainsārā worship another hill called *Bhairapāṭ*. Almost every high or peculiar hill in the Bhūiyā country is worshipped as a *Pāṭ* by some village or group of villages. Thus the Pāuṛi villages of Suākāṭi, Dongapāni, Ṭhakurdih and Jāmdih in the Keonjhar State offer sacrifices to *Kopta Pāṭ*.

The gradual widening of the social organization with the advance in civilization amongst the Bhūiyās is evidenced by the fact that whereas in the Pāuṛi Parganā, although a *Pāṭ* is the tutelary deity of a group of villages, almost every village offers the periodical sacrifices to its own Pāṭ separately,—the Bhūiyās of the different villages of the Kuiṛā Parganā go a step further and all meet together on the Pāṭ pūjā day. The Dihuris and Nāeks and other representatives from all the villages meet at village Kuiṛā before the pūjā of the Pāṭ. There the *Māhākūṛ* or headman of the pastoral caste of Gouṛs supplies a quantity of milk, curdled milk (*dahi*) and clarified butter (*ghee*), and a potter (Kumhār) of village Kolmong supplies earthen vessels for the *pūjās*. These are divided among the different villages, and with these the village elders return to their respective villages, where sacrifices are offered.

The Plains Bhūiyās have a still wider organization, for amongst them a group of neighbouring villages offer sacrifices to their common *Pāṭ* jointly. Thus the sacrifices to the hill-god, *Kālā-pāṭ*, are made jointly at village Lodām by the Bhūiyās of Lodām, Kolāipōsh, Nawāpāṛā, Kanāpāli, Ṭheṭhāipōsh, Nohini-pāṛā, Sukpāli, Ongāpāṛā, Sukhāban, Sagṛiāposh, Ṭeṭengagera, Ṭāngarpāli, Bābni-buṛi, Ṭ.krā, Kendū-dih, Basnār, Kumārdih, Jugihar, Parāgpōsh, Kōṭāpāṛā, Rengālberā, Laupōsh, Ghunsṛipōsh, Bhalenḍih, Dhā-wāḍih, and Mahishchhāpal; and each village brings a goat for sacrifice,—the Kalō or village priest of Lodām officiating as the sacrificer and offering all the goats one after another, to the Pāṭ. In village Kuār, in the Keonjhar State, a hut temple has been provided for the mountain-deity named *Mahā-pāṭ* or the great Pāṭ (cf. the *Marang buru* or *Baṛpāhāṛi* of the Mūṇḍās). This deity has now come to be recognised as a tribal deity by the Pāuṛi Bhūiyās; and tribesmen not only from all over the Keonjhar hills but even their neighbours from the Bonāi and Pāl-Lahera States come to offer sacrifices to this mountain-deity. A great annual festival in honour of this deity is held on a Friday in the month of Māgh (January-February). Some permanent provisions for these sacrifices have been arranged by the Rāj of Keonjhar. The northern Bhũiyās in Chōṭā-Nāgpur, though they no longer recognise and offer sacrifices to special Pāṭs or hill-deities of each village or group of villages, regard *Lugu-Pāhāṛ* (in the Hāzāribāgh District) as their tribal hill-god. Sacrifices are offered by the heads of families to this hill-god or rather to the Mūn-Bīrs or hero-gods or ancestor-gods who are believed to have their seats on this Hill. And either in fulfilment of vows or by way of pilgrimage these Bhũiyās occasionally visit the hill, and then get their heads shaven (in the manner of Hindu pilgrims) and offer sacrifices. Some Bhũiyā psychics under the influence of supposed spirit-possession also repair to this Lugu Hill and some to the Pareśnath Hill and there offer sacrifices.

Among river gods, *Brāhmaṇī Pāṭ* is generally named as a deity by all the Bhũiyās,—Pāuṛis as well as Panchśai-ghariās,—but it is only in one or two bārs of the Pāuṛi Parganā and a few groups of Panchśaighariā Bhūiyā villages that special worship of this deity is observed. All Pāuṛis as well as Plains Bhūiyās speak of "Nadi-Samudra-Brāhmāṇi-Pāṭ" [River-Ocean-Brāhmāṇi-Pāṭ]. Similarly they speak of *Baitaraṇī Pāṭ* as one of their deities; but it is the Bhūiyās of the Keonjhar State, through which State the Baitaraṇī flows, who actually offer sacrifices to the *Baitaraṇī Pāṭ*. The Bhūiyās, like several rude tribes I have known, while they offer sacrifices at some of their pūjās, name all other gods and spirits they can think of, besides invoking the deities then particularly worshipped. Thus the Dihuri of one village told me that at the *Bihiṛā pūjā* he invoked besides Dharam Deōtā, Bāsukī Mātā, Gāi-śrī and Bōṛām, the following other deities as well, namely, Kālō Kamalā, Aṛhā-Buṛhā, Banaspati, Bana-Dūrgā, Ban-Rāi, Bāro-Bhāi Mālār, and Bāgheā-Ṭāngiā. But who these latter deities were the Dihuri could not clearly explain. The *Khaṇḍādhār* waterfall near village Loṛāpāni in Bonāi, is called *Khaṇḍā-Pāṭ* and an annual sacrifice of a white goat is offered to this Pāṭ by the Dihuri of the village. It may be noted that the Northern Bhūiyās in Chōṭā Nāgpur make offerings of milk, molasses and flowers in October to a distinct spirit of vegetation whom they name "Phulmati" (Flower-spirit).

Bahuni or the spirit of surface-springs receives offerings of flowers, molasses and fowls in the months of Āṣāṛh or Śrāban to ensure an unfailing supply of water throughout the year. *Bahūni* is also the spirit of the woods, and offerings of molasses are made in the jungle to this spirit by every cultivator before he begins to clear land for *komān* cultivation on the steep hill-slopes.

The name *Pāṭ* is sometimes applied to the seat of the gods as well as to the gods themselves; and thus we hear of *Pitru Pāṭ* [Pāṭ of the ancestors] and *Lakshmi Pāṭ* [Pāṭ of the Goddess of Wealth].

What strikes me as a most interesting feature of this Pāṭ or Mountain cult of the Pāuṛi Bhūiyās is the taboos observed by them in connection with some of their respective *Pāṭs*. Thus the Pāuṛis who have the Kopta [Pāṭ] Hill for their Pāṭ-deity abstain from eating the pigeon or *Kopta*; those who have the *Sinduira Pāṭ* Hill for their Pāṭ deity taboo the anointing of vermilion or *sindūr* on the forehead of their women and so forth. And it is significant that some Pāuṛis, when asked about their clan, actually name their Pāṭ (E.g. *Kopta* or the Pigeon) as their clan-name. In this connection attention may be drawn to the association, among the allied Birhoṛ tribe, of the emblem of their clan totems with their hill-gods (Buru-bonga).[77]

(*iv*) *General Village Gods.*

Boṛām (also called *Mangalā*) and *Gāi-śrī* (also called *Grām-Śrī*, or *Bāsuṛī*, or *Bāsukī Matā*, or *Thākurāṇī*) are the general village gods who receive offerings at every Pāuṛi village. In the villages of the Pāuṛi areas in the Bonāi, Pal Lahera and Keonjhar States where the village site is changed from time to time, the Bāsuri or Gāi-śrī is represented by a wooden post on one side of the darbār whereas in the villages of Kuiṛā Parganā and the Plains villages where the villagers are all settled agriculturists the *Gāi-śrī* is representd by a *stone* placed along with other stones in a permanent sacred grove called *Jāhira*. Boṛām[78] who is said to be the husband

77 *The Birhōṛs* (1925), pp. 102—107, 122—123.

78 *Boṛam* may perhaps be identified with the Sun-god of the Mūṇḍās and Hōs (*Singbonga*), Khāriās (*Bero or Ponmosor*), Sāntāls (*Chando Bonga or Ṭhakur*). *Gai-Srī* may be identified with the Earth-goddess of most

of Gāi-śrī or Ṭhakūrāṇī or Mangalā, is not specifically represented by any symbol in the Pāuṛi villages, but in the *Jāher* or sacred grove of the Kuiṛā Bhũiyās a stone is placed to represent Boṛām. In the month of Aṣāṛh (July), Gāi-śrī receives a sacrifice either of a black fowl, or of a black fowl and a black goat in alternate years. This offering is meant to induce her to give seasonable rain and good crops. In Chait (March-April) on the Ākhni Pārdhi day, when the Pāuṛis of each village go to the jungles for hunting, the Dihuri offers to Boṛām and Gāi-śrī jointly a few drops of blood of the game as soon as any is bagged. In Māgh or Fālgun (January-February), when the mango blossoms come out, offerings are made to Boṛām and Gāi-śrī by the Dihuri to render innocuous the eating of new fruit, the cutting of trees and bushes and the application of manure to the fields, and generally to avert all evil.

---

of the agricultural Mũṇḍā and Dravidian tribes. As a matter of fact, some better-informed Pāuṛi Bhũiyās do actually identify *Boṛam* with *Dharam*-deõta, and *Gai-sri* with *Bāsuki-mātā* or the Earth-goddess. It may be noted, however, that I found some Hill-Khāṛiās of the Mayurbhanj State in Ōṛissā calling their Jungle deity as Boṛam and their hill deities as Pāṭs and the Supreme Deity as Dharam.

The names *Bāsuki-mātā* (Serpent-mother) and *Basu-mātā* apparently a corruption of *Basumati* or the Earth are used by the Pāuṛi as interchangeable names. And it is not improbable that she was originally a serpent deity.

In Baiśākh (April) an offering of rice is made to Boṛām and Gāī-śrī to make sowing operations free from unseen dangers. Finally, in Bhādra or Āśvin (September-October), offerings of molasses and frankincense are made to Boṛām and Grāmśrī or Gāi-śrī on his field by a Pāuṛi cultivator when he cuts the first sheaves of paddy. Again, two or three days later, when the new rice is first eaten, the Dihuri on behalf of all the villagers sacrifices a fowl to Boṛām and offers to Gāi-śrī a little *jāu* or new rice cooked in a new earthen vessel. Thus are all supernatural dangers that might otherwise arise from the eating of the new rice removed. Ṭhākuraṇī is worshipped in many villages. She appears to be the same as the Mother-goddess Devī or Durgā and is, by some Pauṛis, identified with Gāi-śrī. In some villages there is a hut dedicated to this deity and, in the month of *Agrahāyan*, a clay image of her, purchased from a potter, is set up in this hut temple, and the Dihuri worships her for three days and sacrifices goats or pigs or fowls. During these three days the Dihuri remains fasting in the day-time. On the fourth day, the image is thrown into a stream.

It may not be unreasonable to suppose that Boṛām,

on one side, and *Gāi-śrī* or *Bāsuṛi* or *Bāsuki-mātā* or *Ṭhākurāṇī* or Devī, on the other side, represent the male and the female forces of Nature, or rather the creative and protective aspect of the Deity. It is further interesting to note that the Prajā Bhũiyās and Rāj Koli Bhũiyās all acknowledge a goddess of the name of Pāuṛi Devī as their tribal deity, although the Pauṛi Bhũiyās themselves do not know the name. It appears likely that the Spirit of their original native mountain is now remembered by these Hinduised Bhũiyās as the *Pāuṛi* spirit and many amongst them now identify *Pauṛi Devī* with the great Hindu goddess Devī or Dūrgā. Here is probably another instance of a deity of the primitive tribes being assimilated with Hindu deities.

Thakurāṇī-usha.

In the month of Agrahāyaṇ, a few Bhũiyā families, particularly in the Kuiṛā Parganā of Bonāi, and in the Plains, make a special propitiation called *Ṭhakurāṇī Ushā* every day for a whole month, in fulfilment of some vow, or in expectation of some desired boon, and *Bisri-Ushā* in Māgh for eight days during which Devī is worshipped in a clay image. On the last day of these Ushās or *Bratas*, buffaloes, sheep, goats or fowls are sacrificed to the deity. In another Ushā, known as *Dhūn kuilā ushā*, Mahādeva under the name of *Srī-subana* or *Sōmnath*, and his consort Pārvatī are worshipped for over a month from the eighth day of the new moon in Bhādra to the full moon in Asvin. On the last day of the *Ushā* one or more goats are sacrificed. No image is made. Every evening a number of men and women assemble in the courtyard of the family that celebrate the Ushā and a few young men sing and dance to the primitive music played by an old man or woman with a bow on a rude sounding-board made of an earthen vessel covered up at the mouth with a winnowing basket. As the music proceeds, some of the men often appear to get possessed, and enact a dumb show representing the pranks of mischievous spirits and sometimes the traditional deeds of their hero-gods, while all the others go on singing and drumming. This may be noted in conection with Sir William Ridgeway's[79] contention that in Hindustan, as elsewhere, serious drama arose from the worship of the dead, often deified. This *Ushā* is in vogue among the Plains Bhūi-

---

79 *Drama and Dramatic Dances of Non-European Races* (1915) and *Cambridge University Reporter* (18th May 1920).

yās as well as some other aboriginal and semi-aboriginal families in the Plains. This, like the other *Ushās*, is observed for securing some boon or in fulfilment of some vow.

Lakṣmī is a deity apparently borrowed from the Hindus. She is the guardian of crops and cattle and is the bestower of prosperity. On a Friday, a Bhuiyā cultivator offers molasses and *ārnā* rice to this goddess on his field, and reaps a few sheaves of paddy, brings them home and inserts them into the inner side of the thatch of his hut. While making straw receptacles (*purā*) to store his rice, the cultivator puts inside the first *purā* a betel-nut as an offering to *Lakṣmī*, and after filling this *purā* with rice and plaiting it up, he lights a lamp over it in honour of the goddess.

(v) *Man-Gods*

First and foremost among the family gods of the Pāuṛi are the spirits of his deceased ancestors who have been ceremonially conducted into the house and given seats in the *Bhitar*. These ancestor-spirits or *Pitrus*[80] watch over the well-being of the family. Ex-

80 Cf. the *Haṛam-hoṛōkō* of the Mūṇḍās, the *Haprōm* of the Birhōṛs, the *Ōā-hām* of the Hōs, the *Baṛ-baṛki* of the Juāngs and the *Buṛhā-Buṛhi* or *Māri-masān* of the Khāṛiās.

cept when there is any neglect in making the regular offerings and sacrifices on which they, like other spirits, depend for nutritment, they are uniformly beneficent.

The customary offerings and sacrifices to which the Ancestor-spirits are ordinarily entitled are the following:—

A few drops of liquor are dropped on the ground for them whenever liquor is drunk by the members of the family; an offering of pudding (*jāu*) made of rice-flour and sesamum seeds is given to them at the name-giving ceremony of a Pāuṛi child; a Pāuṛi bride also makes a similar offering of *jāu* to the spirits of her husband's ancestors; when the shade of a deceased member of the family is conducted into the house, offerings of turmeric, rice, frankincense and molasses are made to the ancestor-spirits in the *Bhitar*; similar offerings are made before setting out for the annual Akhni Pardhi hunt in Chait, and on the occasions of the *Am-nuā* ceremony in Māgh-Falgun and the *Nuā-khāi* ceremony in Bhādo-Asvin.

Besides the spirits of one's own deceased ancestors, the spirits of a murdered person is sometimes accepted by the murderer's family as a family god so as to spare the family the troubles that might otherwise be caused by the spirit. Sacrifices are offered to such a spirit at stated intervals.

Sometimes a field is believed to be haunted by the spirit of some deceased or murdered person who causes harm to persons cultivating the field. The owner of the field propitiates such a spirit by giving him an *āsthān* or a permanent seat in the field and promising him periodical sacrifices which are thenceforth regularly offered.

Other man-gods are the *Bāgheā* or the spirit of a man killed by a tiger, and the *Bāuti*, or the spirit of a man killed by a bear. As such spirits are not conducted into the *bhitar* or inner tabernacle of the house, they are believed to wander about at will and try to secure food and nourishment for themselves as best they can. They can assume the shape of a tiger or a bear, as the case may be; and to protect themselves from being destroyed by the *Bāgheā* spirits who appear in the shape of tigers, the Pāuṛis offer fowls to them before they start on a hunting expedition. No *āsthān* is provided for such a spirit.

As the *Bāuti* spirits merely damage the Pāuṛi's crops, no regular sacrifices are offered to them, but occasional vows of sacrifices of fowls are made to them when bears cause repeated damage to the crops of a settlement. The name "Bāuti is also applied to the familar spirits of individuals. *Barāhi-pāt* is the Pig-deity: to prevent pigs and parrots from harming his crops, Pāuṛis sometimes offer sacrifices at the footprints of pigs in the jungles.

Unlike the northern[81] Bhūiyās, such as those of the Hazāribāgh District, the Pāuṛi Bhūiyās have no cult of hereos or *Bīrs*. Risley's conjecture[82] that Rikhmun "was originally the bear-totem of a sept of the tribe" does not appear to have the support of any ascertained facts. No section of the Bhūiyās know of any bear-totem. Even in the list of Bhūiyā totem-names given by Risley [83], the bear does not figure as a clan-totem. The Bhūiyās themselves explain, correctly as it seems, 'Rikhmun' as a corruption of "Rishi-muni". Spirits of some ancient heroes, generally non-Bhūiyās,

---

81 See pp. 30-32 *ante*.

82 Castes and Tribes, Vol. I, p. 112.

83 *Ibid*, Vol. II, App., p. 11.

are vaguely spoken of as deities, but receive no separate sacrifices. Thus it is only on occasions of certain pūjās of the village-gods, when the names of all spirits or deities worth naming are taken by the Dihuri along with the recognized village gods, that we hear the names of *Don Rāi*, *Barā Bhāi Māllār* and a few others who are apparently spirits of deceased men of note. There are two such spirits, however, who have been given 'seats' in the Pāuṛi country and receive offerings of stones. Those are called *Aṇḍya* and *Sāṇḍyā* who are said to have belonged to a *white* (*Puṇḍi*)[84] tribe named the Asūrs who are reputed to have possessed superhuman strength. The tradition goes that in order to attend *jātrās* or dancing festivals they used to walk from Bonāi to Keonjhar and back—a distance of about eighty miles—in one night. One night their enemies (some people, apparently under the influence of Hindu traditions, say the "Devas") succeeded in waylaying and killing them on the boundary line between villages Bōnjō and Jōlō. And there they were buried and stones heaped over them, and every

84 It may be noted that "Puṇḍi" is a Muṇḍāri Word meaning "white" Another Muṇḍāri word I heard among the Pāuṛis is "merōm"—meaning, goat.

passer-by adds a stone or, failing that, a leaf or a twig to the heap in the hope of securing success in his journey.

Such are the principal deities and spirits to whom the Pāuṛi Bhuiyās make regular offerings and sacrifices. Under Hindu influence their conception of some of the deities appears to have become less crude than before. With their increasing contact with the Hindus of the plains, Hindu gods, too, are slowly finding their way into the Pāuṛi pantheon; and it seems probable that within a few decades the Pāuṛi Bhuiyās will be hardly distinguishable from the Hinduized Plains Bhuiyās or Pānchśai Bhuiyās. Indeed, the more well-to-do families of the Kuiṛā Parganā Bhuiyās already approximate the Plains Bhuiyās in their habits and customs, and other families will not be long in doing so. Besides the deities and spirits described above, the Pāuṛis, like other animistic tribes, believe in the presence of a host of impersonal spirits or minor personal agents who may however be controlled, cajoled or tricked into inactivity and quiescence.

Feasts and Festivals.

Some public feasts and festivals mark the turning

points in the annual round of the economic life of the tribe so as to ensure safety and prosperity in their seasonal occupations. A brief account of these feasts and sacrifices are given below.

1 *The Māgh Paroi or Māgh Jātra Festival.*

The Māgh Jātrā festival marks the termination of the agricultural year. It is a festival of rejoicing and thanksgiving for the blessings of the out-going years, and of preparation for entering into the fresh labours of the incoming year with its manifest dangers. The ceremonies and observances in this festival are as follows: An open space outside the setlement is cleaned, and four newly-cut logs of wood brought from the jungle are planted upright in the ground to form a small quadrangle which is roofed over either with logs of wood as in Keonjhar and Pāl Lahera or with grass, leaves and straw as in Bonāi. At mid-day, the Dihuri, with each eye covered up with a rice-flour cake, in some places, but uncovered in others, sets fire to this quadrangular shed while all present shout "Hari-bol". In some Bhūiyā villages (as I found at village Bhonjpali

Hut-burning.

in the Bonāi State) fire on this occasion is kindled by the friction of two pieces of wood; and the hut-burning is done with new fire. All fire in other houses is extinguished, and new fire is kindled from this ceremonial fire. With this new fire *jāu* (rice boiled in milk) is cooked for offerings to the Ancestor-Spirits. On this day, no Pāuṛi Bhūiyā will allow fire to be taken out of his house by anybody. This ritual of hut-burning does not appear to be a rite of purgation or purification to which similar hut-burning by sterile women in several parts of India has been attributed by Crook.[85] The present rite may be a mimetic representation of jungle-clearing for purposes of *Komān* cultivation and is intended to have a magic influence on their agricultural operations. The ashes of this burnt hut are also believed to have a magical virtue. The Pāuṛis of the Keonjhar and Pāl Lahera States note the direction from which the echo of 'Hari-bōl' appears to reverberate, and conduct their *Koman* or *jhuming* operations on that side in the ensuing year, as it is believed to promise success. Every one present puts a mark (*ṭikā*) on his own forehead with the ashes

85 *Man* (February 1919), pp. 18—25.

of this burnt shed. The remaining ashes are taken up by the Pāuṛis present and some take their share home and some keep theirs in the Maṇḍā house. The ashes are believed to bring them luck (*subha*). In the Bonāi State someone carries the Dihuri home on his back and others follow him. Arrived at his house, the Dihuri pours a little water on everybody's feet (this being evidently a relic of an older custom of regular feet-washing), and brings out rice-flour cakes which he distributes to all present. Since morning, the men have all remained fasting, and now every one returns home where an exceptionally good dinner awaits him. But now-a-days, in every villages (as I found in Keonjhar) only the Dihuri observes the fast.

Next morning the Dihuri bathes and goes to the spot where the extemporised hut was burnt and there scatters a handful of paddy-seeds over the ashes and leaves the place. Then two other Pāuṛis of the village go there with a plough; one of them holds the plough and the other drives it over the ashes sown over by the Dihuri, and then go away. The Dihuri with a number of villagers who have remained fasting since morning, go to the *darbār* by the side of which Boṛām and Gāi-śrī have their *āsthāns* (seats). There the Dihuri offers some rice, and sacrifices a few fowls to Boṛām and Gāi-srī and then cooks the meat of the fowls. The Dihuri and the other villagers take each some rice and a new earthen vessel with him to the place, and everyone boils his own rice and eats it with a little of the cooked meat given by the Dihuri.

It is only after this ceremonial burning of newly cut logs of wood and the ceremonial ploughing and scattering of seeds on the ashes, that the villagers may cut wood or fell trees from the jungles, begin new clearings on their hill-slopes, and commence fresh agricultural operations. If anyone cuts wood before the Māgh jātrā festival, sickness to the Dihuri or his cattle is apprehended. Any person who may happen to cut wood before the festival will be required to propitiate the *Boṛām* spirit by sacrificing fowls. Should he omit to offer the sacrifices, the Dihuri will do so himself.

Ceremonial Friendship.

It is particularly on this occasion of the Māgh Jātrā festival that Pāuṛi boys (especially in the Bonāi State) form ceremonial friendships[86] with one another. The different forms of such artificial friendship are known as *Maitra*, *Sāngā*, *Jamḍāir* and *Mahā-Prasād*. The *Maitra* form of friendship is formed between boys who happen to bear the same name. Each presents to the other seven handfuls of *āruā* rice and a few pieces of turmeric and salutes him by saying "Jōhār, Maitra". Subsequently the friends (*maitras*) invite each other to a feast at their respective houses and each presents the other with a new cloth. In the Gāmhā Punāi Parab they exchange *sidhās* or presents of rice, pulse, and other eatables; and on every occasion of a festival, the two *maitras* entertain or make presents of food to each other.

The observances in the *Makar* and *Sāngā* forms of friendship are the same as in the *Maitra* form which differ from the former in the absence of identity of names of the two friends. In the *Mahā-Prasād* friendship, which, too, may be formed at any time of the year but is generally contracted during some festival, one boy puts into the mouth of the other a little *āruā*

86 Similar ceremonial friendships are customary among the Muṇḍās, the Birhōṛs and allied tribes.

rice with a few petals of some flower and then they salute each other by saying, "Jōhār, Mahā Prasād". Clothes are exchanged and each entertains the other to a feast at his house. In a *Jāmḍāir* friendship, which is also formed either on the occasion of the Māgh Jātrā or on the Makar Jātrā festival, a boy puts a tiny *jām* (*Eugenia jambolana*) twig on each ear of the other and then each salutes the other, saying—"Johār, Jāmḍāir". They entertain each other with feasts and exchange presents of cloths as in other forms of friendship. Girls form similar friendships variously known as *Karamḍāir*, *Bairkoir*, and *Makar*. The *Makar* friendship of girls is formed with the same ceremonies as in the case of boys. The *Karamḍāir* and *Bairkoir* forms of friendship are similar to the *Jāmḍāir* friendship of boys with this difference that instead of a *jām* twig, a *karam* (*Nauclia parvifolia*) twig is worn on the ears of *Karamḍāir* friends and flowers of the *bair* (*Zizyphus Jujuba*) are worn on the ears of *Bairkoir* friends. *Karamḍāir* friendships are entered into on the occasion of the *Karam Jātrā* and the *Makar* and *Bairkoir* forms of friendship on the Makar Jātrā day.

On the occasion of these jātrā festivals–the Māgh Jātrā, Makar Jātrā, and Karam Jātrā,—Pāuṛi boys also enjoy themselves in another way. They go in a body from house to house in their village and beg for *piṭhās* or cakes and rice and any other eatables, such as pulse or vegetables, that may be had. They eat the cakes together on the same day, and on a subsequent day enjoy a picnic on the bank of a hill stream, where the rice and other eatables thus obtained are cooked and eaten.

2 The Makar Jātrā Festivals.

This festival, so far as I could learn, is observed only by the Bhūiyās of village Kuirā in the Bonāi State. It is not known among the Pāuṛis of Keonjhar and Pāl Lahera. On the full moon day in the month of *Pouṣ* (December), Bhūiyās from different villages of Kuiṛā Parganā as also some Pāuṛis from Pāuṛi Parganā assemble at village Kuiṛā to celebrate the festival. Those who come from other villages come with cakes and other food for their day's meals, unless they have friends or relatives at Kuiṛā with whom they may have their meals. In every house at village Kuiṛā, cakes are made, and those who can afford to do so kill fowls or goats. In the morning, the Dihuri offers water, molasses, flowers and āruā rice to a sacred stone in an open field outside the village. This stone is called *Nāgeswar Mahādeo*. In the afternoon, on an open space in front of the *āsthān* of Nāgeswar Mahādeo, men dance the *Pāiki* dance. Other tribes and castes of the neighbourhood of Kuiṛā—such as Gouṛs and "Kōls"—also join in these dances. It is after this festival that servants are released from their year's engagement and new servants appointed. The Makar Jātrā and the Karam Jātrā, which are essentially harvest festivals, are really festivals of the Kuiṛā Parganā Bhuiyās among whom wet cultivation of low-land rice is extensively practised, and who appear to have borrowed these from the semi-Hinduized Bhūiyās and other tribes and castes of the plains. The Māgh Jātrā festival appears to be the only genuine harvest festival of the Pāuṛis.

3 *The Karam-Jātrā Festival.*

Unlike the Chōṭā Nāgpur tribes, who celebrate the Karam festival in *Bhādo* (August), when the upland rice has been harvested, a few Pāuṛi families celebrate the Karam Jātrā in Asvin or Kartik or Agrahāyaṇ (October-November) after their lowland paddy has been cut, but before it has been threshed. The following ceremonies are observed. Two or three days before the festival, the Dihuri and Nāek meet at the *darbār* one evening and fix a date for the Karam Jātrā, and notify the date to the villagers, so that they may provide themselves with rice and molasses for the occasion. On the morning of the day fixed, the *darbār* ground is cleaned with cowdung and water, a mud altar is prepared, and a canopy of leaves and twigs is put over it. The Dihuri, who fasts the whole day, goes in the evening to the jungle, cuts a Karam (*Nauclea parvifolia*) branch and brings it to the *darbār*. A number of girls, who have also fasted, go there with *āruā* rice, frankincense and molasses and hand them over to the Dihuri who offers these to the sacred branch. Then the Karam branch is planted on the altar, while women go on making the *huṛhuṛā* sound. The girls now bow down before the Karam branch and say, "O Karam Rājā, O Karam Rāṇī, we are making Karam Dharam". Then same old man who knows the legend (*bākhāṇi* or *kathā*) of Karam and Dharam[87] recites it to the girls. That evening, cakes and other delicacies are prepared at each house. Guests from other villages are entertained at different houses; and feasting, dancing, drinking, and rejoicing form the order of the night. Men alone dance and sing that night.

Next morning the Dihuri, after making ablutions, again offers rice and molasses (*sital*) to the sacred Karam Deity. Then he takes up the branch and hands it over to the boys of the village who carry it from house to house. At each house the women "wash the feet of Karam Rājā" by pouring water at the lower end of the Karam branch and present the boys with cakes. The boys finally immerse the Karam branch in the water of some stream or water-channel, return home, and eat the cakes.

4. *Ākhin Pārdhi.*

This is the annual hunting festival of the Pāuṛis and other Bhūiyās. It is held on the third day of the moon (*Akṣay Tritīā*) in the month of Chait (March). The preceding evening the Dihuri informs the villagers

87 See Chapter XI *post*.

that they are to start on the annual *Akhin* or *Ākhin-Pārdhi* expedition on the following morning. All men wishing to join the hunt, assemble at the ākhrā in the morning, armed with their bows, arrows, and axes. In Bonāi before they start, every man in the party offers a piece of turmeric to Bāsuki Mātā, but in Keonjhar and Pāl Lahera, this is seldom done. The Dihuri leads the party.

Arrived at the jungle, a few men—those reputed as the most daring and fearless—are told off as *ghaṭā-ṛis* who hide themselves behind branches and twigs put up as screens and remain seated with their weapons ready for use. The rest of the party act as *chaṛāhāris*, or beaters, who drive the animals of the forest towards the *ghaṭāṛis*.

As soon as any game is bagged, the Dihuri or other leader takes a little blood of the game and offers it to Boṛām and Gāi-śrī, saying,—"Here we offer you the blood of slain animals. May we have many more now and ever". The man who has shot the animal then offers a little of its blood to his own ancestor-spirits (*Pitrus*).

When the hunt is over, all go with the spoils of

the day to the Nāek's house. There some female of the Nāek's family washes the feet of such of the hunters as have succeeded in bringing down an animal, ceremonially 'kiss' their hands, and anoint their forehead with turmeric paste.

The two hind legs of each game are presented to the Nāek as *ākhni-bheṭi* (present of the hunt), and the Nāek in return gives them either a new cloth or, if he has none, a sum of twelve *annas* for a *barāhā* (pig) or other big animal bagged and four *annas* for each *kuṭari* or small deer or other small animal. The man whose arrow killed the particular animal gets the present of the cloth or money meant for it. The rest of the game is divided amongst the different families of the village.

The quantity of game bagged is regarded as an indication of the good or bad out-turn of the next harvest.

In subsequent hunts, people go singly or with such companions as they choose, and the game is divided amongst the hunters *per capita*, although a little meat is generally presented to each of the families who have not deputed any one to the hunt. Similar annual hunting festivals are customary among most

Mūṇḍā tribes. Festivals of first fruits not only of staple food-crops but also of certain other subsidiary food-products are customary amongst most tribes.

5. *Ām-Nuā.*

The Ām-nuā festival is celebrated in December or January when the mango blossoms have come out. On a day fixed and notified beforehand by the Dihuri, the latter makes his ablutions in the morning, threshes new rice, and, with the *āruā* rice thus prepared and a little frankincense, molasses, mango-blossoms and rice-flour, he goes to the seat of Gāi-śrī, and there offers these to Boṛām and Gāi-śrī. A number of villagers attend the *pūjā*, after having had their ablutions. Then the Dihuri will prepare *jāu* by boiling *āruā* rice in water with mango-blossoms in a stone vessel. A little of this *jāu* is first offered to Gāi-śrī and Boṛām, and then a little is given to every villager present. Until this ceremony has been performed in the village no villager may eat mangoes or other new fruit of the season, or manure his fields.

6. *Tirtiā Muṭi* or *Akṣay Muṭi.*

On the third day of the moon (*Akṣay Tritia* day) in the month of Baisākh, the ceremonial sowing of paddy-seeds is performed to ensure good crops. The *Tirtiā Muṭi* ceremony, as this is called, is performed by each cultivator separately for his own benefit. The man observes continence on the day preceding the ceremony and eats only one meal consisting of *āruā* rice boiled in an earthen vessel and taken in the daytime. Next morning, either his wife or some other woman, who is not in her menses and has not slept with her husband but has observed continence and fasted the preceding night, bathes herself and husks some *āruā* rice. The man too bathes in the morning and carries this *āruā* rice and some paddy seeds to his *kōmān* or clearance on the hill-slope or to other land. Those who have no rice-fields will, all the same, ceremonially sow a few paddy-seeds on the *Tirtiā Muṭi* day on his *bāri* land where merely vegetables, maize, *gōndli* (*Panicum meliare*), *etc.*, are grown. Offerings of *āruā* rice are made to each of the principal deities,–Dharam Deōtā, Bāsu-Mātā, Boṛām and Gāi-śrī,—by placing a handful of rice on his rice field, *kōmān*, or *bāri* land in the name of each. In the case of a rice field, *āruā* rice is also offered to Lakṣmī by placing a handful of it over the paddy-seeds in the basket; those who only grow maize, *gōndli*, etc., and have no rice cultivation, omit this offering to Lakṣmī. Now the man scatters the paddy-seeds and either ploughs the land or just uses his ploughshare to turn up the soil a little. Even if there has been no rain yet and the soil is too hard for ploughing and sowing seeds, still on the *Tirtiā Muṭi* day the Pāuṛi cultivator must not omit this ceremony. Should he do so, he is sure to have bad luck. Similar sowing festivals are celebrated by most other tribes in Ōṛissā.

7. *Bihiṛā or Bihuṛā or Āṣāṛhi pūjā.*

This pūjā is intended to ensure seasonable and abundant rainfall and a bumper harvest. In the month of Āṣāṛh (June-July) the Dihuri calls the villagers to the *darbār* and fixes a day for the performance of Bihiṛā Pūjā. On the morning of the appointed day each villager takes some paddy to him. The Dihuri then bathes, takes the rice, and goes to the seat (*meṛh*) of Gāi-Śrī and prays for abundant rainfall and good crops. The sacrifice of a goat or of a fowl is made alternately every year. In some villages, sacrifices are made on this occasion to other village-gods as well. Thus, at village Jolo, a goat (*pōndṛā*) is offered to

Dharam Deotā, another goat (*bodā*) to Boṛam and a castrated goat to the *Pāts*. This festival corresponds to the festival at transplantation of paddy seedlings among the Mūṇḍās and most other settled agricultural tribes of Chōṭā-Nāgpur and Ōṛissā.

8. *Gamhā Pūnai or Ganthā Pūnai.*

Two or three days before the full moon in the month of Śrāban (August) the men of the village assemble at the *darbār* and request the Nāek and the Dihuri to borrow on their behalf some rice and molasses for the Gāmhā Punāi festival, the loan to be repaid at the next harvest. At this time of the year, most Pāuṛis have no rice or other grain left in his house. A day or two before the full moon the Nāek and Dihuri procure the necessary rice, etc., or advance them from their own stock, if any, and the villagers who need them divide these amongst themselves according to their respective requirements and means of repayment. The day before the full moon, paddy is threshed and husked in every house, and those who possess any cattle give them some salt to eat and anoint their horns with sesame oil. On the full moon day, *piṭhās* or cakes are prepared in each house with rice-flour, and a hearty meal of boiled rice, pulses, etc., is prepared and eaten. In the evening such Pāuṛis as possess any cattle, wash their hoofs when the cattle return home from the jungle, anoint their foreheads with turmeric paste and feed them with raw rice and a kind of fried rice called *khai*. Lamps are lighted in the cattle-sheds that night. On the *Gāmhā Punāi* day and the day preceding it, their cattle are given absolute rest by the Pāuṛis.

9. *Bār and Nuā-Khiā Festivals.*

The Bār and Nuā-Khiā ceremonies are intended to make the reaping and eating of the new rice innocuous. On a day, fixed beforehand at the *darbār,* the Dihuri bathes in the morning, pours libations of water and makes offerings of rice, molasses and frankincense to Bōṛām and Gāi-śrī. He then proceeds in company with other villagers to the gōṛā or upland paddy fields of the village and cuts a few sheaves of gōṛā paddy from their fields, including his own, if he has any. Each cultivator now goes to his own field, offers a little *ārua* rice, water, molasses and frankincense to Dharam Deōtā and cuts a few sheaves of paddy which are taken home and kept suspended from the roof; and *johār,* or salutation (by bowing) is made to these sheaves. Subsequently they reap their gōṛā (upland) crops. Two or three days later the Dihuri goes to the *darbār*, sacrifices one or more fowls to Bōṛām, cooks the meat and eats it alone. Then, in a new earthen vessel, he boils new *gōṛā* rice supplied by the villagers, offers this *jāu* first to Gāi-śrī, and then to his own ancestor-spirits. He now first eats a portion of the *jāu* himself and gives the remnant to other members of his family to eat. After this, the other villagers may eat the new rice. Before doing so, every Pāuṛi must offer a little of it to his own ancestor-spirits in the *bhitar* of his house. Here, it may be noted that the principal deities (such as Bōṛām or Dharam and Bāsukī-mātā or Ṭhākurāṇi and the Pitrus) of the Pāuṛi Bhūiyās still receive homage from the Plains Bhūiyās, and most of the same festivals are still observed by both, though the Plains Bhūiyās have also adopted some of the rites and deities of their professed Hindu faith. Thus instead of the sacrifice of fowls and animals, offerings of milk, ghee and sweets are offered by the Plains Bhūiyās to some of their deities such as Dharam or Bōṛām and Bāsukī-Ṭhākurāṇī.

10. Other Observances regarding Crops, etc.

Among the Pāuṛis of the Bonāi State, when all the rice of a Pāuṛi has been threshed, he takes up a handful and places it on the threshing-floor and leaves it there. The first rice beer (*hāṇṛiā*) of the year is prepared in every Pāuṛi house when the new gōṛā rice has been threshed, and a little of this *hāṇṛiā* together with seven rice-flour cakes is first offered to the ancestor spirits at the threshing-floor (*kharā*). After that, whenever *hāṇṛiā* is prepared, a little of it is first offered to the ancestor-spirits. Before a Pāuṛi proceeds to thresh his lowland rice (*bil-dhān*), he offers on the threshing floor a little liquor (*hāṇṛiā*) prepared with old rice to his ancestor-spirits.

The Last Sheaf and Last Fruit.

The last few sheaves of lowland paddy is left standing on the field when the rest is harvested. If a Pāuṛi has more than one such rice-field, it is the last sheaves of the field reaped last of all that are left standing, These sheaves are called *Khet bāṛhilā*. This is not definitely explained by the people as meant for the Corn-spirit.

The last jack fruit is left on his tree and not plucked by the Pāuṛi, and so also the last fruit on his mango tree is not plucked by himself or by any other member of his family. It is said that if the tree is denuded of all its fruit, the mother (tree) will look about for its children (fruit) and feel disappointed and grieved.

Founding a New Settlement.

In the selection of a site for a new settlement the Pāuṛi employs a form of divination. The Dihuri, takes a bath, and places a handful of *āruā* rice on the site intended to be occupied and covers over the rice with a new earthen vessel and fixes it down on the ground by plastering the rim of the vessel with clay.[88] Next morning, the Dihuri again bathes and goes to the spot and examines the rice. If on scrutiny he finds that no insect or ant has eaten up or disturbed any portion of the rice, then it is considered an auspicious site; otherwise a new site is sought out. When the site is found to be auspicious, the Dihuri cuts down a log of wood and

88 Their neighbours, the more primitive Juāngs, follow the same form of divination for the purpose. But instead of one handful of rice, three handfuls of rice are placed side by side and covered up with three new earthen pots.

plants it upright in the centre of the site. This post is called the *Śubha Khūṇṭā* (auspicious post) and also the *Gāi-śrī Khūṇṭā*—the post sacred to Gāi-śrī. It stands out about four feet above ground. The Dihuri, with his face to the east as in all pūjās, offers rice and molasses, in the names of Gāi-śrī, Bāsukī-mātā, Boṛām, and Dharam Deotā,—and prays, "May we live here in health; may we have success in clearing the forest, and get enough to eat".

The foundation of a new settlement and also of a new house must be laid either on a Wednesday or on a Friday. Mondays and Tuesdays are also not inauspicious, but Saturdays are particularly unlucky. When the village site is selected, each family selects a site for the family dwelling and plants a *Śubha-khūṇṭā* or auspicious post in the centre of the selected site. This forms one of the posts to support the roof, and to this post a small mango twig is tied with unbleached thread. The compartment of the hut where this *Śubha-khūṇṭā* stands is selected as the *bhitar* where the ancestor-spirits have their seat. When a newly married couple sets up a new house, the Dihuri places inside the hut an earthen pot with its bottom upwards under which the ancestor-spirits are to reside and receive offerings and libations.

If the old Gāi-śrī Khūṇṭā post is blown away by the wind or is otherwise uprooted or destroyed except through natural decay, the village site must be forthwith changed. Another occasion for changing a village site is the exhaustion of the soil after a few years' cultivation of vegetables, maize and other crops in their *Kōmāns* or clearances.

In some Pāuṛi villages, as in village Suākāṭi in the Keonjhar State, may be seen planted in front of the *Maṇḍa-ghar* a long bamboo pale painted white with rice-flour-paste and surmounted with a circular shield or umbrella made of plaited bamboo splinters and adorned all round its rim wfth a garland of pith. About two feet lower down, the pole is wound round with another bunch of pith garlands decorated with tinsel adornments such as small mirrors and combs. And about the same distance further down, the pole is similarly decked with pith-garlands and tinsel trappings. The entire pole is called the "*Chhatra-Khunṭ*" or the umbrella-pole, and the umbrella-like top is called the "*Thākurāṇi Chhatra*" or the umbrella of the goddess Ṭhākurāṇi. On top of this umbrella flaps a flag decked also with garlands of pith. This pole with the umbrella and the flag on it is carried in procession to the hut-temple of the goddess *Ṭhākurāṇi* at the time of the periodical propitiation of that deity.

II. Magic.

The Pāuṛi Bhūiyā's religion proper, as we have seen, consists in a belief in unseen supernatural beings believed to direct and control the course of nature and of human life, and in various rites and ceremonies designed to establish friendly relations with such powers with the object of securing good luck and preserving, strengthening, and ennobling life. The Pāuṛi also believes in the presence all around him of impersonal powers, forces, and tendencies which are either unembodied, or are inherent in certain men, animals, and other material objects, such as plants, stones, etc., and even in certain words and numbers. The ways and means adopted to ward off or control these powers or to press them into service for the preservation, and enrichment of life constitute the Pāuṛi's Magic. This is what is called white Magic. Whereas Faith and

Hope forms the keynote of Religion as well as of White Magic, and Fear and Suspicion form the keynote of Black Magic, among the Pāuṛis as among other tribes.

All illness is believed to be caused by some supernatural power,—either by a deity for some offence of omission or commission on the part of the patient or of some member of his family, or by some evil spirit (Chūṛūṇi or Masāṇi) or some evil power set in motion by some maleficent magician or witch, or by the 'evil eye' of some malicious person.

When any illness is due to the visitation of some deity, the services of the Dihuri or village-priest are requisitioned to propitiate the offended deity. And with appropriate sacrifices, offerings and libations the Dihuri seeks to propitiate the deity and remove the illness.

The *Ancestor-spirits* generally bring on sickness to their descendants if their sacred tabernacle or *bhitar* happens to be defiled by contact with some ceremonially unclean person or object. In such a case the head of the family will implore forgiveness and pray to them to re-enter their earthen-pot (which is their appointed abode) and there offer to the ancestor-spirits *jāu* or rice boiled in milk in a new earthen-pot.

If the *Pāṭ* spirit is responsible for the sickness a vow is made to offer him either a goat or a fowl in case of cure.

In cases of epidemic to men or cattle, the Dihuri offers libations of water in the names of all the spirits of his village and native hill and also to the deities Boṛam and Gāi-srī. Dharam-Deotā and Dhartī-mātā are the only deities who are uniformly beneficent and never cause any sickness or other harm. The principal supernatural agents of sickness and death are the *Masāṇi* spirits and the *Bāuti* spirits, besides the 'evil eye' of certain malicious persons and the sorcery of wizards and witches. *Masāṇis* are the malevolent spirits of those deceased persons whose spirits have not been conducted back to their respective houses on account of the unholy mode of their death. *Bāuti* spirits are the familiar spirits of certain individuals whose crops or fruits or *jhums* and other possessions are guarded over by these familiars. They are said to be spirits of persons devoured by bears. There are some minor spirits whose evil attentions cause no serious harm. Thus the Chitrangi spirit is said to cause nightmares. As has been stated in a previous *Chapter* the afflicted person has only to turn round in his sleep and the *Chitrangi* spirit leaves him.

Certain persons are believed to have an innate evil influence which emanates from their eyes, and harms a person towards whom it is directed. Thus the sight of certain individuals in the morning before one commences his day's work or a journey or other undertaking is calculated to bring ill luck. Some people acquire the evil eye through training under a Pāngni or witch. When such a person sees another engaged in eating some dainty *dishes*, and mutters to herself, "Oh, how nice it would be if I could have had such delicacies for myself," the person eating the food is sure to fall ill. When a Pāuṛi, particularly a child, suffers from nausea, flatulence, or diarrhia, the ailment is generally attributed to the evil eye (*najar*). To neutralize the bad effects of such a *najar*, the services of a Rāūnṛiā or magician are requisitioned, and the Rāūnṛia seeks to cure the patient through spells or the coercive magic of words. If words of power fail, the Rāūnṛia seeks the aid of a *Betal* spirit which is the familiar spirit of Rāūnṛiās.

Pāuṛi Magicians are of four classes, known respectively, as Pāngnis, Ḍāinis, Rāūnṛiās, and Gūṇīs. The first three classes of magicians have their familiar spirits or *Bāutis* to whom they sacrifice in secret, and who are believed to take away their votaries' lives whenever they neglect to offer the proper sacrifices to them in time. The Gūṇīās only cure snake bites and some other wounds; and this they do through spells, combined with blowing on the patient with their mouth and making passes on him with their hands. Pāngnis and Ḍāinis are women who learn their art in secret from others who know it. Generally a Pāngni learns the art from her mother. While all other people are asleep, a Pāngni instructs her daughter as to the spells to be used to effect malicious and anti-social purposes. Ḍāinis learn their art from other Ḍāinis at dead of night in some secluded spot where they sit down naked. They sometimes dance together at night in a state of nudity. Thus the power of the Pāngnis and Dāinis to cause harm is derived from the use of certain spells or words of power, coupled with their own will-power, and also from their familiar spirits. A Ḍāini is credited with the power of sucking another person's blood from a distance. Rāonṛiās, it is said, can cure diseases and other troubles inflicted by Pāngnis and Ḍāinis, but can do no harm to others. Rāonṛiās find out whether any particular disease has been caused by a witch or by some evil spirit. Their method of discovering this is as follows:—A reed called *sir-khal* is broken into halves and then the pieces are measured with the span of the hand. If they measure just three spans each, it is not a case of spirit-attack but is attributed to the evil eye or some other cause. While measuring the reed, the Rāonṛiā silently prays to Boṛām that if it be a case of spirit-attack the reed may show it by lengthening itself. The names of different *masāni* spirits of the village are also taken while measuring the reed; and the last name taken when the measuring is just finished, is believed to be the name of the spirit responsible for the trouble. The spirit is subsequently expelled by the *ningchhā* ceremony which consists in waving four times round the head of the patient a handful of sun-dried rice and powdered turmeric tied up in a leaf and throwing it away and at the same time addressing the spirit and commanding or exhorting it to go away with such words as the following: "Here, take thy share [of offering], and leave this 'body' (the afflicted person). Do thou stay away and live in peace and quiet." Some Rāūnṛias, it is said, have powerful familiar spirits with whose aid they can subdue the familiar spirit of a Pāngni and foil the Pāngni's efforts.

If a Bhūiyā on his way to the jungle to hunt or to bring fuel-wood or to gather roots, fruits and vegetable, or when going on some other business, happens to meet a Pāngni he apprehends failure in his expedition.

The methods employed by the magician to inflict disease death and trouble to man or cattle or crops may be called offensive magic, whereas the use of charms, amulets, and other devices to ward off disease, death and other calamity proceeding from supernatural sources may be called defensive or protective magic. The most common method of defensive magic is the use of charms and amulets. The most common amulets to protect children as well as adults from the evil eye and the evil attention of mischievous spirits employed by the Hill Bhūiyās are made of certain vegetable roots of their native jungles which must be gathered on the last day of the lunar month of Āsvin (September-October). The application of soot between the eye-brows of a child to ward off the evil eye is also in vogue.

CHAPTER XI.

FOLKLORE, OMENS AND SUPERSTITIONS.

1. *Folk Tales.*

Like other tribes in the lower culture, the Pāuṛi Bhūiyās possess a store of traditional knowledge regarding their own origins and those of their gods, the course of nature, the properties of things, the habits of other creatures, and so forth, which their old men recount to the younger generation in the form of folktales, riddles and proverbs. A few specimens of such folk-lore are given below.

(i) *The Story of Creation.*

In the beginning there existed only God or *Dharma* whose visible representation was the Sun with the Moon. Then there appeared an ocean of water of the depth of seven times the height of a man with upraised hands (*sāt-tāṛ pāṇi*); and out of depths of the ocean up came a mass of mud to a height of fourteen times the height of a man with upraised hands (*chowda-tāṛ-panka*). Then Dharma on this mud-bank created a man and a woman known respectively as Parihār Buṛhā and Baṛāmaṇi Buṛhi. The mud-bank (earth) began to shake and tremble (*ṭalmal halā*). God saw from heaven that such an earth was not fit for human habitation. Then He made clay figures of a tiger and tigress (*Rāi bagh* and *Rāi baghini*), infused life into them, and ordered them—"Go, kill the human couple—and put their blood and flesh on the four corners of the Earth so as to make it firm". The tiger and tigress did as they were ordered. The blood and flesh of the original human couple settled down in the four corners of the earth as iron-pillars supporting the earth; and the earth became hardened like stone. Then God created another couple who became, in due time, parents of seven sons and seven daughters. From these seven couples descended the different peoples of the earth. And Parihār Buṛhā and Baṛāmaṇi Buṛhī became the gods Baṛam and Baṛāmaṇi or Buṛhā-buṛhī. The god *Jhankar* is the son of Baṛam and Baṛamaṇi or Buṛhā-buṛhi or Mangalā. The Earth or *Medinī* is the same as the goddess Basuṛi or Ṭhākurāṇi or Bāsukī Mātā.

(ii) *Miraculous Birth.*

The Pāuṛi Bhūiyās believe that their first ancestor sprang miraculously out of Mother-Earth and hence the tribe is named "Bhūiyā" or "Earth-born". They believe that they have always lived on the ridge of the difficult hills on the borders of the Keonjhar, Pāl Lahera and Bonāi States that form their home to this day. But unlike their neighbours and congeners the Juāngs, the Bhūiyās do not point to any particular portion of the hills as their original birth-place. The Juāngs, as I found, have a tradition of a rain of fire (*Lālāi-guḍ*) which destroyed the earth. After the fire-rain had subsided, so said my Juāng informants, the first man issued out of the Earth near the source of the Baitaraṇi river not far from the present village of Gōnāsikā. The first man was the progenitor of the Juāngs; then arose the progenitor of the Bhūiyās whom the Juāngs claim to be their younger brothers. Though Pāuṛi Bhūiyās have no tradition of any migrations, the Northern Bhūiyās of Chota Nagpur have a tradition of their former home at or near "Maghā Maner" or the village Maner now in the Patna District of Bihār. Some of these Northern Bhūiyās of the Hāzāribāgh district of Chōṭā Nāgpur told me the following traditional story of a miraculous birth, which is obviously an adaptation in conformity with Bhuiyā ideas of blood being the source of life, of the Hindu epic story of the birth of Sītā, the bride of the hero of the Rāmāyaṇa:—

When the Bhuiyās dwelt at Maghā Maner, they were called *Rikhs* because they used to live on wild roots and fruits of the jungles as the Hindu *Rikh-Mūns* (Rishis and Mūnis, or ascetics) used to do. Rājā Janak of Janakpur sent his *sipāhis* or peons to demand rent from the Rikhs (or Bhuiyās) for the jungles where they used to gather their food. The Rikhs assembled together and, after deliberations, some of them drew out blood from their own thighs and filled an earthen-pot with this blood and closed up the mouth of the vessel by gluing a lid on to it. Over the lid was inscribed or drawn a symbol which purported to be an imprecation of a terrible curse upon any one except the queen who might open the lid. The queen of Janak Rājā accordingly uncovered the lid,—and out of the blood of the Bhuiyās sprung a bonny female baby who came to be called Sītā. In time Sītā grew up into a most beautiful young maiden.

King Janak had a big wooden bow lying in one of the rooms of his palace, and an amount of dust had accumulated over it. Sītā ordered one of her maids to sweep the dust from that part of the floor after removing the bow to one corner. The maid replied,—"It is enormously heavy. There is none here strong enough to remove it." At this Sītā quietly went to the bow and unostentiously moved it aside. When Rājā Janak who had been out hunting returned home, he was astonished at seeing that the bow had been removed from its former position, and enquired who could have done it. On learning that this feat was accomplished by Sītā, he issued a proclamation to the effect that he would bestow Sītā in marriage to the person who might prove a match for Sītā's strength and that the trial of strength was to take place on such-and-such date at the Janakpur palace. Princes from far and near assembled on the appointed day, and one after another they tried to move the bow but failed,—till at length Prince Rāmchandra proved equal to the task. So he was duly married to Sītā. And this is why the Bhuiyās to this day have a saying amongst them—"Rāmjīkō āsan Rikhkō duār", by which Rāmchandra and Sītā are connected with the Rikhs or Rikhiāsan Bhuiyās.

(iii) *The story of Karam Rājā.*

The Pāuṛi Bhuiyās celebrate the Karam festival in October or November when the following legend of the origin of the institution of the Karam festival is recounted:–There was once a rich man who had seven sons and seven daughters. Once the man told his wife, "I shall go out to distant places for trade. Prepare for me some *bhūk-nāṛus* (large globular pills which prevent hunger) and *Shūsh-nāṛus* (large globular pills which prevent thirst)." The wife prepared the *nāṛus* and the man took them with him and started on his trading voyage. After successful trading he returned home with his boat laden with precious metals and other valuable marchandise and anchored his vessels at the boundary of his village, on a *Karam pūjā* day and called out to his wives and sons' wives to come and honour the vessel with ceremonial worship (*bandan*). But the women were then dancing round the seven Karam branches and the men were playing the *changu* and *māndar* drums so that none paid heed to his summons. He waited and waited for them till his patience was exhausted. He then went home in a huff and struck down the seven *Karam* branches and the seven mud-pulpits and the drums. No sooner was this outrage on the Karam deity committed, than his trading vessel with all its valuable contents disappeared under the water, all his cattle were devoured by tigers or otherwise died or strayed away. All search for his lost wealth proved futile and at length the man went to an astrologer to discover the cause of his misfortune and its remedy, if any. The astrologer declared that his losses were the Divine punishment for his impious outrage on the Karam-Rājā (or the Karam-king, i.e. the Karam-god) and that the only remedy was to appease Karam Rājā and pray for the restoration of the lost wealth as a boon (*bar*). He then went home and asked his wife to prepare *bhūk-nāṛus* and *sūsh-nāṛus* for him as he wanted to go to the abode of Karam-Rājā. His wife made the *bhūk-naṛus* and *shūsh-naṛus* as desired, and he started on his journey to the sea where Karam-Rājā has his seat. Arrived there, he humbly prostrated himself before the deity.

The deity was pleased and asked him what he wanted. The man inquired, "Why has my wealth disappeared? And how shall I get it all back?"—The Karam Rājā replied "You were punished for your sacrilege. Go and make seven pulpits and bring seven branches of the Karam tree and plant them on those pulpits, and take seven *māndal* drums there, and let your seven wives and seven sons and seven daughters-in-law (sons' wives) remain fasting and dancing and singing for seven days and seven nights (in my honour), and then your lost wealth will be restored to you". The man returned home and did as he was directed. And at the end of seven days and seven nights thus spent in *Karam-pūjā* he got back his lost wealth.[89]

(iv) *The Story of a Transformation.*

An old woman had domesticated a favourite parrot. The parrot once flew out on a pilgrimage and returned with a nectarial fruit (*amrita phal*) reputed to avert death and old age. The women kept it carefully in the house. A cobra saw the fruit and stung it with its fangs and it rolled down. A cat saw it falling down

89 It may be noted that different versions of the *Karam* legend are in vogue among different tribes of Oṛissā and Chōṭā-Nāgpur.

and, taking it to be a rat, devoured it and instantly died. The woman thought that it was a poisonous fruit with which the parrot wanted to kill her. She buried the cat, and out of the grave sprang a tree which bore beautiful fruits. Another old woman who was living with her seven sons and their wives was disgusted with her life because her daughters-in-law slighted her. She listlessly plucked one of the fruits and ate it, and, lo and behold! she was forthwith transformed into a young woman of exquisite beauty. The other woman who owned the parrot and the fruit saw this wonderful metamorphosis and she too plucked and ate a fruit from the tree and was similarly transformed into a maiden with eternal youth.

(v) *The Ever-fresh Garland.*

A newly-married couple found it difficult to make both ends meet. The wife insisted that her husband should go to some distant town to earn a decent livelihood. The husband was unwilling to leave his young wife alone. The wife thereupon wove a wreath of flowers and gave it to her husband saying, "Keep this with you. As long as you find this keeping fresh, so long you may be sure that my chastity will remain intact." The husband went to the capital of a Rājā under whom he took service as a *Paṭnāik*. Once a peon of the Rājā was sent by the husband to take some money to his wife at her village home. The peon on his return reported to the Rājā how exquisitely beautiful the Paṭnāik's wife was. The Rājā tried to seduce the wife but all his efforts failed. The wreath of flowers always kept fresh. And the Paṭnāik, on his return home, was satisfied that his wife was ever steadfast in her fidelity to him.

(vi) *The Courage of an old Gouṛ Woman.*

An old woman of the pastoral Gouṛ (milkman) caste used to sell curds. One day on her way home through the jungles after selling curds in other villages, she saw a bear eating white-ants by thrusting itself into a large ant-hill. The Gouṛ woman covered up the mouth of the anthill with his curd-vessel, and pressed it hard so that the bear might not come out. She remained pressing down the bear from morning till noon by which time two other caste-fellows of hers who were returning that way with their buffaloes came that way and she requested the two men to help her. She sent one of the two men to cut down and fetch two thick tree-branches to kill the bear with; and herself with the other Gouṛ pressed down the bear in the hollow of the ant-hill. When the other Gouṛ returned with thick branches, the two men killed the bear by striking at its neck therewith.

The Pāuṛi Bhūiyās have a number of other folk-tales illustrating the peculiar characteristics of certain beasts of their forests as also of certain castes and tribes with whom they come in contact. Thus they have stories showing how the Pāuṛi Bhūiyā can outwit the tiger or the bear in his native jungles, and also other stories in illustration of the proverbial stupidity of the Pān or weaver tribe, the cunning of a man of the Bhaṇḍāri or barber caste, the simplicity of a Guṛia or confectioner and the cupidity of the *Mahājan* or merchant and money-lender.

2. *Folk Medicines.*

The Hill Bhūiyā does not attribute all ailments of the body to supernatural causes. He recognises that some ailments are due to natural causes and are amenable to remedies supplied by his native hills and jungles. Thus, to cure tooth-ache he uses tooth-picks of certain jungle plants known as *Bandari* and *Bija*. To cure ear-ache he squeezes the juice out of the leaves of the *Āmri* tree and mixes it with salt and strains the mixture through a piece of fine cloth, heats it and drops it into the affected ear or ears.

To cure aching of one side of the forehead, the root of the *Ghuddu* tree is pounded along with turmeric and is applied as a paste over the affected part of the forehead; or, some lime-stone with one grain and a half of black pepper and either the leaves or flowers of the *Banrāsi* plant, together with a pinch of salt and turmeric-powder are pounded together and used as snuff by the patient.

To cure bloody Dysentery, a root of the *sāṛbhānga* plant is washed several times in water and pounded and mixed with *Shānti* powder and taken on three consecutive days.

To cure indigestion, dried *Agni-jaṛ* plant and *Shānti* are pounded together and the powder is taken.

To cure Cholera, the *Pitāṛu* plant is pounded and eaten.

To cure hydrocele of children, seven bits of *Hemidesmis* root are heated red-hot and the swollen areolar tissues are branded with these red-hot roots at seven points.

To cure hydrocele of adults and children, a fowl is taken to the foot of a *Malli* plant where the red fleshy protuberance near the tail of the fowl is broken off with the hand so that blood falls on the plant; and seven bits of this plant are cut off and heated and with these red-hot pieces of the *Malli* plant, the areolar tissues are branded at seven points, one with each piece.

To cure snake-bite, a string is lightly fastened above the affected part, a bit of the *Kurchi* or *Indrajab* plant is chewed by the patient so as to drink its juice, and the chewings are applied over the wound.

To cure dog-bite, seven *Jandās* or long ants and seven of the noxious insects that attack *rahar* plants, are pounded together with a little oil extracted out of the corolla of the *Mahua* (*bassia latifolia*), and a part of the mixture is taken internally and a part applied as an ointment over the wound.

To cure bleeding piles or hemorrhoids, the root of the *Bakumda* plant is pounded in *ghee* (clarified butter) and heated in a pan over the fire, and wrapped up in cloth with which the hemorrhoids are fomented.

It may be noted that the Pāuṛis take blood of goats and fowls or other birds and animals killed, (except those sacrificed to deities or spirits), heat the blood over a fire and when it coagulates, eat it as food; but no curative or other properties are attributed to it.

3. *Dreams.*

The Pāuṛi Bhūiyā believes in the significance of dreams as foretokens of good or bad luck. A few instances of such beliefs are given below. If a person dreams of a snake, he should avoid stirring out of his house on the following day, so far as possible, for such a dream portends some mishap.

To dream of a horse or elephant or cow augurs good luck.

To dream of the buffallo portends death.

To dream of the bear portends failure of the dreamer in some undertaking.

To dream of a pea-fowl crying indicates success of the dreamer.

To dream of money or of gram protends affliction with sores.

To dream of the construction of a new house forebodes certain death.

To dream of annointing oneself with oil forebodes illness to oneself or one's family.

To dream of human excrement forebodes illness to the dreamer.

To dream of drinking the syrup of mollasses forebodes illness to the dreamer.

To dream of a tiger indicates that the dreamer will meet a king.

4. Omens.

The Pāuṛi Bhūiyās observe many **omens** of which the following are most common:—

While starting on a journey either for a wedding or other purpose the sight of an elephant or a kite (*Miloss iclinus*) with a white head is a good omen.

The sight of an elephant or a kite with a white head (*sankha-chil*) augurs some unexpected gain.

If you see a crow cawing with its face to the east, you will either meet with a king or with an old friend.

If a party going for a marriage meet on their way either a small deer of the species called *Kuṭrā* jumping across the road, or a snake or an empty vessel on the road, or a parrot flying across the road, the marriage party must return home. If on three successive journeys, some evil omen or other is seen, the marriage negotiations have to be broken off.

The appearance of a comet portends pestilence and extensive havoc among men and cattle.

5. *Riddles.*

Question:—Its stature is low; its head is bare; it is the brother of the Water-deity; and it eats everything except the Fire-god: What is that?

Answer:—The white ant, which is a tiny creature and whose habitation (ant-hill) is low and bare-topped; which infests damp places, and eats almost everything except fire.

Q.—What is the creature which is born first and grows its legs later?

A.—The frog.

Q.—What fruit is that which ripens after its kernel comes out ?

A.—The *Bhelwa* (*Semicarpis anacardium*) fruit or the marking-nut.

Q.—Who is the deity who has no temple but sits on a white *newar*-bed with birds flying all around ?

A.—Dharam-Deota or the Sun God. (The rays of the sun are spoken of as birds flying, and its disc is white as a *newar* bed).

Q.—What is that which is born with a cap on its head with which Srikrishna charmed the cowherd-girls (Gopīs), with which Rāmchandra killed Rāvana, and which is now-a-days used for vegetable-curry ?

A.—Bamboo,—over the young shoots of which an earthen vessel is placed like a cap by the Bhuiyās and some other tribes in order to get an esculent to make vegetable curry with; of which (bamboo) Srī Krishna's flute is made; of which the bow, with which the Hindu epic hero Rāmchandra shot his fatal arrow at Rāvana was made; and whose tender shoots are used for curry.

6. Nature-Lore.

The Sun (Beṛo) is identified by the Pāuṛi Bhūiyās with their Supreme Deity or Dharam-deotā; and after morning bath the Bhūiyā salutes (johār) the Sun. The Moon when it appears in the evening is also saluted by some Bhūiyās, saying, "Johār, Jana māmu," i.e. "I salute thee, O maternal uncle Jana." Thus the Moon (Jana) is regarded by the Pāuṛi Bhūiyās as their maternal uncle (*māmu*). The Sun (Beṛo) has the Moon (Jana) for his younger brother, and the lightening (Bijli) for his son. All the other Stars are the daughters of the Moon, but the Milky Way (Bāṛniā tārā) is called the son of the Moon.

The Evening Star is called the 'Wicked Star' (*Khaṛuā tārā*) for, it is said, she reports to the Yama Rājā (God of Death) which boys and girls are good and which are bad and the Yama Rājā carries away the naughty children. [This was perhaps originally meant to act as a deterrant to naughty children]. The Morning Star (*Pohāntia tārā*) is believed to have beneficial influence on the threshing of rice, and therefore the Pāuṛi Bhūiyās thresh their paddy before dawn when the Morning Star is visible, as only rice threshed then will be plentiful. If threshed before this Star is visible, the quantity of rice will somehow turn out to be below expectation.

Comets are called tailed (jhāliā) Stars. The rainbow is called *Rām-Jana* (Rām's Star) and is believed to obstruct and stop rain.

The god Indra is believed to bring rain or rather rain-clouds as a loan from the Ocean and lives on the loan for six months in the year (from *Jaisṭha* to *Pous*, i.e. from middle of June to middle of December) as many Bhūiyās have to live on loans of rice, etc., during those months. For the next six months (Māgh to Baiśākh) the debt is repaid by Indra to the Ocean-god (as is done by Bhūiyā debtors to their own creditors). Earth-quakes are said to occur when the tortoise which supports the Earth on its back turns from one side to the other. Among the Pāuṛis, I came across no tradition regarding the eclipse of either the Sun or the Moon. But when an eclipse is seen Pāuṛi women (presumably in imitation of Hindu women) make the ululation or *hur-huri* (*ulu-ulu*) sound by waving their coiled tongues; and both men and women put out their steel and iron implements as also any broken pieces of

Fig. 17. Preparing for the Sāp-Pari Dance.

iron that they may have, in the open space or pathway in front of their huts. With iron thus exposed, some people get a *chūṛkāthi* or curved iron implement made, and in cases of stomach-ache, head-ache and aching of any other part of the body, heat the *chūṛkāthi* and apply it to the affected part as it is supposed to be an effective remedy to cure the pain.

7. *Games and Pastimes.*

The chief amusement of Pāuṛi Bhūiyā youth of both sexes is dancing and singing. Games are mostly left to the younger boys and girls and to the children. The following are among such games:—

(1) *Bhomrā.*—The pastime of spinning the top (*bhõmṛā*) is a favourite one with Pāuṛi children. The spinning top is roughly carved out of wood by their elders and a fibre-string is used to hold and spin it round.

(2) *Bāṭi khel.*—This game is played with marbles made of sand and molten lac. Two parties, each consisting of one, two, or more players, stand at some distance on opposite sides of a circle drawn on the ground. Each party, takes up as many marbles as the number of its members. One party

places its marbles at the centre of the circle. One boy of the other party starts the game by shooting his marble with his fingers towards the circle, so as to come close to it. He then takes his aim with this marble at a marble of the other party so as to push the adversary's marble towards his own party. If he succeeds in pushing his adversary's marble to where the boys of his own party are seated, his party wins all the marbles of the adversaries. If he fails, another boy of his party repeats the process from the beginning. When the boys of one party fail in pushing a marble of their adversaries to their side, they lose the game, place all their own marbles in the circle for the other party to try their skill at similarly pushing their adversary's marble to their own side.

(3) *Bāgri khel.*—In this game, too, the players divide themselves into two parties of three, four, or more each. The two parties take their stand on opposite sides at some distance apart. One boy of either of the parties starts the game by running towards the other party while reciting

hurriedly without taking breath some distich like the following:—

" *Maṛā khunji jāi, ḍamarū bājāi,*
Kanak ghanṭiā nauṛe;
Bagh-chhāl khanḍē piṭhrē pakāi,
Kirtan karū thhāi."

The boys of the other party run in all directions to avoid the touch of this boy. If while repeating such a verse in one breath the boy succeeds in touching a boy of the opposite party and in returning to his own party without being caught, his adversary who was 'touched' by him is regarded as 'dead'. If, however, the former is caught by an adversary before he returns to his own party, he is regarded as 'dead'. And the 'dead' players cannot take further part in the same game. In this way, every boy tries his skill till all the boys of one party are 'dead' before those of the other party, and then the former party is declared to have lost the game. When one party is thus defeated, its members go over to the opposite side of the circle leaving their side for the winning party.

(4) *Chhūṛ.*—Boys form into two parties of four each. One party is supposed to be keeping guard over a store of salt. The other party tries to rob and eat the salt. The boys of the former party seek to prevent the approach of those of the other party by stretching their hands by way of defending the store of salt. The robbers seek to take the salt by somehow avoiding the guards. If the party of guards succeed in slapping one of the robbers, the latter lose the game and change places with the former. Girls also play this game either among themselves or in company with the boys.

(5) *Nuknuka.*—This is a game played generally by two girls. A low long ridge is constructed with sand or dust by one girl who manages unobserved to conceal a small wooden peg in one part of the ridge and smooths out the whole ridge so as not to betray the place of concealement. The other player is then required to place her hand on the exact spot where the peg has been concealed. If she succeeds, it will be her turn to conceal the peg unobserved for the other to find it out.

(6) *Dhapa.*—This is another game played by unmarried girls. Two girls sit down facing each other and play the game with seven small pieces of stones. One girl takes up the stones on the palm of her right hand, throws them up and tries to catch as many of them as she can on the back of her palm. If none is caught she loses the game and the other girl tries her hand. If the first girl can catch one or more of the stones in this way they are kept by his side and with the rest she repeats the same process till all are similarly caught on the back of her palm whether by ones or twos or more at a time. If she fails any time to catch on the back of her hands any of the stones, she loses the game. Then the other girl begins the game in the same way as the the last one did. And so the game goes on.

8. *Dances.*

Like other primitive tribes the Hill Bhuiyās are passionately fond of dancing and singing. Dances and songs, more than any thing else, bring zest to the Pāuṛi's otherwise generally dull and cheerless life. These form the chief source of enjoyment in the hard and dreary existence of both dancers and spectators. Besides being a means of intense emotional satisfaction and crude artistic expression, the tribal dances serve as an expression of social solidarity and rejoicing, and a means of promoting courtship and marriage, and occasionally a means of inducing in individuals of a psychic temperament a kind of auto-hypnotism which is believed to be spirit-possession.

Besides its social and religious significance, the tribal dances appear also to have a magical import as well as some economic value. Indeed the dance is associated with and reflects almost the whole of the Pāuṛi's life. In the open space in front of the Maṇḍa-ghar of the village may be seen, night after night, particularly in moon-lit nights, young men and women untiringly engaged in dancing till a late hour and sometimes till the small hours of the morning. On occasions of periodical religious festivals and social festivities—particularly weddings,—and on occasions when young men or young women from some 'Bandhu' village come for dancing and for wooing or for being wooed, dances and songs go on for two, three or more consecutive days and nights almost without break.

Generally it is the men who sing songs and play upon their *chāngu*-drums, while the women are the principal dancers who take up the songs started by the men and dance to their tune. The Pāuṛis have various kinds of dances, in most of which the dancers adopt a stooping posture, in some of which they dance in an erect posture; in some the girls and women veil their faces and in others they dance with their faces unveiled; in some the movements are slow and in others brisk, in some the dancers are arranged in one or more rows, and in some forms of dances they move in a circle; in some forms of dances, again, a large number of men take part, and in others a smaller number.

Though the Pāuṛis themselves have no notion of the original objects of these dances, some of these dances may be presumed to have some magical object similar to those of the corresponding dances among their neighbours the Orāons [90] of whom a small sprinkling are to be found near many of their settlements, holding a much lower status than in their native Choṭā-Nāgpur plateau. But as the greatest and the most

90 See, S.C. Roy, *Oraons of Chōṭā-Nāgpur*, pp. 275 ff.

exciting occasions for Pāuṛi dances are the dancing-meetings of the bachelors of one village and the maidens of another, many of their dances would appear to be suggestive of courtship and wooing. The partial and complete veiling of the faces of the girls, and the young men gallantly advancing with brisk but measured steps towards the girls and the girls, in their turn, coquettishly flitting backwards and again advancing a little forward, may not improbably symbolise this.

In the *Sāngi Nāṭ*, which is the "Chāngu Nāṭ" *par excellence* and which has more than one variety, a large number of men and women, young as well as adult, take part. The women veil their faces with one end of their *sāṛi* cloth, and dance in a stooping posture holding each other's hands, and moving three steps forwards and then backwards. The men sing and play upon their *changu* drums standing at right angles to the line of the women. But at intervals, as if by way of exhibition of gallantry, they advance a few steps forward and confront the line of the female dancers who thereupon recede backwards.

The *Udkā Nāṭ* is another form of dance in which, too, the female dancers veil their faces, and dance in a

Fig. 15. *Sangi* (stooping) dance in which the dancers veil their faces.

Fig. 16. The Stooping Dance.

stooping posture, each holding the hands of the dancer to her right and the one to her left and each with her feet similarly joined respectively with those of her two contiguous companions.

In the *Dega Nāṭ*, which is said to be another form of the *Udkā Nāṭ*, the girls dance without veiling their faces. They hold each other's hands as they dance in a stooping posture with one foot placed in front of the other, moving in a line and now and again wheeling round in a circle.

The *Ghechā Pāri Nāṭ* is another stooping dance in which the dancers do not veil their faces. They arrange themselves in two rows, one confronting the other. Each girl holds the hands of the girl standing opposite to her in the other row.

The *Tuki Nāṭ* or Girls' dance *par excellence*, in which, however, not only little girls but both young and old women may take part, is distinguished by the agility of its movements, whereas in the *Buṛi Nāṭ*, in which not only old or elderly women but all may join, the movements are particularly slow so much so that it is also called "the bashful dance".

These are the more important ordinary dances of the tribe, some of which are either identical with or similar to the dances of several other tribes of the Central Hill-belt of India. But the most interesting *Pāuṛi Bhūiyā* dances for the anthropologist as also for the stranger visiting their hills are the dances in imitation of the movements of various animals and reptiles and birds of their native hills and forests, such as the tiger, the bear, the elephant, the deer, the snake, the vulture, the *gunduri* bird, the cock, and the dove. Some of these imitative or dramatic dances would seem to have originally had some magic motive behind them, but the Bhūiyās of our days appear to have no notion of it.

In this part of the country, it is only their close neighbours, the more primitive Juāngs, who have the same dances; but it is not quite certain whether one of the tribes borrowed them from the other, or whether they both inherited them from a common original ancestral stock. The fact that the songs that accompany these dances among both the tribes are composed in the Ōṛiyā language which the Pāuṛi Bhūiyās speak and that the Juāngs have no corresponding songs in their

Fig. 18. *Bora Pari Dance*

The heads of the dancers represent the black frame of the *Bora* snake which gulps down whatever comes its way.

own Juāng language, might perhaps indicate that the animal dances were developed by the Pāuṛis from whom the Juāngs borrowed them.

In the *Sāp-pāri Nāṭ* or Snake Dance, a number of women kneel down on the ground in a straight row, bend forward their bare heads so as almost to touch the ground and, in tune with the sound of drums and songs, slowly swing their heads sideways with short turns in imitation of the zigzag movements of snakes.

In the *Bōṛā-pāri Nāṭ* or Bōṛā-snake Dance, the dancers similarly imitate one of those huge black Bōṛā Snakes that can hardly move their unwieldy bodies but lie inert, stretching their bulky length, and devour any creature that comes their way.

In the *Bāgha-pāri Nāṭ* or Tiger Dance, a few female dancers, dancing in a stooping posture, represent deer grazing, and a man represents a tiger attacking the deer.

In the *Bhāl-pāri Nāṭ* or Bear Dance, a number of female dancers represent a party of persons whom a man representing a bear attacks.

In the *Mrigi-pāri Nāṭ* or Deer Dance, a party of female dancers represent a herd of deer grazing in the forest, and a man is shown as shooting an arrow at them.

In the *Hāthi-pāri Nāṭ* or Elephant Dance, a few women, each with a twisted cloth hanging down in front of her head to represent an elephant's trunk and each with a boy on her back to represent the rider on the elephant, dance with the heavy leisurely gait of elephants.

In the *Gidha-pāri Nāṭ* or Vulture Dance, the dancers represent vultures wheeling round a carcase and one after the other pecking at it.

In the *Guṇḍāri-pāri Nāṭ* or Sparrow dance, a number of girls with light steps briskly dance about in a stooping posture to represent little birds frisking about.

In the *Mūrgi-pāri Nāṭ* or Cock-Dance, girls with cloth sticking out of their heads as Cocks' combs dance in imitation of cocks.

9. Songs.

The Pāuṛi Bhūiyās, like most other primitive tribes, are intensely fond of song and music. But their musical instruments are few and simple, consisting only

Fig. 19. The *Hāthhi Pari* or Elephant Dances.

[Three women with cloths suspended from their head to represent trunks, are dancing each with boy riding on back]

of the invariable *chāngu* drum which they themselves manufacture with *Karkār* wood for the frame and a piece of goat's or baboon's skin for the sounding board, and occasionally a bamboo flute. Stringed instruments are practically unknown.

The themes of the Pāuṛi's songs, too, are limited to the common objects of their environment—the birds and beasts of their native hills and the crops of their forests, and the elemental feelings of the human heart, particularly the emotion of love. They have also acquired a store of songs relating to the love of Krishna and Rādhā which they appear to have borrowed from their Hindu neighbours of the Plains. A specimen of this class of songs is the following:—

Dinē Banamālī[91] *jaithili kheli,*
Kadamb[92] *mūlrē helē;*
Vrishabhānu jemā seṭhāku āsitē
Benī nayana dekhile Krishna harasha mana.

Translation.—

In day time did Banamāli go [on his flute] to play.
At the foot of the *Kadamb* tree;

91 Banamāli is another name of Krishna.
92 *Kadamb* is the *Nauclea parvifolia*.

Soon as Vrishabhānu there appeared,—

Her sweet eyes gladdened Krishna's heart.

The following song about the bear of his native forest is sung by the Pāuṛi Bhūiyā at the *Bhāl-pari-nāṭ* or Bear-dance:—

Āilā-rē buṛhā Bhālu; bhairo khāilu hālu hālu;

Rūmē jhūmē Bhālu paṛāilā ban-ku.

Chanchithili bāis-ṭhengā bhāluke piṭitē,

Rūmē jhūmē Bhālu paṛāilā ban-ku.

Translation.—

The old Bear came and *bar* fruit gorged,

Then flouncing into the forest it fled.

To kill the Bear, bamboo clubs I had scraped;

But flouncing into the forest it fled.

Specimens of genuine Pāuṛi love-songs have been already given (see *ante*, pp, 155-57).

Dalton[93] has given metrical translations of a few snatches of these love-songs. He was so impressed with their songs that he wrote: "They have certainly more wit, more romance, and more poetry in their composition than is usually found amongst the country folk in India."

93 Dalton, *Ethnology of Bengal*, pp. 143-144.

CHAPTER XII.

CONCLUSION.

(i) *A general View of Hill Bhũiyā Culture.*

In the preceeding chapters I have given a rough sketch of the life-activities of the Hill Bhũiyās—a tribe of rude and relatively simple culture. To see the tribe's life as a whole, we must picture to ourselves their life-activities, their joys, sorrows, and aspirations, on the background of their physical and social environment and their tribal history.

Although at some remote period they appear to have been a dominant people in what are now Keonjhar, Pāl Lahera and Bonāi States where their importance is still recognised by their native rulers and the people in general, the Pāuṛis have for centuries now secluded themselves in their present mountain homes and have cut themselves off from close or continued contact with their more civilised fellowmen. Though they appear to have seen better times, they are now obliged, as we have seen, to depend mostly on their natural environment and the rude work of their own hands and the simple devices of their own brains for the means of sustaining life and, so far as possible, making it worth living.

Circumstanced as they now are, the Pāuṛi Bhūiyās could not be expected to develop or maintain a very complex culture. Living as they do, amid the various terrors of jungle and hill,—with mysterious supernatural powers believed to be hovering around them in earth, air and water, with alien human communities down in the Plains below, with certain evil-minded creatures among their human neighbours and also in the animal world around them, believed to possess uncanny powers,—it is natural that the sub-conscious mind of the primitive Pāuṛi should be filled with an anxiety to avoid bad luck and secure good luck, safety, and strength to himself, his family and his community, through alliance with the good powers and avoidance of the evil powers, visible and invisible, surrounding him.

In relation to their human environment their need for economic strength led Pāuṛi families to combine in

Fig. 20. *Gidha Pari or Vulture Dance.*

[One woman is lying down personating the carcase of an animal and another stooping to personate a Vulture and pecking at the carcase.]

settlements or shifting villages, and Pāuṛi villages to combine into *bār* organizations (pp. 93 ff., *ante*) which are socio-political federations of groups of such villages under a common headman, and the tribe as a whole to combine as a man, on extraordinary occasions of common danger, real or fancied, to combat some apprehended or actual peril.

In their villages, the younger people are amenable to discipline and obey the directions and orders of the village elders who constitute the village Panchāyat. The *Maṇḍa-ghar* and the *Darbār* ground are the centres and symbols of organised village life,—and the Dihuri and the Nāek or Pradhān represent the authority of the society over the individual.

These village headmen always act in the spirit of public opinion and enforce the will of the entire community,–for the Pāuṛis, like the other Mūṇḍā tribes, are essentially democratic in spirit. The Panchāyat really includes all the adult members of the community.

Religious feeling, fostered by the common or congregational *Pūjā* of the village deities, supplies the cement for the social integration of the village, as the common *pūjā* of the *Pāṭ* or hill-god serves as the cement to bind the *Bār* federation together as a social unit, and the *pūjā* of such tribal or general deities as the *Mahā-pāṭ* at village Kuār in the Keonjhar State, the worship of *Konto Kuāri* in the Bonāi State, and of *Maṇḍal Pāṭ* in the Kuiṛā parganā of that State, serve to strengthen tribal consciousness and tribal solidarity.

More or less secluded from the outside world, the Pāuṛi clings close to his family, his village, his Bār, and his tribe. His attitude towards his children is one of great affection and even indulgence; and the children, on their part, show great filial affection. Towards the female sex the Pāuṛi is generally considerate. The wife is, as a rule, the mistress of the house and generally exercises considerable influence over her husband and other members of the family. Pāuṛi marriages are generally love-marriages; and in most cases domestic life among the Pāuṛis is fairly happy. The consideration and esteem in which they hold their women-folk appears to be indicated by the expression "*Mā-bhūn*" (literally, mothers and sisters) which is used collectively to mean the female-folk of a Pāuṛi village.

The religious bond that binds the family closer together is the fear and worship of their ancestor-spirits. These are the tutelary deities of the family; and to them a corner of the cooking apartment in each house is consecrated; and there libations of liquor and offerings of food are regularly made to them in each family, particularly before every domestic, socio-religious or religious ceremony.

In their relations with their immediate non-Bhūiyā neighbours on their hills,—namely, their congeners the still ruder Juāngs, the comparatively recent immigrants of the primitive 'Kōl' (Ho and Mūṇḍā) and Ōraon tribes who look up to the Pāuṛis as the 'lords' of the hills, and the Ōṛiya-speaking pastoral Gouṛ caste, with probably a strain of Āryan blood in their veins, who supply them with milk and *ghee* required for their *Pūjās*. Even in their relations with occasional alien visitors from the plains below, the Pāuṛi Bhūiyā is habitually friendly and hospitable. In fact, the Pāuṛi is remarkable for his ready hospitality and never-failing geniality in ordinary times, but he is fierce and revengeful when he suspects evil intentions or foul play.

When their Rājā or any person of consequence

visits a Pāuṛi village, the *mā-bhūn* or women of the village, represented by a few matrons and maidens, come out to greet him and wash his feet. A small wooden stool or a new palm-leaf mat or both are placed on the ground for the guest, and his feet are washed by the *mā-bhūn* with turmeric water, and a pumpkin is presented to him in token of respect and good-will of the villagers.

To their Chhatri "Rājā" who lives in the Plains below, the Pāuṛis are ordinarily friendly and loyal, so long as they are not exasperated by some real or supposed wrong. But when they are goaded beyond endurance by a sense of injustice or oppression, they combine as a man to remedy the grievance, by open revolt if necessary.

At every stage of their economic life, the first care of Pāuṛi society is to ensure the protection and blessings of the gods. When a new village site is selected, the first thing that the community does is to instal *Gāī-śrī* or the tutelary deity of the proposed village at the centre of the selected site by ceremonially setting up a post (*Subha khuṇṭa* or auspicious post) as the deity's symbol.

As in other Mūṇḍā tribes, the spirits of their deceased ancestors are the tutelary deities of each family and, as we have seen, a corner of the cooking apartment in each house is consecrated to them. As each house has thus its tutelary deities so, too, has the whole village its tutelary village deities named *Gāi-śrī* or *Ṭhākurāṇī* and her husband *Boṛām* or the Sun-God.

The main economic pursuits of the Pāuṛis, such as jungle-clearing for purposes of *kōmān* or *Jhūm* cultivation (pp. 233 ff, *ante*), sowing of paddy-seeds (p. 244 ff. *ante*), harvesting of rice (p. 240 ff. *ante*), hunting (p. 241 ff. *ante*), the eating of the first mango and other fruits of the season (p. 244 ff, *ante*), and the eating of first fruits of rice (p. 248 ff, *ante*), must be blessed and sacralised, as we have seen, by ceremonially associating the deities with them.

As in economic activities, so, too, in other activities and situations in life, the deities and spirits must be invoked to bless them. In this way the whole of Pāuṛi life is one of dependance on the supernatural world. The religious ritual that ushers in every important economic and social activity is intended to place the

Pāuṛi community in rapport with the beneficent supernatural powers and energies so as to secure good luck in the undertaking and to frustrate the maleficent powers and thus avoid ill luck.

Religion with the Pāuṛi is not an affair of mere gross utilitarianism or a seeking after material advantages, nor is his religious feeling one merely of fear. The joyous emotions of love and hope also have their place in his religious complex. In this the closer association in the past of the Pāuṛis with the Hindus would appear to have been of help. Their ideas of the gods would appear to be a little more refined than that of most of their other primitive neighbours. The numerous songs relating to the love of the human soul for the Eternal Spirit typified by the songs of the love of Krishna and Rādhā which the Pāuṛi Bhuiyās take intense delight in singing are obviously borrowed from their Hindu neighbours in the *Plains*. Though the deeper spiritual meaning of these songs is unknown and generally unintelligible to the modern Pāuṛi, all that he feels and cares for is that these are songs of power which thrill his mind with the vital religious emotions of hope and joy, with a consciousness of temporary spiritual uplift and of a higher and a more dynamic life.

Like his economic and his social life, his Morals have also their foundation in Religion—in the fear of the supernatural world and in the instinctive association of purity and holiness with the spirits and gods. Even most of what we call his "superstitions" would appear to be the blind gropings of the subconscious mind after the Eternal Source of all Power and Life,—an instinctive, though vague, attraction towards Light and Joy, the Good and the Beautiful, and an instinctive aversion towards all that jars against his innate, though undeveloped, sense of Beauty and Goodness, Life and Light.

Thus the key-note of the Pāuṛi's life would appear to be the desire, mostly sub-conscious, of placing himself in harmonious relations with his human neighbours and his environment generally, and, above all, with the invisible supernatural world from which are beleived to emanate mysterious spiritual energies that are responsible for all happenings in the phenomenal world—all that make for human happiness and misery, good luck and bad luck. Owing to his lowly culture and his crass ignorance, however, he has not yet discovered the right value of things and the right path by which he may reach the goal of his desires.

(ii) *A General View of Plains Bhūiyā Culture.*

The Plains Bhūiyās of Oṛissā who have long been in close contact with Hindu castes of a comparatively higher culture have, as might be expected, advanced one or two rungs higher in the cultural ladder than their Pāuṛi congeners. The fact that in the northern (Telugu, Kanarese and Tulu) areas of the Draviḍian country, a certain amount of mesocephaly and leptorrhiny is found[94] and that among the Plains Bhūiyās of the Mayurbhanj State 14.9 per cent of leptorrhine and brachycephalic elements have been detected[95], may indicate that a modicum of Draviḍian racial element has entered into the racial make up of the Plains Bhūiyās of Oṛissā. This may, I think, account for the impression of Campbell and Dalton (see pp. 29 ff. *ante*) of the Draviḍian origin of the Bhūiyās.

---

94 Thuston, *Castes and Tribes of Southern India*, vol I. p. XII, and p. LII.

95 *Journal of the Asiatic Society of Bengal*, XXV, pp. 158 ff. See *ante* p. 52.

Whether a Draviḍian element has entered into the racial composition of the Plains Bhũiyās or not, certain elements of their culture may perhaps be taken to point to Draviḍian influence. Thus, the Plains Bhũiyās of Oṛissā generally claim to belong to the Nāgas or Nāg *gotra* or stock, though different sections of them have each what they call a number of different *Khilis*[96] (probably a variation of the Muṇḍāri term *Kili*, meaning, clan or sept). They say that the Bhũiyās of Mayurbhanj, Keonjhar and the neighbouring States belong to the Dudhiā Nāg *gotra*, those of the Gāngpur State and of the adjoining British district of Sambalpur to the Gāngu Nāg *gotra*, those of Chōṭā Nāgpur to the Chuṭiā or Choṭā Nāg *gotra*, and those in the Central Provinces to the Bhaiñsā Nāg *gotra*. This may not improbably

96 Thus I found the following *Khilis* among the Plains Bhũiyās of the Mayurbhanj State:— (1) *Sardi*, (2) *Kāt*, (3) *Garli*, (4) *Naladri*, (5) *Bāi*, (6) *Nāṭ*, (7) *Pānsiāl*, (8) *Banial*, (9) *Gal*, (10) *Kanta*, (11) *Muguri*, (12) *Banāi*, (13) *Namgi*, (14) *Bānkā*, (15) *Koliāl*, (16) *Koṛa*, (17) *Kenduālī*, (18) *Bārhā*, (19) *Arkhei*, (20) *Jerengi*, (21) *Bālmāṇḍi*, (22) *Jaipuri*, (23) *Taṛri*, (24) *Aṛandi*, (25) *Puting*, (26) *Baṛhei*, (27) *Kukṛā*, (28) *Kondhai*, (29) *Telli*, (30) *Puting*, (31) *Bheṇḍāli*. Some Plains Bhũiyās also claim to belong to *Bhōj baṁś*—apparently a name borrowed from the Hindus. In this connection it may be stated that some Hinduised Muṇḍās of the *Jom-Tuṭi* clan now claim to belong to the Bhoj-Rāj *gotra* or *Bhōj-bams* (as the *Muṇḍāri* word *Jom*, like the Samskrit word *Bhojan*, means 'eating'.) (See S.C. Roy's *Mundas and Their Country*, p. 411). Similarly, as mentioned in p. 30 above, some Bhũiyās of Oṛissā claim to belong to *Pawanbams* or to be descendants of Pawan, the Wind-god who is said to have been the father of *Hanumān*, the so-called 'Monkey-god' of the Hindus.

refer to the traditional claim of the Plains Bhūiyās of Oṛissā to their racial affinity with the Nāga branch of probably the Draviḍians of the Proto-Mediterranean race.

As among some Draviḍian castes so, too, among the Plains Bhūiyās of Ōṛissā, the mother's brother of the bride conducts the bride by the hand to the marriage platform and seats her in front of the bridegroom. The close affinity of the Plains Bhūiyās with the pre-Draviḍian Pāuṛi Bhūiyās, on the other hand, is pointedly indicated by, among other facts, the recognition of *Pāuṛi Devī* or the goddess Pāuṛi as the tutelary (*Iṣṭa*) deity of the tribe. In their ceremonial eating of the first fruits in the month of Bhādra, in their annual offerings to the manes of their male ancestors in the month of Āsvin and female ancestors in Kartik, and in their *Makar saṁkrānti* festival in the month of Pauṣ,—offerings of milk, molasses, sweets and plantains are made to the Pāuṛi deity. Though the Hinduised Plains Bhūiyās now seek to identify Pāuṛi Devī with the benignant Hindu goddess Dūrgā, it appears very probable that she was in origin the Deity of the Hills (Pāhāṛ) which formed their original home before they had separated from the Pāuṛi or Hill section of the tribe.

In economic life, the Plains Bhūiyās have long taken to regular cultivation of lowland rice in irrigated and terraced fields. A section of them, known particularly as Pāik Bhūiyās or Khanḍāit Pāik Bhūiyās, once formed the militia of the States in which they respectivly live, and they still have the battle-axe or sword (*Khanḍā*) as their tribal emblem (*Santak*).

With their comparatively advanced economic progress, certain families of Plains Bhūiyās have risen to positions of considerable local importance as landed proprietors, such as *Garhātias* or owners of forts, *Ohdārs*, *Ganzhus* and the like. Even among the lesser magnates, recognition of distinctions of social rank is expressed by the different *sangyās* or titles such as *Ṭhākur*, *Sāhu*, *Photkār*, *Sāont*, *Mānjhī*, *Sārtiā*, *Behārā*, *Rāut*, *Kōṭwār*, *Mahāpātra*, and so forth (*Vide* pp. 101 ff. *ante*).

As with the *Pāuṛis* so too with the Plains Bhūiyās, all their important economic pursuits have to be bessed ansid acralised by benedictory religious ceremonies. Bedess observing such festivals of this nature as are observed by the Pāuṛis, namely *Māgh Parab*, *Ākhin Pārdhi*,

Ām-nuā-Khiā, Tirtia Muṭi, Asāṛhi or *Bihiṛā Pūjā, Gāmhā Punāi,* and *Dhān-nuā-Khiā,* the Plains Bhūiyās have further adopted a few Hindu festivals in vogue amongst the general Hindu population of Ōṛissā. Thus they observe the *Kojāgar Purṇimā* festival on the full moon day of the month of Kārtik (October-November) and the *Chitau Parab* on the new moon day of the month of Śrāvan (July-August), besides various *vratas* or *oṣās*.

In their social organisation, too, as I have said, the Plains Bhūiyās have worked out a wider organisation than the inter-village *Bār* federation of the Pāuṛis. The Plains Bhūiyā area in each State or District or Parganā is divided into *Piṛs,* and several Piṛs constitute the Deś or 'country'. Each *Piṛ* has its own *Panchāyat* or social, administrative and judicial council with such office-bearers as Paṭ-nāik or Bhal-bhāi, Pāni-pātra, and Chhāṭiā or Dākuā. The *Chhāṭiā* is the messenger of the *Piṛ*, the *Paṭ-nāik* or *Bhal-bhāi* presides over and, in some cases, records the proceedings of the Panchāyat, and the *Pānipātra* eats the first morsel of food at a tribal feast of the *Piṛ*. These posts are honorary and ordinarily hereditary. The Panchāyat of a *Piṛ* is also called the *Deś* (*lit.*, country,) or *Deś Panchāyat*, and the questions which it is now generally called upon to decide are those relating to adultery and marriage or sexual union with socially ineligible mates (*strī-badh*, *lit*, woman-slaughter), causing death (generally accidental) to a cow (*gō-badh*), and the contamination of leprosy (*māchhi-pātak*) which is believed to be the divine punishment for some dire sin committed either in this life or in some previous life.

When the Deś-Panchāyat cannot unanimously decide a question, or it is otherwise deemed necessary to obtain the decision of the whole tribe resident in the Parganā or State, the matter is referred to a higher tribunal consisting of the representatives of all the different Bhūiyā *pirs* of the Parganā or the State, as the case may be. The Mahāpātra who is the social head of the tribe resident in the Parganā, convenes a meeting of this wider union known in the Mayurbhanj State as *Danti sabhā*. The Mahāpātra who is the tribal head of an entire Parganā is, in the Mayurbhanj State, elected by the tribe as a whole, and the appointment is confirmed by the State. Similar assemblies of the Plains Bhūiyās of the Keonjhar, Bonāi and Pāl Lahera States are known as *Gaddis*, in which not only representatives from the different Pirs of the particular Parganā or State concerned come together but even representatives from the neighbouring States also attend. In these States there is no officially appointed president like the Mahāpātra of Mayurbhanj, but usually the oldest among the village headmen jointly guide the deliberations of the tribal assembly (See *ante* pp. 102-104). Similar meetings of the tribal heads from different *Pirs* are held in the Plains Bhūiyā areas all over Orissā on occasions of marriage-festivals or funeral festivals in the houses of well-to-do Bhūiyās who can afford to invite and entertain them.

As for social virtues, the Plains Bhūiyās have the same attachment to their family and children, the same fidelity and attraction towards their village, their Pir, and their tribe, and the same feeling of loyalty and obedience to the authorities as the Pāuris,–though their comparative complexity in life would appear to have to some extent impaired the simplicity, straightforwardness, truthfulness and even hospitality and allied virtues for which their Pāuri brethren are to this day particularly noted.

In his socio-religious ceremonies, the Plains Bhũiyā has adopted a few rites and customs from his Hindu neighbours and renounced or modified some of the grosser features of his old tribal rites. In Plains Bhũiyā marriages, a Brāhmaṇ priest is called in to perform the *Hōm* ceremony or offering of oblations to the Deity represented by Fire. Divorce is permitted only when the wife proves unchaste. No bar is placed on the remarriage of a widow or a divorced wife, except that she can marry only a widower. As among the Pāuṛis, female relatives (*mā-bhun*) accompany the bridal procession along with male relatives and tribe-fellows to the bride's house. But, unlike the Pāuṛi bridegroom, a Plains Bhũiyā bridegroom has to receive initiation (*guru-karṇa*) from a Brāhmaṇ religious preceptor (*guru*) who invests him with the sacred thread and whispers into his ears the name of the particular god who is to be his tutelary deity (*Iṣṭa Devatā*).

This cult of a personal god requires the Bhũiyā, like every other Hindu, to regard his *Iṣṭa Devatā* as his Ideal, his Guide and Monitor and his Protector through life. Though in most cases this duty is more honoured in the breach than in the observance, this personal aspect of religion marks a step in advance, and differentiates the religious ideal of the Hinduised Plains Bhūiyās from that of the Hill Bhūiyās and other primitive tribes with whom religion is essentially an affair of the community and its practical concerns and mental needs rather than an affair of the individual and his spiritual needs.

In such religious ceremonies as those of eating the first fruits of his fields or the first vegetables and fruits of the season, the Plains Bhūiyā besides making offerings to his ancestral spirits and village deities also makes offerings to his *Iṣṭa Devatā* or tutelary deity. In some of the States, the Plains Bhūiyās have adopted *gotra* or clan-names in imitation of the Hindus. These are usually totemistic, such as *Kachchhap* (the tortoise), *Komasṭa* (a small bird), *Nāga* (the cobra), *Mayūr* (the peacock), *Barāha* (the boar), and so forth. Some Rājkoli Bhūiyās claim to belong to the *Bhōjbaṁś* which they interpret as *Bhujanga-baṁśa* or serpent stock and thus claim affinity with the "*Nāg-vaṁśī Kshatriyas*"

The conception of the gods and the mode of worship of the Hinduised Plains Bhūiyā would also appear to have undergone a little improvement upon the ideas and methods of the Hill Bhūiyā. His identification of some of his original tribal deities with certain Hindu deities, such as the Pāuṛi Devī with the Goddess Dūrgā of the Hindu pantheon and the adoption of such Hindu deities as Lakshmi, the Goddess of Prosperity (whom the Plains Bhūiyā worships particularly on the full-moon night in the month of Āsvin) would indicate that the cult of wholly benignant deities has come to supplement, though not wholly supplant, his belief in the older spirits of malignant and partly malignant and partly benignant attributes. It may, however, be noted that through Hindu influence, some of the deities of the Hill Bhūiyās, too, are now regarded as more beneficent than maleficent.

As for the mode of worship, the Hinduised Plains Bhūiyā has given up sacrificing fowls and animals, except occasionally a goat, to his deities; and his usual offerings to his deities now consist of milk, molasses and sweets, fruits (ordinarily plantains) and flowers, fragrant sandal-paste, and the burning of frankincense. A tribal priest is still appointed to propitiate the village gods. By way of preparation for every Pūjā, the Kālọ or Dehuri has to observe a preliminary fast, and to live a life of abstinence and ceremonial purity during the days of worship. In this matter the Plains Bhūiyā priest is even more punctilious and strict than his Pāuṛi colleague.

An effective instrument for the dissemination of Hindu religious and moral ideas among such Hinduised backward communities as the Plains Bhūiyās has been the discipline of the *Vratas* or *Oṣās*. These consist of certain periods of ceremonial fasting and abstinence followed by worship and the recital of *Kāhinīs* or long-winded religious stories illustrative of the happy consequences and good luck attending on virtuous conduct and devotion to some deity and the ill-luck and miseries resulting from evil conduct and godlessness. Plains Bhūiyā women, in imitation of their other Hindu neighbours, observe the *Ṣaṣṭhi Ōṣā* particularly in the month of Aśvin, the *Tārinī Ōṣā* in Aṣāṛh, the *Mangalā Ōṣā* in Chaitra, the *Daśaharā Ōṣā* in Āśvin or Kartik, and the *Jitbāhan Ōṣā* in Āsvin. Some Plains Bhūiyās—men and women–also observe the *Sōmnāth vrata* in the month of Bhādra. At the concluding stage of some of these *vratas*, the services of a Brāhmaṇ priest may by requisitioned. The *Dhankuilā Ōṣā* is observed by barren women desirous of children. These *vratas* constitute an effective popular method of imparting moral instruction and religious discipline and habits of abstinence to backward sections of the Hindu population.

(iii) The Pāuṛi and Plains Bhūiyā Cultures Compared.

In this way, the Plains Bhūiyās have acquired from their Hindu neighbours a somewhat richer store of moralizing stories, saws and sayings, a somewhat improved religious and social discipline and a somewhat higher conception of the gods and a partially improved mode of worship; and there has thus been a slight improvement in the traditional material that enters into their mental operations. Yet the average Plains Bhūiyā hardly shows any marked improvement over his Pāuṛi congeners in the principles of classification of experience and in the social and emotional associations of sense-impressions and habitual activities.

In this characterisation I have left out of consideration the few families of big landed proprietors among the Oṛissā Bhūiyās who have, through several generations of assimilation of Hindu culture, now become quite distinguishable from the average Bhūiyā and almost indistinguishable, both in his virtues and vices and general mental characteristics and culture, from their Hindu neighbours of the same or similar social standing and similar upbringing,—thus suggesting the futility of all attempts to correlate race with mental capacity and culture.

Differences in occupation and social environment, have, as we have seen, produced some difference in the cultural condition of the Plains Bhūiyās from that of the Hill Bhūiyās. Under better social and physiographical environment, the Plains Bhūiyās have attained a little higher economic development and a somewhat better material culture, and a wider social organisation. Yet the ordinary Plains Bhūiyā and the Pāuṛi Bhūiyā would, as I have said, appear to possess much the same fundamental categories of thought and classification of the facts of experience. Although, a slight difference in physical characteristics would appear to have been brought about probably through a slight strain of Draviḍian admixture in the Plains Bhūiyās, there is hardly any appreciable difference in mental characteristics between them and the Pāuṛi Bhūiyās.

If the Pāuṛi is more easily roused to political excitement and revolt, it is due to ignorant apprehensions and conclusions resulting from a lack of proper knowledge and of adequate experience of the outer world beyond his native hills, and not to a comparative lack of control over his impulses and passions. He is as capable as individuals of other communities of inhibiting his impulses and natural inclinations in matters in which social traditions and regulations demand it, as, for instance, in the observance of the various taboos imposed by tribal custom. If he is wrong in some of his conclusions, his logic is not at fault, but his premises, based as they often are on inadequate or mistaken knowledge, are in error. If he is ordinarily indolent and apathetic, it is because his needs and interests are limited and easily satisfied and he is more optimistic and consequently less provident and prudent than his more progressive neighbours of other tribes and castes. In matters which really interest him, he is capable of applying his mind with as much attention, assiduity and perseverance as individuals of more advanced communities. If he is more conservative than the Plains Bhūiyā it is because he is more ignorant and has had lesser opportunities of seeing and knowing the world outside his native hills.

The old conservatism of the Pāuṛi is, however, gradually wearing away. With the increasing number of *hāṭs* or markets just beyond the borders of the Pāuṛi country, he no longer waits for traders to come to his village, but himself takes his grains for sale to the nearest markets of the Plains below and thereby secures better profits, and purchases not only articles of necessity, such as salt and kerosine oil, but also, if funds permit, articles of what are luxuries to him, such as a cloth umbrella and even a hurricane lantern. There appears also an increasing tendency towards adopting wet cultivation of paddy, though this can never extend to any large extent as lands capable of such cultivation are small in area and isolated in location, and thus only a few can take up such land, and, what is worse, crops of such small isolated plots of land in the midst of jungles stand greater risk of depredation by wild elephants and other animals. In other matters, too the Pāuṛi's increasing contact with other castes and tribes is gradually widening his mental outlook and wearing away certain old prejudices and fears. But he still preserves much of his native simplicity and innate sense of self-respect and independence of spirit and his accustomed exuberance of life. In this respect he compares favourably with the Plains Bhūiyā in whose life some amount of complexity and artificiality appears to have impaired these old tribal characteristics. His more intimate contact with neighbours of a comparatively higher culture and his natural desire to imitate them has inevitably introduced this complexity and artificiality into the life of the Plains Bhūiyā. This has indeed led to some economic and social progress, but has also to some extent impaired his primitive virility and zest in life, though he no longer appears to have any actual feeling of pessimism or social discomfort on that account. The Pāuṛi Bhūiyā's contact with the comparatively recent Pre-Draviḍian settlers in his hills, such as the Santāl, the Hō ('Kōl'), the Orāon and the Goṇḍ, has not yet appreciably affected his economic and cultural life. In fact, the Pāuṛi disdains to have any social intercourse with these immigrants who have settled on his hills by his sufference. It is also by the Pāuṛi's sufference, if not by his special leave and favour, that these new-comers have taken up waste lands on his hills for more intensive cultivation. A few Pāuṛis have indeed been prompted by the example of these more industrious new-comers to take up the cultivation of rice in irrigated terraces. Owing, however, to the paucity of suitable lands on their hills, such cultivation has not been, and cannot be, generally adopted.[97]

The States authorities have wisely refrained from interfering with his accustomed ways and habits and ancient customs and ideas which are the outcome of the Pāuṛi's tribal genius and history, and which have so far answered his economic and social, mental and emotional needs fairly well. His native forests have been spared such exploitation as has caused great economic distress to some primitive tribes elsewhere. There has yet been no proselytizing attempt on the part of missionaries of higher religions to impose upon him utterly unfamiliar (albeit higher) ideas of religion and a new way of life that not unoften involves, through injudicious discipline, a loss of that interest in life which is the primary factor in the welfare of a people. The Pāuṛi has also been generally spared the attentions of the recruiting agents of tea-plantations in Assam and the Duars and large industrial concerns nearer home whose owners generally feel little interest in their employees except as labour-machines, and where they are prone to pick up vices and diseases from which they have been so long happily immune.

The only important cultural influence that has for countless generations very slowly and imperceptibly infiltrated into the Pāuṛi's indigenous system of thoughts and feelings, ritual and belief, customs and habits, is that of his Hindu neighbours; but such influence, though it has affected his religious life to some extent, has made very little impression on most other aspects of his life.

---

97 Thus, at the Revenue Settlement of the Bhūiyā *Piṛs* of Keonjhar in 1907-8, it was found that the total number of houses in those *Piṛs* was 3633 of which 2139 had ploughs and 1494 houses owned no ploughs, and the total number of ploughs was 2207½. Twenty years later, in the last Settlement in 1926-8, the total number of ploughs was found to be 2545½, the total number of houses with ploughs 2453 and without ploughs 1478. Thus there has been an increase of 338 ploughs in twenty years; and only 16 more houses or families have discontinued the exclusive use of the primitive digging-stick or *ānkusi-bāḍi* for agricultural purposes and taken also to plough-cultivation.

APPENDIX A.

By Ramesh Chandra Roy M. Sc.

[ABBREVIATIONS USED:—*Face:*— ov.=oval; sq.=square; pent.=pentagonal; Rd.=Round. *Forehead:*— +=Retreating; -=straight *Lips.*— +=everted (slightly or moderately); th.=thick. *Prognathism:*— +=slight or moderate; ++=extreme; -=nil.]

I. Statistical Analysis of one hundred adult Pāuṛi Bhũiyās.

Measurements.		Mean.	Probable Error to Mean.	Standard Deviation.	P.E. to S.D.	Coeff. of Variation.	P.E. to Variation.
Stature	in cms.	157·31	±·33	4·94	±·24	3·14	±·15
Head-Length	in mms.	186·82	±·44	6·52	±·31	3·48	±·18
Head-Breadth	„	136·55	±·29	4·23	±·20	3·10	±·15
Head-Height	„	116·21	±·35	5·23	±·25	4·51	±·22
Nasal-Length	„	44·77	±·19	2·85	±·14	6·37	±·31
Nasal-Breadth	„	39·24	±·24	3·55	±·17	9·05	±·48
Least-Frontal Breadth	„	101·39	±·28	4·20	±·20	4·14	±·64
Nasion Prosthion Length	„	68·47	±·25	3·68	±·18	5·38	±·26
Nasion Gnathion Length	„	112·14	±·39	5·79	±·28	5·16	±·25
Bizygomatic Breadth	„	130·09	±·32	4·79	±·23	3·68	±·18
Bigonial Length	„	92·72	±·33	4·94	±·24	5·33	±·44
Cephalic Index		73·29	±·18	2·64	±·13	3·60	±·17
Altitudinal Index		62·31	±·22	3·27	±·16	5·25	±·28
Nasal Index...		87·93	±·66	9·75	±·46	1·11	±·54
Facial Index		86·19	±·34	5·02	±·24	5·82	±·28

II. Anthropometrical Measurements

No.	Village.	Name.	Stature (1)	Head Height (2)	Head Length. (3)	Head Breadth. (4)	Altitudinal Index $= \frac{2}{3} \times 100$	Cephalic Index $= \frac{4}{3} \times 100$	Least Frontal (5)	Bi-zygomatic (6)
1	Koinsar	Sadananda	156·5	11·0	19·3	13·1	57·0	67·9	10·0	12·8
2	,,	Lakhan	166·2	11·5	17·9	13·6	64·2	76·0	10·4	12·9
3	,,	Dhimu	161·0	11·3	17·9	13·5	63·1	75·4	10·2	13·2
4	,,	Rudhan	160·7	12.6	19·7	15.2	63·9	77·2	10·8	13·4
5	,,	Nandu	159·8	12·1	19·7	14·0	61·4	71·1	10·3	13·1
6	Jamdihi	Muchia	153·0	11·2	18·2	13·2	61·5	72·5	9·8	12·1
7	,,	Khendu	146·5	11·1	18·3	13·2	60·7	72·1	10·5	12·6
8	,,	Kunshu	148·3	11·1	18·7	13·2	59·3	70·6	9·8	12·9
9	,,	Nidhi	153·0	11·4	19·9	14·2	57·3	71·4	10·0	12·9
10	Jamtor	Mohono	153·2	11·8	18·3	13·4	65·5	73·2	9·3	12·2
11	Jamtor	Naba	148·5	11·7	18·5	13·4	63·2	72·4	9·5	12·7
12	Suakaṭi	Chandou	169·3	12·3	18·1	14·1	67·8	77·9	10·6	13·3
13	,,	Nandi	151·1	12·6	18·2	13·5	69·2	74·2	9·5	12·7
14	,,	Gura	159·6	12·4	18·6	13·8	66·7	74·2	11·1	13·7
15	Chandi	Nayan	154·1	11·3	18·1	13·5	62·3	74·6	10·1	12·8
16	Lapdha	Garia	152·5	11·6	19·4	13·2	59·8	68·0	9·9	12·9
17	,,	Dhama	158·6	11·1	19.3	13·9	57·5	72·0	11·1	13·4
18	,,	Chandro	158·4	11·2	18·7	14·1	59·9	75·4	10.0	12·3
19	,,	Karu	161·8	11·4	19·7	14·7	57·9	74·6	10·3	13·4
20	Echinda	Ravan	154·5	10·5	17·8	13·4	60·0	75·3	10·0	13·3

of adult male Subjects.

Bi-gonial (7)	Nasal Length (8)	Nasal Breadth (9)	Nasal Height (10)	Nasal Index =9/8×100	Nasion Prosthion Length (11)	Nasion Gnathion Length (12)	Facial Index =12,6×100	Bi-orbital Length (13)	Circumference of the head (14)	Face (15)	Forehead (16)	Lips (17)	Facial Prognathism.
9·1	5·0	4·2		8·4	7·2	12·4	96·9		55·0	pent.	+	+	+
8·7	4·7	3·7	1·3	78·7	6·8	11·5	89·2	10·9	53·3	ov.	+	+	–
9·7	4·4	3·9		88·6	7·2	11·1	84·1		53·1	sq.	+	th.	+
9·8	4·8	4·7	1·7	97·9	7·5	11·8	88·1	10·7	57·1	ov.	+	"	+
9·6	5·1	4·4	1·6	86·3	7·5	11·6	87·9	10·3	51·2	"	+	+	+
8·7	4·4	3·9		88·6	6·3	11·0	90·9		54·0	"	+	th.	+
9·0	4·1	3·8	1·4	92·6	6·6	10·0	79·4	10·4	52·2	pent.	–	"	+
9·5	4·4	3·9	1·4	88·6	6·3	11·0	85·3	10·8	54·0	ov.	+	"	+
9·9	4·3	3·8	1·3	88·4	6·7	10·7	83·0	10·5	55·6	pent.	+	+	–
9·8	4·6	3·3		71·7	7·0	11·1	91·0		52·1	ov.	+	+	+
8·0	4·2	3·7		88·1	6·8	11·2	88·2		54·5	"	+	+	+
9·3	4·2	4·0	1·4	95·2	7·2	11·7	87·9	10·4	55·1	"	+	+	+
8·9	4·7	4·0		85·1	6·9	10·7	84·3		54·2	"	+	th.	+
9·6	4·8	4·3		89·6	7·0	11·3	82·4		53·5	"	+	"	+
10·0	4·7	3·7		78·7	6·6	10·8	84·4		52·5	"	+	+	+
9·2	4·7	3·8	1·2	80·9	6·9	12·0	93·0	80·5	56·0	sq.	+	+	+
10·2	4·7	4·3	1·1	91·5	6·7	11·3	84·3	10·6	57·2	"	+	+	+
9·2	4·3	4·0	1·3	93·0	6·6	11·0	89·4	11·0	52·3	ov.	+	+	+
9·5	4·1	3·7	1·2	95·1	6·5	11·2	83·5	11·1	56·4	sq.	+	+	–
9·0	4·2	3·9	1·2	88·1	6·4	10·7	80·4	10·3	51·4	ov.	+	+	+

II. Anthropometrical Measurements

No.	Village.	Name.	Stature (1)	Head Height (2)	Head Length (3)	Head Breadth (4)	Altitudinal Index =2/3×100	Cephalic Index =4/3×100	Least Frontal (5)	Bi-zygomatic (6)
21	„	Rama	162·8	11·8	19·2	13·3	61·5	69·3	9·9	12·8
22	Kaipur	Daba	162·5	11·3	19·3	13·1	58·6	67·9	9·9	13·3
23	Suakati	Chema	160·4	11·8	20·2	14·3	58·4	70·8	10·2	15·1
24	Kaipur	Rasura	157·2	11·7	19·3	13·9	60·6	72·0	10·0	12·9
25	Doroj	Kendra	154·3	11·1	18·9	13·5	58·7	71·4	10·0	12·2
26	„	Lambudar	151·5	11·4	18·1	13·4	63·0	74·0	9·7	12·5
27	„	Kulia	161·7	12·2	19·5	13·8	62·6	70·8	10·0	12·9
28	„	Duku	156·6	10·9	18·9	13·2	57·7	69·8	9·7	12·7
29	„	Sira	159·5	11·4	19·6	14·2	58·2	72·5	11·4	12·8
30	„	Vigo	162·1	11·5	19·8	14·3	58·1	72·2	11·0	13·6
31	„	Gopi	154·5	11·2	17·4	13·8	64·1	79·3	10·2	12·8
32	„	Darsalie	156·3	11·8	18·4	13·7	64·1	74·5	9·6	13·1
33	Deora	Pindka	169·5	12·4	18·5	13·8	67·0	74·6	10·8	13·4
34	„	Milu	153·3	10·9	18·0	14·1	60·6	78·3	9·9	13·9
35	„	Nadhura	159·4	11·5	18·2	13·8	63·2	75·8	10·2	13·0
36	„	Bomia	156·0	11·8	18·3	13·4	64·5	73·2	10·3	13·2
37	„	Zira	159·8	12·1	18·9	13·5	64·0	71·4	10·0	12·6
38	„	Mongsira	166·2	11·2	18·4	13·3	60·9	12·3	10·1	12·6
39	„	Hari	156·3	10·4	19·3	14·2	53·9	73·6	10·7	13·3
40	„	Choni	162·0	11·1	18·4	13·8	60·3	75·0	10·2	13·9

of adult male Subjects.

Bi-gonial (7)	Nasal Length (8)	Nasal Breadth (9)	Nasal Height (10)	Nasal Index =9/8×100	Nasion Prosthion Length (11)	Nasion Gnathion Length (12)	Facial Index =12/6×100	Bi-orbital Length (13)	Circumference of the head (14)	Face (15)	Forehead (16)	Lips (17)	Facial Prognathism.
9·4	4·1	3·9	1·4	95·1	6·9	11·1	86·7	10·8	54·3	ov.	−	th.	−
8·9	4·0	4·1	1·3	102·5	6·7	10·9	81·1	10·3	56·0	pent.	−	+	+
9·1	5·1	4·2	1·6	82·4	7·5	12·3	93·9	11·0	57·2	,,	+	+	+
9·0	4·6	4·0	1·4	87·0	6·7	10·8	83·7	10·4	56·1	,,	+	+	+
8·4	4·7	3·8	1·1	80·9	7·2	10·7	87·7	10·5	52·8	ov.	+	+	−
9·6	4·8	3·8	1·5	79·2	6·4	10·3	82·4	10·4	54·6	,,	+	+	+
9·5	4·3	4·2	1·0	97·7	6·5	11·6	89·9	10·6	56·5	sq.	+	+	+
8·5	4·6	4·0	1·2	87·0	6·5	11·2	88·2	10·5	54·2	pent.	+	+	+
9·4	5·1	4·4	1·7	86·3	6·9	11·3	88·3	11·2	56·0	sq.	+	+	+
10·9	4·8	3·9	1·4	81·2	7·5	12·4	90·5	11·3	58·3	,,	−	+	+
9·3	4·7	3·8	1·3	80·9	7·2	11·9	93·8	10·5	52·1	Rd.	+	th.	−
8·4	4·2	3·8	1·1	90·5	6·5	9·8	74·8	10·0	54·1	sq.	−	+	−
9·1	4·5	4·1	1·4	91·1	6·9	11·1	82·9	10·9	52·3	ov.	+	+	+
9·5	3·9	3·9	1·3	100·0	7·1	11·0	80·3	10·8	53·1	pent.	+	+	+
9·4	4·6	3·6	1·3	72·3	7·0	11·7	90·0	10·1	53·0	,,	−	+	+
9·6	4·6	3·8	1·2	82·6	6·7	11·6	87·9	10·7	53·5	,,	+	th.	+
8·9	4·0	3·7	1·3	92·5	6·5	11·2	88·9	10·6	53·3	ov.	−	+	−
8·9	4·4	3·7	1·5	84·1	6·6	11·5	91·3	10·3	52·2	pent.	+	+	+
9·2	4·8	3·9	1·5	81·2	7·4	12·3	92·4	10·1	56·0	ov.	+	+	+
9·7	5·0	4·2	1·5	84·0	7·4	12·2	83·4	10·5	55·6	,,	+	+	+ +

II. Anthropometrical Measurements

No.	Village.	Name.	Stature (1)	Head Height (2)	Head Length (3)	Head Breadth (4)	Altitudinal Index =2/3×100	Cephalic Index =4/3×100	Least Frontal (5)	Bi-zygomatic (6)
41	Deora	Chemtu	165·3	11·9	18·1	13·4	65·8	74·0	9·9	13·0
42	„	Kunja	152·6	11·4	17·4	13·8	65·0	78·7	9·7	12·4
43	„	Gopo	155·9	11·6	18·3	14·2	63·4	77·6	10·7	13·8
44	„	Dutia	157·6	12·1	19·0	13·3	13·7	76·0	10·2	13·0
45	„	Sadan	164·1	11·9	17·8	13·5	66·9	75·8	10·2	12·6
46	„	Dhania	157·4	12·2	19·3	13·8	63·2	71·5	10·3	12·4
47	„	Sibo	155·7	12·0	19·3	13·5	62·2	70·0	10·4	13·4
48	„	Girbo	157·7	12·6	18·7	13·5	67·3	72·2	10·2	13·5
49	„	Budhu	162·1	12·2	18·6	13·4	65·6	72·0	10·1	13·0
50	„	Sugnati	155·4	11·5	18·2	12·8	63·2	70·3	9·7	12·4
51	„	Kandha	162·3	12·1	19·1	14·4	63·4	75·4	10·6	13·5
52	„	Hodu	156·2	11·8	18·9	13·3	62·4	70·4	10·1	13·3
53	„	Babhan	152·8	11·6	18·5	14·2	62·7	76·8	10·1	13·9
54	„	Lochu	153·2	11·0	17·5	13·3	62·9	76·0	9·3	12·8
55	„	Banjam	154·1	12·4	18·6	14·4	67·7	77·4	10·9	13·7
56	„	Jugi	152·3	11·6	18·4	13·3	63·0	72·3	9·8	12·8
57	„	Goria	161·7	11·1	18·7	13·7	59·4	73·3	9·8	12·9
58	„	Gadha	166·4	12·5	18·9	13·6	66·1	72·0	10·5	12·8
59	„	Chandu	159·6	11·8	19·3	13·5	61·2	70·0	10·6	13·1
60	„	Kusri	165·0	12·5	19·6	13·8	63·9	70·4	10·2	12·3

of adult male Subjects.

Bi-gonial (7)	Nasal Length (8)	Nasal Breadth (9)	Nasal Height (10)	Nasal Index =9/8×100	Nasion Prosthion Length (11)	Nasion Gnathion Length (12)	Facial Index =12/6×100	Bi-orbital Length (13)	Circumference of the head (14)	Face (15)	Forehead (16)	Lips (17)	Facial Prognathism.
9·5	3·7	3·6	1·1	97·3	6·0	10·5	80·8	10·8	54·0	sq.	+	+	+ +
8·5	4·4	4·0	1·3	90·9	6·7	10·4	83·9	10·5	52·0	ov.	+	+	+
9·0	4·3	3·9	1·6	90·7	6·3	11·2	81·1	10·5	56·5	pent.	+	+	+ +
9·4	4·7	4·2	1·5	89·4	6·6	11·6	89·2	10·0	54·5	sq.	+	+	–
9·2	4·6	3·7	1·2	80·4	7·1	12·4	98·4	10·2	53·2	,,	+	+	+
9·5	4·7	3·8	1·5	80·9	7·5	11·4	91·9	10·3	54·1	,,	+	th.	+
9·5	4·1	3·9	1·4	95·1	6·5	11·0	82·1	10·4	54·5	ov.	+	,,	+
9·5	4·7	3·8	1·4	80·9	6·9	11·1	82·2	10·5	53·5	sq.	+	+	+
9·2	5·0	3·5	1·4	70·0	7·7	12·1	93·1	10·2	55·0	ov.	+	th.	+ +
9·0	4·4	3·7	1·1	84·1	6·8	10·6	85·5	10·3	50·0	,,	–	+	+ +
9·7	4·7	3·2	1·4	89·4	7·9	12·1	89·6	10·9	57·0	sq.	+	+	+
9·2	4·2	3·7	1·5	88·1	7·2	12·2	91·7	10·8	54·2	,,	+	+	–
8·9	4·5	3·6	1·2	80·0	7·3	12·0	86·3	10·7	54·0	ov.	+	+	+
9·1	4·3	3·7	1·6	88·1	6·7	10·4	81·3	10·0	51·5	pent.	–	+	+
9·5	4·3	3·7	1·2	86·1	7·0	11·5	84·6	10·5	55·0	sq.	+	+	+
8·9	4·4	3·7	1·6	84·1	6·9	10·5	82·0	10·4	54·1	pent.	+	+	+
9·5	4·5	3·6	1·7	80·0	6·8	10·7	83·0	9·5	55·8	ov.	+	+	+
9·4	4·6	4·0	1·5	87·0	6·6	10·7	83·6	10·6	53·8	sq.	+	+	+
10·2	4·7	3·8	1·2	80·9	6·9	11·8	90·1	11·4	54·5	,,	+	+	+
10·2	4·7	3·9	1·5	83·0	7·5	11·7	95·1	10·5	58·0	pent.	+	+	+

II. Anthropometrical Measurements

No.	Village.	Name.	Stature (1)	Heap Height (2)	Head Length (3)	Head Breadth. (4)	Altitudinal Index =⅔×100	Cephalic Index =4/3×100	Least Frontal (5)	Bi-zygomatic (6)
61	Deora	Dhatar	155·3	11·7	17·4	13·5	67·2	77·6	10·0	12·8
62	„	Budhan	156·5	11·3	17·9	12·8	63·1	77·5	9·9	13·0
63	Jagor	Kalu	159·6	12·3	18·4	13·7	66·9	74·5	9·9	12·4
64	„	Achu	157·7	10·5	19·5	13·9	53·9	71·3	10·1	13·0
65	„	Suna	154·8	11·7	17·6	13·4	66·5	76·1	9·8	11·9
66	„	Tuka	163·1	11·5	18·7	13·9	61·5	74·3	9·8	12·9
67	„	Kusan	151·3	11·6	17·7	13·8	65·5	78·0	10·5	13·4
68	Khunta Gata	Dasan	159·9	12·2	19·3	13·8	63·2	71·5	10·4	13·5
69	„	Kendhu	158·8	11·9	17·7	13·5	67·2	76·3	10·1	12·2
70	„	Panra	159·9	11·2	18·6	13·3	60·2	71·5	10·8	13·7
71	„	Ruda	162·3	11·7	18·5	14·2	63·2	76·8	10·0	12·6
72	„	Daspuna	155·0	11·5	18·3	13·4	62·8	73·2	9·9	12·4
73	Kasna	Budhan	157·1	11·4	17·5	13·3	65·1	76·0	10·1	12·7
74	Kandi	Ratna	166·9	12·5	19·1	12·8	65·5	67·0	9·2	12·8
75	„	Nandu	164·0	11·3	18·5	12·9	61·1	69·7	10·0	13·1
76	„	Chuna	151·9	11·2	18·7	13·9	59·9	74·3	10·1	12·9
77	„	Pratop	163·2	11·8	18·1	13·0	65·2	71·8	9·2	12·4
78	„	Sukra	146·2	11·1	18·1	13·7	63·3	75·7	10·0	13·1
79	Suakati	Sira	156·5	11·6	18·6	14·2	62·4	76·3	10·2	13·1
80	„	Pasu	156·6	11·2	19·1	13·2	58·6	69·1	10·3	13·8

of adult male Subjects.

Bigonial (7)	Nasal Length (8)	Nasal Bredth (9)	Nasal Height (10)	Nasal Index =9,8×100	Nasion Prosthion Length (11)	Nasion Gnathion Length (12)	Facial Index =12,6×100	Bi-gonial Length (13)	Circumference of the head (14)	Face (15)	Forehead (16)	Lips (17)	Facial Prognathism.
8·6	4·0	3·4	1·3	85·0	6·4	10·2	79·7	11·0	50·5	sq.	+	th.	−
9·0	4·4	3·9	1·4	88·6	6·6	10·7	82·3	10·8	51·5	,,	+	,,	−
9·4	4·2	3·1	1·6	73·8	6·7	10·7	86·3	10·5	53·4	pent.	−	+	+
9·2	4·4	4·0	1·5	90·9	7·1	11·2	86·2	10·6	56·0	ov.	+	+	+
9·2	4·4	3·6	1·2	81·8	6·6	11·0	92·4	9·8	52·0	pent.	+	+	+
9·0	4·1	4·0	1·4	97·6	6·7	10·3	79·8	10·6	53·5	sq.	+	+	+
8·5	4·5	3·8	1·3	84·4	6·8	11·3	84·3	10·5	52·5	,,	−	+	−
8·5	4·4	4·0	1·1	93·0	7·0	10·9	80·7	10·7	56·0	ov.	+	+	−
8·4	4·6	3·9	1·1	84·8	6·6	10·7	87·7	10·1	51·5	,,	+	th.	+
9·8	4·6	4·0	1·2	87·0	7·2	11·2	81·8	10·2	53·5	sq.	+	+	+
9·2	4·8	4·1	1·4	85·4	7·4	12·7	100·8	8·8	54·5	pent.	+	+	−
9·2	4·5	3·7	1·3	82·2	7·1	11·1	89·5	9·5	53·0	,,	+	+	+
8·4	4·3	4·3	1·1	100·0	6·4	10·5	82·7	9·7	51·2	ov.	+	+	−
8·2	4·8	3·9	1·2	81·2	7·0	11·5	89·8	10·0	53·5	pent.	+	th.	+
9·2	4·5	3·9	1·3	86·7	7·1	11·3	86·2	10·8	53·0	ov.	+	+	+
9·9	4·0	3·6	1·1	90·0	6·4	11·0	85·3	10·1	53·8	sq.	+	th.	−
9·0	4·5	3·4	1·2	75·6	6·6	11·1	89·5	9·7	52·5	,,	+	+	+
9·2	4·2	3·9	1·2	92·9	6·1	10·8	83·0	10·5	52·0	pent.	+	th.	+
9·1	4·1	3·9	1·3	95·1	6·9	10·8	83·0	11·2	54·1	,,	+	th.	+
9·9	4·7	4·5	1·2	95·7	7·1	11·5	83·3	10·7	53·8	sq.	+	+	+

II. Anthropometrical Measurements

No.	Village.	Name.	Stature (1)	Head Height (2)	Head Length. (3)	Head Breadth. (4)	Altitudinal Index $= \frac{2}{3} \times 100$	Cephalic Index $= \frac{4}{3} \times 100$	Least Frontal (5)	Bi-zygomatic (6)
81	Suakati	Dharia	154·8	12·2	18·8	14·1	64·9	75·0	10·6	13·2
82	„	Paran	159·8	12·6	19·1	13·9	66·0	72·8	10·4	14·5
83	„	Asura	153·5	11·3	18·2	13·9	62·1	76·4	10·2	12·8
84	„	Mangsira	162·7	11·8	18·3	13·7	64·5	74·9	10·2	13·3
85	„	Sadhu	162·6	11·4	18·7	13·8	61·0	73·8	9·7	13·3
86	„	Indra	158·0	12·3	18·3	13·6	67·2	74·3	10·0	12·8
87	„	Kandhi	158·7	11·9	19·2	13·3	62·0	69·3	10·2	13·0
88	„	Noria	155·2	11·1	18·7	13·3	59·4	71·1	11·1	12·9
89	„	Kusia	157·1	11·2	19·1	14·4	58·6	75·4	10·4	13·4
90	„	Nanthu	158·2	10·5	18·0	13·4	58·3	74·4	10·4	13·5
91	„	Baniya	153·0	11·5	19·6	14·2	58·7	72·5	10·3	13·2
92	„	Somaro	168·8	11·1	18·9	13·6	58·7	72·0	9·9	13·8
93	„	Milu	148·3	10·6	18·7	13·6	56·7	72·7	9·7	12·8
94	„	Kundh	153·4	12·1	18·5	13·2	65·4	71·4	9·9	12·8
95	„	Irau	159·9	12·2	20·1	14·2	60·7	70·7	11·1	13·7
96	„	Nisa	154·6	11·5	18·6	13·7	61·8	73·7	9·9	13·4
97	„	Kusmbu	161·9	10·9	18·9	13·6	56·6	72·0	9·9	13·3
98	„	Sapra	149·1	12·5	19·1	13·7	65·5	71·7	9·7	12·1
99	„	Kudh	157·2	12·0	19·8	14·2	60·6	71·7	9·8	12·2
100	„	Sakam	160·5	11·7	18·6	13·6	62·9	73·1	10·1	13·4

of adult male Subjects.

Bi-gonial (7)	Nasal Length (8)	Nasal Breadth (9)	Nasal Height (10)	Nasal Index =9.8×100	Nasion Prosthion Length (11)	Nasion Gnathion Length (12)	Facial Index =12.6×100	Bi-orbital Length (13)	Circumference of the head (14)	Face (15)	Forehead (16)	Lips (17)	Facial Prognathism.
10·1	4·3	4·1	1·3	95·3	6·6	10·5	79·5	11·1	55·0	sq.	+	th.	+ +
9·7	4·0	4·3	1·5	107·5	6·3	10·6	73·5	10·4	51·5	Rd.	+	+	–
8·6	4·2	3·8	1·4	90·5	6·4	10·2	79·7	10·7	51·0	ov.	–	+	+
9·0	4·6	3·9	1·3	84·8	6·6	10·4	78·1	10·6	53·8	„	–	+	+ +
9·8	4·6	4·0	1·4	87·0	7·3	11·8	88·7	10·6	53·4	Rd.	+	+	+
9·9	4·2	3·9	1·5	92·9	6·7	11·3	88·3	9·4	50·9	ov.	+	+	+
9·2	4·4	4·1	1·8	93·2	7·0	10·9	93·8	10·8	54·0	pent.	+	+	+
10·5	4·1	3·8	1·3	92·7	6·5	10·8	83·7	10·3	54·5	sq.	+	+	+
9·1	4·8	3·8	1·4	79·2	7·2	11·8	87·9	11·0	54·1	ov.	+	th.	+
9·7	4·4	3·9	·9	88·6	6·7	10·9	80·7	10·6	52·0	sq	–	„	–
9·6	4·4	4·4	1·4	100·0	6·6	10·8	81·8	10·9	56·8	ov.	–	+	+
9·1	4·6	4·0	1·3	87·0	7·1	11·7	81·2	10·8	54·5	„	+	th.	+
9·2	4·8	3·9	1·1	81·2	6·9	11·5	89·8	10·6	54·0	„	+	+	–
8·7	4·6	3·7	1·3	80·4	6·6	10·8	84·4	10·5	52·5	sq.	+	+	+
9·2	4·7	4·1	1·5	87·2	6·7	12·5	84·0	11·5	56·0	ov.	+	+	+
9·1	4·5	4·1	1·3	90·1	6·8	11·2	83·6	10·5	53·1	„	+	+	+
9·3	4·4	4·0	1·2	90·9	7·1	11·3	85·0	10·8	55·0	„	+	+	+
9·4	4·4	4·2	1·4	95·5	6·3	11·9	98·3	10·1	56·5	sq.	+	th.	+ +
9·3	4·6	4·3		93·5	6·8	11·4	92·6	10·5	57·8	ov.	+	„	+
9·5	4·5	4·2		90·4	7·0	12·5	93·2	10·4	53·5	sq.	+	+	+

APPENDIX B.

Local Accounts of the PLAINS BHŪIYĀS of the Orissān State of Gangpur.

The author is indebted to H.D. Christian, Esq. Superintendent of the Gangpur State, for the following accounts of the Plains Bhūiyās of that State collected by him at my request. The first four accounts were given by the leading Hinduised Bhūiyā Zamindars of the State. Special interest attaches to the Hinduised Bhūiyā's own idea of his tribe as indicated in the subjoined notes of these Bhūiyā Zamindars.

Mr. Christian who has been long amongst the Plains Bhūiyās and has knows them intimately, in his covering letter dated the 14th September, 1934, forwarding the subjoined accounts to the author, wrote as follows :—

"The Bhūiyās here are divided into two endogamous groups—the Khaṇḍāit or Pāik, and Prajā. To the former belong the Zamindars, tenure-holders, and all Bhūiyās who are *gaonṭiā* of villages, being in fact the barons and landed gentry; they are Hindu. The Prajā Bhūiyās are definitely lower in the scale both socially aud materially and are cultivators and labourers; for practical purposes they are animist. The

Zamindar of Himgir, a Khaṇḍāit Bhūiyā, in his letter, it will be seen, classes Khaṇḍāit as Āryan, and Prajā as non-Āryan. The principal ceremony among the Khaṇḍāit is the ear-boring just as among the Rajput it is the sacred-thread investment. The Zamindar of Sarapgaṛh (a Khaṇḍāit Bhūiyā), it will be seen, says that all the Bhūiyās are non-Āryan. The Bhūiyās pay great respect to the Nāg or serpent and are reported to be averse to killing it. The Bhūiyās have generally buried their dead, though the upper classes are now taking to cremation."

Account no. 1.

"The Bhūiyās of Gangpur State have two divisions; first, Khaṇḍāit or Pāik; second, Prajā Bhūiyā. The Khaṇḍāit or Pāik were so called because they used to fight with Khaṇḍā (swords sharpened on both sides) and also one-edged swords and they were able to protect their rights and properties and themselves from enemies.

"The Khaṇḍāit or Pāik Bhūiyā gradually migrated into Gangpur State through Ōṛissā from Central India by groups during the reign of some of the descendants of Yajāti Keśarī. One man of each of the said groups became the leader or foremost man of the State. The groups are known as follows:– Daś-Ghariā, Panchāś-Ghariā, Chār-Ghariā, Chhai-Ghariā, Bāro-Ghariā, Chhai-Nāyak, Daś-Ganjhuan, Panchāś-Dal, Panaraśai-Ghariā, *etc.* The Gotras of the Khaṇḍāit Bhūiyā or Pāiks are *Nāg* and *Kachhapa.* According to the family dynasties, the Khaṇḍāits bore the following Bargas (titles), viz., *Manjhi, Pradhan, Naik, Malik, Sa, Amat, Barāik, Ḍaṇsanā, Kālo, Bhoi,* etc. The greater part of the State was being enjoyed by the Khaṇḍāits as Zamindari, Parganādāri, Ganjhuāni, Māfidāri, Jāgirdāri, Gaunṭiāi, and Raiyati, as is even now the case.

"The Khaṇḍāits contract marriage with families related to them and also with those that are not related but are living not far from them. According to convenience and status, marriages take place among the Khaṇḍāits of different groups. Rice and vegetables are taken from other groups only when there are relationships between one another. As between groups which have no connection with one another, only the taking of cooked vegetables is allowed for the first time, and when connection of some sort is established rice is also permitted to be taken.

"The adoption or continuance and propriety of particular rites and customs depend on the decision of the social head of each group. The social customs of different Khaṇḍāit families vary according to their respective status. These customs relate to Birth, Naming, First rice-eating, First hair-cutting, Ear-boring, Marriage, and 'Second-Marriage' Ceremonies. All these ceremonies are now performed according to the Hindu Shāstras with the help of Brāhmaṇs. The Vaishnavas are the hereditary religious preceptors of the Khaṇḍāits. The dress and ornaments of the Khaṇḍāits were similar to those of other civilized castes, but at present even these are the same with those prevalent in the country. Tattooing is quite optional with Khaṇḍāit females.

"The Khaṇḍāits were too much attached to their Kshatriya rulers and hence they came to be classed among civilized castes. The Khaṇḍāits do not take liquor and fowl. They take rice, *etc.*, only from the hands of Brāhmaṇs and Kshatriyas. Fighting and cultivation were the chief occupations of the Khaṇḍāits. At present the Khaṇḍāits are living solely upon cultivation.

"The Prajā Bhūiyās are known as 500-Ghariā. They are regarded as non-Āryans. They perform all their family rites among their own clan. They do not require any Brāhmāṇ to perform their marriage and funeral ceremonies. They take liquor and fowl like other non-Aryans. Their chief occupations are cultivation and daily labour. They do not know how to use arms. They are similar to be Pabia, Bhūiyār, Goṇd, Lohrā, Kōl, and other jungle tribes."

Sd/- Chandan Singh Gartia.
Zamindar of the Himgir Estate.

<u>*Account no. 2.*</u>

"1. We are Khaṇḍāit but not Bhūiyā. We are called Bhūiyā simply because we are landholders.

"2. We have each got our *gotra* but I cannot describe them.

"3. Marriage within the same clan is always permissible, and we can marry in higher clans such as Kshatriya, but cannot do so in any lower clan.

"4. The characteristic tools and implements of our clan are guns, swords and shields.

"5. All our ceremonies are performed by Brāhmaṇ priests.

"6. The original home of the Khaṇḍāit is said to be the Jodh land near Jhanked in the district of

Cuttack and people of our tribe are to be found in the Bamra and Bonai States also."

Sd/- Harihar Singh,
Zamindar of the Nagra Estate.

Account no. 3.

"The Bhūiyās inhabiting Gangpur at present are of two classes: first, the *Khaṇḍāits* or *Pāik Bhūiyās*, secondly, *the Prajā Bhūiyās*. Because the Khaṇḍāits were well-versed in using arms and weapons they were experts in warfare and could uphold their rights. That is why they have acquired the title of Khaṇḍāits.

"The Khaṇḍāits poured into Gangpur first in batches passing through Ōṛissā proper during the reign of a successor of Yajāti Keśarī and began to settle down here. As they came in groups, the captain or head of each group was known as *Gadee*. Their divisions are as follows:—Daś-Ghariā (*lit.*, consisting of 10 houses), Panchāś-Ghariā, Chār-Ghariā, Chhai-Ghariā, Bāro-Ghariā, Chhai-Nāik, Daś-Ganjuāl, Pānch-sai-Ghariā and Panra-śai-Ghariā, *etc.* The Nāg (Cobra) and Kachhap (Tortoise) are their *gotras*. Each stock has its own surname, such as, Mājhi, Pradhān, Nāik, Mallik, Sā, Amat, Ḍoṇsaṇā, Baṛāik, Kālo, Bhoi and others. These Khaṇḍāit Bhūiyās had been and have been enjoying the major portion of Gangpur as Zamindārs, Parganādārs, Ganjhus, Gāonṭiās, Māfidārs, Jāgirdārs, and Raiyats.

"Each division of the tribe at first used to marry in its own division and also sometimes into a neighbouring group to whom they might be related. By and by, different divisions came to observe their own marriage ceremonials which came to have distinctions according to their convenience, circumstances and class and other considerations, only some either taking cooked rice or curry or both from other classes at social feasts. The heads of the divisions are responsible to see that the tribal customs are duly observed in accordance with ancient formalities. In course of time they came to be divided into three classes each of which now observes its own social customs. The social customs, such as, *Nāmkaraṇ*, *Anna Prāsana*, *Chuṛā Karaṇa*, *Karṇa Bedha*, *First marriage*, and '*Second-marriage*', are performed by Achārya Brāhmaṇs according to the Hindu *Karma kāṇḍa* (prescribed ritual). *Dikshā-grahaṇa* (initiation) is only accepted from a Brāhmaṇ of the preceptor line according to the tenets of the Vaishnavas.

Their garments, ornaments, and similar other things resemble those of advanced castes. Though tattooing ("Gudhna") is not the social custom, yet such of the women as desire to follow the local custom generally get themselves tattooed of their own accord in imitation of females of more advanced tribes.

"As the tribe has always been in contact with the Government of higher Kshatriya kings, it has been reckoned, both in the past and present, among one of the civilised castes in this district. They never take such forbidden food and drink as flesh of fowls, wine, rice cooked or served by any other caste except those of Brāhmaṇ and Kshatriya. Both in the past and at present profession of arms and cultivation have been their main occupation. Because they were always habituated to the use of swords and similar other weapons, they became known as Khaṇḍāits or Pāiks. In course of time, since the promulgation of the Arms Act, the practice of arms and weapons has disappeared. Now as the only means of our livelihood, cultivation is left to us. At present most of our tribesmen, who can find no occupation, are continually swelling the number of the unemployed. In many places, pressed for want of money, many of them have become coolies and degraded to a very low stage of society. Their old punctiliousness in observing their social and tribal customs, which was the chief mark of their social superiority, having slackened, they are sinking low in the scale of castes. Their fore-fathers before coming to Ōḍra Deś or Ōṛissā, were living, some in Central India and others in South-west Kalinga.

"Next to them are the Prajā Bhūiyās, also known as the *Pānch-śai-Ghariā*. Their social observances are to a great extent just like those of the aborigines. They perform all their social customs without the help of Brāhmaṇ priests, but in accordance with their old tribal laws. They do not feel the need of Brāhmaṇs either on auspicious occasions or in other crises such as marriage, parturition of women, or death. They, like the other aboriginals, take wine and flesh of fowls. They engage themselves in cultivation and day-labour (*majuri*). They have or had no arms and weapons except implements of cultivation. They are always afraid of losing their lives. When these Bhūiyās came to this country, they were such jungly aboriginals residing sparsely hither and thither as the Vabiya,

Bhūiyār, Khand, Luhoora, Kol and other tribes."

Sd/- Gajraj Singh.
Zamindar of Sargipali.

Account no. 4.

"The Bhūiyās came to this State from Ōṛissā and belong to non-Āryan tribes. There are two sub-divisions in the Bhūiyā caste, viz., (i) Khaṇḍāit or Pāik Bhūiyā and (ii) Prajā Bhūiyā.

"1. The Khaṇḍāit or Pāik Bhūiyās used to fight in ancient times with Khaṇḍās (sword with both ends sharpened) and also ordinary swords and were considered as brave soldiers in those days. They used to protect their rights and privileges by their own bravery. They also used to wear the sacred thread, and still do so only on occasional ceremonies. They are descendants of Yajāti Kesarī, the famous King of Orissa.

"2. The different groups are known as follows:— 4-ghar, 6-ghar, 12-ghar, 10-ghar; 50-ghar, 6-Naik, 10-Gonjhuan, 500-ghar and 1500-Dal.

"3. The *Barags* are known as follows:— 1. Manjhi, 2. Nāik, 3. Patel, 4. Mallick, 5. Daṇsana, 6. Sāh, 7. Āmat, 8. Bhoi, 9. Biswal, 10. Pradhān, 11. Rāut, 12. Chataria, 13. Bhitria, 14. Samrath, 15. Kālo 16.

Bahera, 17. Dehri, 18. Baṛāik, 19. Adha. The Khaṇḍāits are all of *Nāgeswar* gotra or clan.

"4. (*a*) *Marriage customs:*— Early marriage is in vogue among the Khaṇḍāits and also a ceremony of 'second-marriage' on the attainment of puberty by married girls. There are no hard and fast rules or restrictions about it. Their marriages are performed according to the Hindu Shāstras with the help of Brāhmaṇs, and certain local customs are also observed. A marriage within the same *gotra* or clan is permitted but not into a division other than one's own. Widow marriage is strictly forbidden among the Khaṇḍāits or Pāik Bhūiyās.

"(*b*) *Funeral customs:*—Funeral ceremonies are performed according to the Hindu Shāstras and there are no special tribal customs regarding it.

"5. *Description of tools, implements, specific dress:*— The males used to wear *chapkan,* white or yellow *Pāgṛee, Dhoti* and *Chādar.* They used swords only. The females wear *Sāṛi* and *mukuṭ,* all of yellow colour.

"6. Their females wear ornaments just like those of civilised castes, and there is no restriction against wearing any kind or make of ornaments.

"7. Tattooing is not compulsory among the Khaṇḍāit caste by way of a distinguishing mark. Some like it and some not.

"8. The Khaṇḍāits are prohibited to drink liquor and to take fowls.

"9. The principal foods among the Khaṇḍāits are rice and vegetables, *etc.* They take rice, *etc.*, cooked by Brāhmaṇs only. The chief occupations are cultivation or Pāikari (Soldier's work). Their present occupation is cultivation.

"10. The Khaṇḍāits came or migrated from Kurukshetra i.e., north-west direction of their present habitat.

"11. The Prajā Bhūiyās are called 500-*Ghariā*. Their customs regarding marriage and funeral ceremonies are very different. They are just like low-caste people and perform those ceremonies themselves and not according to the Hindu Shastras through Brāhmaṇs. They take liquor and fowls like other low-caste people. Their chief occupation is cultivation; and some are day-labourers.

"12. The Khaṇḍāits cannot take food nor drink water from the hands of Prajā Bhūiyās. Marriage also could not be performed except in their own caste.

Sd/- Danardan Singh
Zamindar of Saraphgarh.

Account no. 5.

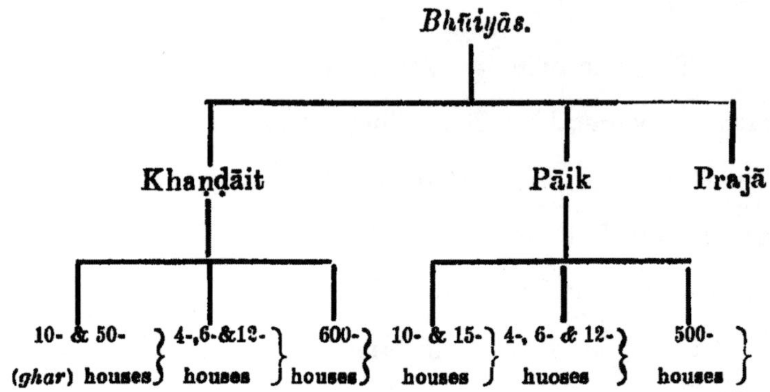

Bhūiyās are the primitive inhabitants of India and belong to non-Aryan tribes. From the Mayurbhanj side they gradually spread to Sambalpur, Gangpur and Jashpur sides. Formerly the Bhūiyās were working as Sepoys of the ancient settlers and a few of them were engaged in cultivation. Bhūiyā Sepoys were using 'khaṇḍā' (sword sharpened both sides) and common swords and *paikar* (an iron or brass plate to parry strokes of sword which is called *Dhal* in other local languages). Thus those who used Khaṇḍā became Khaṇḍāits, those who used sword and *paikar* became *Pāyak* or *Pāik* and those who cultivated land became *Prajā* Bhūiyās. Khaṇḍāit and Pāik Bhūiyās are nominally two, but they really form one clan, and the Prajā Bhūiyā, though an offshoot of the Bhūiyās, forms a separate 'caste'.

Sub-divisions:— The Khaṇḍāit and Pāik Bhūiyās are again sub-divided into three groups according to the number of houses as shown in the table given at the top.

Gotra:— The Manjhi i.e., Bhūiyās of 10- & 50-houses (*ghar*) are of *Kachhap* (tortoise) Gotra, and the rest belong to *Nāgasa* (snake) Gotra.

The Praja Bhūiyās are also of *Nāgasa* Gotra.

Barga (*Title*):— The following are the Bargas of the Bhūiyās:— (1) Manjhi (2) Nāik (3) Paṭel (4) Mallik (5) Daṇḍasana (6) Sāh (7) Āmat (8) Bhoi (9) Buija (10) Pradhan (11) Biswal (12) Rāut (13) Chataria (14) Bhitiria (15) Samaratha (16) Ganjhu (17) Pardhia (18) Kālo (19) Deheri.

Dress:— The Bhūiyās used to wear *kachha* which was then a war dress. The females used to wear *Luga* in up-country fashion, but now-a-days they have altogether changed the style, and are wearing clothes just in the fashion of other castes and tribes of their country. At present there is nothing to distinguish the Bhūiyā from a high class Hindu.

Ornaments:— The Bhūiyās use all the ornaments which are used in their country. They have only taken *Chauri Mundi* as their special head-ornament. It is a compulsory ornament of the Bhūiyās. Other ornaments, such as, *Bandaria, Kataria, Taṛ, Baha, Suta,* for the arms; *Ḍanḍi, Guna, Bari, Ratha,* for the nose; *Ganthia, Betala, Bali,* and *Jhalara* for the ears; and *Pairi* for the legs; and *Gunchi* for the waist, are used according to the status of particular Bhūiyā families.

Tattoo marks:— Tattooing is not a distinguishing feature of the Bhūiyās. It is quite an optional thing with them, and solely rests on the choice of the women although it is very much in vogue in this part of the country. The females are tattooed on their chests just below the collar bone, on their arms, upper and inside elbow, upper palm of the left hand and just above the ankle joints, They are tattooed before they are married, generally when they are 10 or 12 years of age or even earlier and in some cases later. Men are not tattooed.

Marriage customs:— There is no peculiar custom in the marriage rites of the Bhūiyās. They do not practise child-marriage. Boys are married generally at the age of from 18 to 20, and a girl when she reaches the age of puberty, that is, at the age of from 14 to 16 years. Their marriage relationship is confined to their own community. Bhūiyās of the Daś-ghariā and Panchāś-ghariā divisions may marry girls from the other two divisions but they do not dine with the latter sections. Bhūiyās of the last two groups marry girls from the first group and dine with them. Similar is the case with the second and third groups. No inter-marriage is permitted between the Khaṇḍāits and the Prajā Bhūiyās.

Funeral customs:— All Bhūiyās used to bury their dead bodies. Now-a-days some Bhūiyās of high status, such as Zamindars, burn their corpses. Like other high class Hindus they apply oil on their limbs on the third day after cremation. On the tenth day they perform the *śrāddha* ceremony. On the eleventh day they make gifts to Brāhmaṇs and take *Āmish* (fish) after taking *Hōm Ghrita* (clarified butter used for the *Hōm* oblations). On the 12th day they give a feast to Brāhmaṇs and their own caste-fellows and thus they finish the ceremony.

Deities and Cult:— Bhūiyās have no special tribal deity or special cult. They worship all the deities that high class Hindus do. All temples and shrines are open to them. Brāhmaṇs accept Pakwarma (bread and sweets etc.) and water at the hands of the Paik and Khaṇḍāit Bhūiyās as they are counted among the Vaiśya class. This is not the case with the Prajā Bhūiyās. Brāhmaṇs, Kshatriyas and Vaiśyas do not take water or cooked food at the hands of Prajā Bhūiyās.

Musical Instruments:— The Bhūiyās have got no special instrument of their own for music. But the Gayans (Bhāṭs) are their special musicians. The Bhāṭs visit every Bhūiyā's house on occasions of marriage or funeral ceremonies and sing songs to the tune of the *Khanjani* (a small piece of hollow wood covered with leather on one side and used as an instrument of percussion).

Sd/- S. S. Sahai,
Sub-Inspector of Police, Himigr.

Account no. 6.

The Bhūiyās are of two sections:- *Pāik* and *Prajā*

Bhūiyās. There is no interdining and inter-marriage between Pāik and Prajā Bhūiyās. The former are superior to the latter, and Brāhmaṇ priests perform all ceremonies in their houses. The former have certain sub-divisions such as four-Ghariās, six-Ghariās, ten-Ghariās, twelve-Ghariās, 500-Ghariās and 1500-Ghariās. They have only *Nāgasa* and *Kacchhapa* Gotras. There is inter-marriage and inter-dining according to sub-divisions. The Prajā Bhūiyās have only one division and they are of 500-Ghariā. They have only one Gotra namely, *Nāga* or *Nāgasa*. They have no particular customs or usages for tatoo marks. The women only take them at their pleasure. The Pāik Bhūiyās, too, have the same practice about tatoo marks. These are taken only for beauty's sake.

Sd/- B. Bohidar, Tahsildar.

INDEX.

A Correction.

At page 50, line 10, for 'square' read 'oval', and p. 50, line 11, for 'oval' read 'square'.